A BOUNDED LAND

COLE HARRIS

A Bounded Land

Reflections on Settler Colonialism
in Canada

UBCPress · Vancouver · Toronto

29 28 27 26 25 24 23 22 21 20   5 4 3 2 1

Printed in Canada on FSC-certified ancient-forest-free paper
(100% post-consumer recycled) that is processed chlorine- and acid-free.

Library and Archives Canada Cataloguing in Publication

Title: A bounded land: reflections on settler colonialism in Canada / Cole Harris.
Names: Harris, Cole, author.

Description: Includes bibliographical references and index.
Identifiers: Canadiana (print) 20200306790 | Canadiana (ebook) 20200306855 |
ISBN 9780774864411 (hardcover) | ISBN 9780774864428 (softcover)
ISBN 9780774864435 (PDF) | ISBN 9780774864442 (EPUB) |
ISBN 9780774864459 (Kindle)

Subjects: LCSH: Canada – Colonization – History. | LCSH: Indigenous peoples –
Colonization – Canada – History. | LCSH: Indigenous peoples – Canada – Social
conditions. | LCSH: Indigenous peoples – Canada – Government relations – History. |
LCSH: Canada – Ethnic relations – History. | LCSH: Canada – Race relations – History.

Classification: LCC E78.C2 H37 2020 | DDC 305.897/071 – dc23

Canadä

UBC Press gratefully acknowledges the financial support for our publishing program
of the Government of Canada (through the Canada Book Fund),
the Canada Council for the Arts, and the British Columbia Arts Council.

Printed and bound in Canada
Text design: Irma Rodriguez
Set in Devanagari and Museo by Artegraphica Design Co. Ltd.
Copy editor: Lesley Erickson
Proofreader: Jonathan Dore
Cartographer: Eric Leinberger

UBC Press
The University of British Columbia
2029 West Mall
Vancouver, BC V6T 1Z2
www.ubcpress.ca

For Muriel,
also our children
Douglas, Colin, and Rachel

Contents

Acknowledgments

I can no longer accurately identify the many intellectual debts, spread over more than half a century, that underlie these writings. Specific acknowledgments accompany the most recent of them (and appear before the relevant endnotes for each chapter), but a comprehensive general acknowledgment is impossible. On the other hand, I can identify the general circumstances in which most of this writing has been situated – the context, as it were, that has facilitated the whole undertaking.

A large part of that context has been the intellectual environment created by faculty and graduate students in and beyond the Geography Department at the University of British Columbia, a rich ground for the cultivation of ideas.

Financial support for much of my research has come from the Social Sciences and Humanities Research Council. Compared to most of the sciences, my work does not require heavy funding, but smallish regular grants have been exceedingly useful and deeply appreciated. The Council is a crucial Canadian institution.

It is important that UBC has a successful university press. It does and I have wanted to publish there. In return, my books, this one among them, have been splendidly copy-edited and designed. Such a press, at hand, is a much-appreciated resource. And I have had the singular opportunity to work over the years with two outstanding design cartographers: Geoffrey Matthews at the University of Toronto, and Eric Leinberger at UBC. Eric has drafted or redrafted all the modern maps in this book.

Finally, all my work has been situated within the support, variously offered, of my immediate family, which is why this book, my last considerable work, is dedicated to them.

A BOUNDED LAND

Introduction

PUBLISHED IN VARIOUS locations and for various audiences over the last fifty years, the writings republished here all deal with settlers and their descendants and with those they substantially displaced – in short, with settler colonialism. They all have analytical edges and are broadly related to one another. But tucked away in various publications and often embedded in more empirical investigations, many of them have been nearly invisible. Nor has it been possible to consider them as a coherent body of thought. Although that thought has evolved over the years, common assumptions run through these various writings. If the more analytical of them are assembled, something of the broad architecture of settler colonialism may appear – the premise that underlies this collection.

By "settler colonialism" I mean, simply, that form of colonialism associated with immigrants who became the dominant population in the territories they occupied and, in so doing, displaced the Indigenous peoples who previously had lived there. The coming of settlers was variously buttressed by military force; commercial and, later, industrial capital; and the administrative apparatus of a state. But in the long run, the durability of settler colonialism rested on the creation of resident, settler populations. Colonies that were based on economic exploitation, managed by an expatriate elite, and controlled by force of arms reverted to the Indigenous population when the elite and its military supports withdrew, whereas, in settler colonies, recently transplanted populations, now in control of the territories they occupied, survived and often flourished as imperial support declined. Moreover, as connections with former homelands weakened, and as lives and societies were recontextualized in different settings, immigrants and their descendants considered these new settings home.

Settler colonialism has a long history – the Greeks established settler colonies in places around the Mediterranean rim some 2,500 years ago. In this book, however, I deal with the settler colonialism associated over the last several centuries with the European outreach into the non-European world. It was one of the means by which, at the height of its global influence, Europe came to dominate more than three-quarters of the world. More specifically, and with the exception of forays into New England and South Africa, I focus here on Canada. Yet settler colonies have some common shape; to write about settler colonialism in one place is to say something about its character in another.

The writings that follow are situated within the broader pattern of the European coming to northern North America, of which settler colonialism was only one mode. Throughout the sixteenth century and well beyond, commercial capital created a European presence along much of the Atlantic coast. Thousands of fishermen came year after year to seasonal cod fisheries, dried cod ashore, and returned to dozens of ports from southern England to Portugal. Only slowly and unremarkably – as a few men were left as caretakers of fishing properties, as small merchants began to operate in Newfoundland, and as a few women joined them – would small resident populations appear in some fishing harbours. In these scattered and often largely invisible ways, the European settlement of Newfoundland began, but it would be many years before anything like an established settler colony emerged. Late in the sixteenth century, another form of commercial capital, the fur trade, entered the St. Lawrence River where, prompted by the French crown, it too would eventually draw settlers. A trading company was granted a royal monopoly in 1627 and mandated to establish a proprietary colony and bring four thousand colonists in fifteen years but could not meet these conditions. In 1663, when the French crown revoked the company's charter, barely two thousand transplanted people lived along the lower St. Lawrence. Thereafter, the Crown managed this incipient colony (Canada). In the Bay of Fundy (Acadia), the fur trade also drew settlement, though on a scale even more modest than in Canada.

Yet Canada and Acadia were the first settler colonies in the large North American space that would eventually come to be known as Canada. Acadia, which attracted not many more than three hundred immigrants and was perched between French and British positions in North America, was always a frail creation. Canada, settled over the years by some ten thousand immigrants who left descendants, became a substantial colony. By the end of the seventeenth century, it contained two small towns, a countryside that stretched for many miles along the river, and the basic components of French society: government officials, soldiers, merchants, members of religious orders, tradespeople and workers of many types, seigneurs (holders from the Crown of large land grants that they were expected to subgrant) and, more numerous than all the others, peasants living on land held from the seigneurs. By the middle of the eighteenth century, more than fifty thousand people lived in this French colony.

Almost from their beginning, Canada and Acadia were enmeshed in the protracted struggle between France and Britain for North America, a struggle in which Britain, with far more North American colonists and a larger navy, was in the stronger position. Acadia fell repeatedly to the British, for the last time in 1710. Three years later, the Treaty of Utrecht confirmed its new status as a British possession, along with Newfoundland and Hudson Bay. To the north, south, and east, Canada was hemmed in. In these narrowing circumstances, France built a massive fortress, Louisbourg, on Cape Breton Island, intending it to protect the Gulf of St. Lawrence; it fell to an Anglo-American force in 1745, was returned, and fell again in 1758. The Acadians, their loyalty suspect, were deported. Aided by Indigenous allies, the French fared better in the Interior, but Quebec fell the following summer, Montreal a year later. Canada was now in British hands. Fifteen years later, the British colonies along the Atlantic seaboard revolted; when that war ended, Britain had lost all her former seaboard colonies but, ironically, held the heart of New France. What the French called the *pays d'Illinois*, the huge, fertile basin of the upper Mississippi Valley, which France claimed but had barely occupied and British diplomacy had not held, passed to the new United States. The southern border of British North America was drawn near, and often beyond, the northern continental limit of agriculture.

In these circumstances, space was available for new settler colonies – New Brunswick, Nova Scotia, and Prince Edward Island in what had been Acadia, and Lower and Upper Canada in the St. Lawrence Valley. Lower Canada already had a sizable settler population; elsewhere, almost all potential farmland was open for settlement. It attracted Loyalists fleeing the United States, American land seekers who happened to fetch up in British North America, and, particularly after the Napoleonic Wars, an enormous outpouring of people from the British Isles, the majority probably Irish (more Protestants than Catholics) but also a great many Scots (particularly from western Scotland) and English (particularly from the Midlands).

In Britain, the source of the majority of these immigrants, industrialization was shifting the locus of work from workshop or farm to factory, from countryside to city. What Marx called independent producers were becoming factory hands. Older ways of life and the economies that underpinned them resisted as they could, but the economies of scale of factory production were inexorable. Returns for handwork were falling; those who had managed a living with a tiny plot of land, a cow, and a hand loom held out as they could but usually capitulated. In the burgeoning cities, they faced the squalid, life-threatening conditions that Engels, Dickens, Gaskell, and many others vividly described. Moreover, the long assault on local, customary-use rights to land, associated with the gradual expansion of the common law and with enclosures dating from Tudor times, had gained much momentum in the late eighteenth and early nineteenth century. Most land was enclosed, the common law was pervasive, market economies were ascendant, and the rights of private property were firmly established. For most people – Scots confined to tiny crofts on the coast after their former villages and fields had been converted into sheep runs, Irish peasants whose labour for a year earned the right to rent (but not to rent) one acre of arable land – the countryside had become constricted and largely inaccessible space. For many of these people, an alternative to British factories and slums was emigration to a British North American colony.

In many ways, this was a deeply conservative migration. People sought to maintain themselves as independent producers by crossing an ocean, tackling a forest the likes of which they had never seen, and establishing a farm – a gamble at every turn. Many died in the attempt, but overall the forest yielded, at least in patches, and farms were established – niches for several more generations of independent producers. In 1871, when Britain's population was more than half urban, 80 percent of Ontarians (Upper Canadians) were rural, and Toronto, the largest city, only had 3.5 percent of the provincial population. Prince Edward Island was 97 percent rural. Migration had provided the opportunity to acquire land. In some places, the timber trade and the work camps associated with it dominated, but, overall, new countrysides and established farm families were the principal creations of these settler colonies. Although industrial capital had helped push people from Britain, it had not made these countrysides. Rather, they were the work of a great many now largely anonymous people who acquired farm lots, took on a forest, and after years of pioneering, confined it to woodlots on family farms.

By 1871, almost all accessible farmland had been taken up, and many of the young, unable to replicate family farms in British North America, were moving to the United States. In Quebec (Lower Canada), clergy seeking to protect language and religion, and in Ontario, businessmen seeking to expand their markets, sought to staunch this flow by encouraging a northward migration into the fringe of the Canadian Shield. They promoted colonization roads and variously encouraged settlement. For the relative few attracted to these schemes, the almost invariable result was a desperate struggle with intractable land, dire poverty, and, if the parents managed to hold on, the quick departure of the young. The land was simply too hard. It was becoming clear that, agriculturally, British North America was severely bounded space, quite unlike the vast, expanding heartland of the United States.

Beyond these constricted settler colonial spaces, the fur trade extended European influences inland, in so doing creating a sprawl of trading posts and relying on Indigenous peoples to bring furs, and often provisions, to the posts. Early in the nineteenth century, the trade reached the Pacific; by mid-century, in what French traders called *le petit nord,* north and west of Lake Superior, the fur trade was more than two hundred years old. There and elsewhere, it altered Indigenous ways and local ecologies, but it required Indigenous labour and skills and, unlike settlers, rarely competed with Indigenous peoples for land.

The Canadian Pacific Railway, built in the early to mid-1880s, opened up land for agriculture. Suddenly, there was more space for pioneering and independent producers, but the Prairies were difficult space, not because of a daunting forest but because of the close boundaries of aridity and cold. To quit an industrial town in the English Midlands, settle on the bald prairie well removed from any neighbour, and survive a bitter winter in a sod hut was a precarious undertaking. Thinking sturdy peasants would fare better, the federal minister of the Interior favoured immigrants from eastern Europe. Although its composition differed from any in eastern Canada, another substantial settler colonial space emerged, this one soon tangled in corporate interests associated with railways, grain elevators, brokerage firms, and the like, but also bounded northward, usually by cold.

In British Columbia, where mountainous terrain meant far less space for agricultural pioneering, industrial capital rather than settlers became the most aggressive new user of land. Fish canneries along the coast; logging camps almost wherever there was good, accessible timber; mining camps and mining towns – these were the common forms of new settlement, and most of them, quick to deplete a resource and vulnerable to technological change and fluctuations in commodity prices, were short-lived. Where agricultural settlement occurred, it was usually more enduring, but in British Columbia, as around the southern edge of the Canadian Shield, pioneers pushed into corners of intractable land, struggled, and gave up. Beyond all of this new western development was the larger part of British North America, where the fur trade lingered and other forms of European influence could barely reach.

But in places where newcomers settled, prior ways were being re-contextualized. To live on a long-lot farm in a row of similar farms along the lower St. Lawrence, or along a concession-line road in Upper Canada, or on a quarter section in Saskatchewan, was to live in circumstances with no close European equivalent. Everything was somewhat altered: the physical environment, the emerging human landscape, the composition of the surrounding population, innumerable details of daily life, and perhaps most basically, the relative value of land and labour. These differences reworked European cultures and social structures – the creative side of settler colonialism. At another scale, and for the purposes of settler colonialism, Canadian space was bounded. Whereas a generous relationship with an ongoing land underlay the United States, Canada was underlain by pinched relationships within bounded patches of land that stretched discontinuously across the continent – a structural difference between the two countries. The circumstances of Indigenous peoples in early Canada depended, in good part, on whether they lived within or beyond the land that settlers could use.

Settler colonialism requires land and takes it from Indigenous peoples, who had usually used it for thousands of years, knew it intimately, and claimed it as their own, a displacement that raises enduring moral issues. In 1839, Herman Merivale, then a professor at Oxford and before long undersecretary at the Colonial Office (where, more than anyone else in the Britain of the day, he managed an empire), concluded, based largely on his knowledge of Australia and the United States, that settler dealings with Indigenous peoples were full of deceit, rapine, and killing. But what to do about it? The problem, he thought, was that the interests of settlers and Indigenous peoples were opposed, that power lay with the former and that they took what they wanted. A solution seemed to be to appoint officials, responsible to the Colonial Office, who would lay out reserves and control settlers. But would this work? Settlers would eventually covet and take reserve land; moreover, they would demand responsible government, it would be granted, and settlers would then control land policy. The only long-term solution, he thought, was what he called amalgamation, the intermarriage of Indigenous peoples and settlers and the creation of a merged society. Towards the end of his life, he doubted that even this would work and feared that there was no solution to what he called the "Native question."

Merivale's analysis is a fair fit with settler colonial Canada. He was right that the interests of Indigenous peoples and settlers were opposed; right, for the most part, that power lay with settlers and their governments; and right that this imbalance of power facilitated the taking of land. Even treaties were efficient, relatively inexpensive forms of taking. He was right that settlers would covet and take land reserved for Indigenous peoples and right that settlers would acquire responsible government and, with it, the control of land policy – hence in British Columbia Indigenous attempts to bypass this control and reach the executive – the Crown – in Britain. Merivale thought that the alternative to amalgamation was probably the extinction of Indigenous peoples. In this he was wrong, but like others of his day he assumed that a modernizing world would have a single, very European, face.

However, away from the pockets of immigrant settlement, in the great majority of the territory that became Canada, Merivale's analysis does not apply. Population densities were exceedingly low, and in most places there were few, if any, settlers. For the most part, this had been the territory of the fur trade and, when that trade declined, it drew industrial capital in the form of sawmills and mines, missionaries, and, eventually, government officials, but not many settlers. The population, small and dispersed as it was, remained largely Indigenous. Moreover, most people lived where their ancestors had always lived and, until well into the twentieth century, followed many traditional ways. When the outside world impinged, as it did, they were buffeted by the uncertainties and social pathologies associated with primary resource industries; the utopian visions, variously derived from Christian certainties and Enlightenment philosophers, that led to residential schools; and regulations and bureaucratic efficiencies emanating from the settler colonial state. Yet, through all of this, Indigenous peoples remained, and today their populations, no longer checked by the biological yield of the land, are growing rapidly. The large majority of the population of Canada is derived from immigrants and is part of the settler colonial project, but the large majority of the land of Canada has not fit this project. Canada is a country that became possible because of settler colonialism, but settler colonialism in this country has been a bounded project. For all the penetrations of the outside world and the territorial claims of the

Canadian state, the land beyond the boundaries of immigrant settlement has remained substantially Indigenous.

THE FOLLOWING WRITINGS are engaged with these matters. They emerged out of an interest in settler colonialism and its effects that has extended over some sixty years. I cannot say that, at the beginning, I had any clear idea of where I was going. I was interested in early Canada and curious about my own position in the country. What was it to be a Canadian, and where did my life fit in relation to the lives of ancestors who had come from Britain and to a country that, in good part, was French-speaking? That curiosity, I suppose, forms the background of these writings. I had done a combined degree in geography and history at the University of British Columbia and in 1959 went to the University of Wisconsin to study under Andrew H. Clark, then America's pre-eminent historical geographer. Clark took me under his wing, historical geography at Wisconsin was exciting, and I loved being there. Clark, who had written on the human and biological invasion of the South Island of New Zealand and was interested in the comparative study of mid-latitude European settlements overseas, asked me, as his research assistant, to find out what I could about the Acadians, the French settlers in the Bay of Fundy. It was there, tentatively and with no larger sense of direction, that my investigations of settler colonialism began.

Acadia involved me with the French beginnings in North America, and I decided to write a doctoral thesis on early Canada, the French colony based on the lower St. Lawrence River. I planned to write on the evolution of agriculture, but as I got into the archives I found myself confronted by feudal law and custom that I did not understand, and I ended up writing a thesis on the seigneurial system. It had little to do with my thesis proposal – ever since, I have been skeptical about most thesis proposals – and I only slowly realized what I had on my hands: a study of how French law and socioeconomic relations changed when suddenly recontextualized overseas.

There were jobs for historical geographers in those days. When I found myself at the University of Toronto, I began to make inquiries about the early nineteenth-century settlement of Upper Canada. Before long, John Warkentin at York University and I came together to write a text on the historical geography of pre-Confederation Canada. Beyond it was a much larger challenge of synthesis, the *Historical Atlas of Canada,* a project launched in the cartographic laboratory at the University of Toronto. We proposed a six-volume atlas, which, fortunately, the Social Science and Humanities Research Council rejected. But the council did support a three-volume atlas, and I became editor of the first volume (to 1800), a project that consumed me for almost a decade. I had returned to the University of British Columbia, where, the atlas finally behind me, I turned to the study of settler colonialism when Indigenous issues were increasingly to the fore. I wrote a book of essays on settler society in Indigenous space and another on the working out of the Indian reserve system, the means by which Indigenous peoples were dispossessed of almost all their land. When well retired, I wrote a denser, more nuanced book than its textbook predecessor on pre-Confederation Canada.

Throughout these years, I thought of myself as a historical geographer, although, in studying places and times with which few geographers were familiar, my immediate intellectual dependence was often on historians. To all intents and purposes, I worked at the interface of these disciplines. My debts to historians are large and often personal. I did not know what I was doing when I arrived in Quebec City and plunged into the archives. Historians rescued me. On one occasion, I asked the archivist at the Séminare de Québec, a distinguished, elderly man, if I could see the account books for the seminary's seigneurie, Beaupré, and was told there were no such books. Jean Hamelin, a young history professor at Laval University, took me back to the seminary to be properly introduced, go through the polite formalities and, eventually, see the account books. Fernand Ouellet, whose book on the social and economic history of Quebec from 1760 to 1850 had opened up the study of those years, was equally helpful. He invited me to his house, where, over a diminishing bottle of Scotch, he explained in no uncertain terms why he had so little use for the bourgeoisie in the Upper Town. Moreover, he had been recently fired as provincial archivist (for engaging in research rather than administration) and seemed sardonically proud of the mode of his going: "Ils m'ont fait rouler. C'était magnifique." Later, I got to know the historian Louise Dechêne; I worked closely with her on the atlas and considered her among the finest scholars I knew. I admired the meticulousness of her archival research; her deep respect for the ordinary people of early Canada, whose hard lives she so well understood; and the conduct of her university life. She asked for little, worked hard, and published sparingly but well.

And yet, for all my involvement with and dependence on historians, the writings that follow are inflected by the fact that I am a historical geographer. They have more of space and place – of land and environment – about them than most historical writing; are more engaged with social theory than has been characteristic of Canadian historiography; and are probably a little more reckless, a little more inclined to skate on thin ice, than fits the measured caution of most good historians. These inflections have advantages and disadvantages, but if one is interested in settler colonialism, which is about the detachment of some from their land and its repossession by others, and if, particularly, one seeks a comparative grasp of different instances of settler colonialism, then these inflections are exceedingly helpful.

AS I HAVE MENTIONED, my interest in social change in immigrant societies is partly personal. My mother's Scotch-Irish ancestors were in Upper Canada in the 1820s. Much closer at hand, my English paternal grandfather (from Calne, in Wiltshire) and his Scottish wife (from Fyvie, near Aberdeen), both of whom I knew as a boy, established a mountainside farm in the Kootenays of British Columbia in the late 1890s. That farm is still in the family, and the lives lived on it have been British in some ways, not in others. When in Britain, I am well aware of the provenance of some of my ancestors and that I am neither English nor Scottish. But what had changed, and why? That is the question I brought to the Acadians, to the Canadians along the lower St. Lawrence, and eventually to the British Columbian society in which I grew up. It has been my point of departure for the study of settler colonialism, and it has dominated all my early work on the topic.

Having several protracted opportunities to consider the sweep of early Canada, I was increasingly struck by what seemed to me the obvious fact that immigrant lives there were situated in quite different types of settlement: towns, countrysides dominated by family farms, and work camps associated with the staple trades. Lives were very different in each of these settings, and for each setting it seemed possible to work out their characteristic patterns. Moreover, it seemed to me that most of these containers were situated in closely bounded space – rock and cold to the north, a border with the United States to the south – and that the combination of a few characteristic containers in bounded space had produced a particular pattern of early Canada, one with wide and enduring ramifications. Off and on over the years, I have returned to such musings.

It was after I had Volume 1 of the *Historical Atlas of Canada* behind me that I first seriously considered the means and effects of the settler colonial dispossession of Indigenous peoples. I was then back in British Columbia, and the issue of Indigenous title was in the air and the courts, in part because of the constitutional entrenchment of Indigenous rights in 1982. When I was offered a temporary chair in Canadian studies and a light teaching load for two years in return for three public lectures and a book, I turned to a study of the reserve system, the official means by which Indigenous peoples had been detached from almost all of their land. That study drew me into the modi operandi of dispossession, at least as they worked in British Columbia in the late nineteenth and early twentieth centuries, and towards the circumstances of Indigenous life in a settler colonial society. For the first time, I felt the Indigenousness of the province in which I had grown up. The result was a new book and other writings that edged closer to Indigenous worlds than anything I had previously written.

SUCH ARE THE MAIN themes of this collection of writings on settler colonialism. Put most starkly, they address the immigrant experience in early Canada, the organization of immigrant space, and the contraction of Indigenous space. They are organized in five parts.

Part 1 consists of three short pieces that treat what may be thought of as the initial conditions for a subsequent colonialism. The first is an account of an encounter between people previously unknown to each other and situated in vastly different lifeworlds. When the fur trader–explorer Simon Fraser descended the river later named after him, he met the Nlaka'pamux, who thought him Coyote, the Great Transformer who had made the world and was now returning to remake it. In retrospect, the Nlaka'pamux were right about the change that would ensue, but I use this meeting to represent all the other first encounters between newcomers and those who say they had always been there across the span of what became Canada. The second describes how Europeans began to imagine and conceptualize land that had been outside their experience, in so doing shifting it into a simple register they could grasp and bypassing Indigenous understandings based on intricate, long-accumulated local experiences of land and life. And the third, which deals with the spread of smallpox and other infectious Old World diseases in the southwestern corner of British Columbia, is but an example of the horrific carnage wrought by the viruses and bacteria that accompanied Europeans overseas. Settler colonialism in Canada, as elsewhere in the western hemisphere, was accomplished in the wake of this tragedy and on severely depopulated land.

Part 2 provides three local examples of immigrants or their descendants settling land and putting it to uses derived, broadly, from Europe. In Acadia in the seventeenth and early eighteenth centuries, settlement spread throughout, and eventually beyond, the marshlands around the Bay of Fundy. A few immigrants became, by the middle of the eighteenth century, a population of more than ten thousand living, for the most part, in small houses at the upland edge of their diked farmlands. They were a peasantry, but no French peasants spoke French or lived quite as they did. In a corner of the northwest Atlantic, they had become a distinct people.

In Champlain's day, the Petite-Nation was a small group of Algonquins living well up the Ottawa River, but in the early nineteenth century Petite-Nation was a seigneurie owned by Louis-Joseph Papineau, one of the leaders in Lower Canada of the Rebellion of 1837. Most of the people who settled his seigneurie were *habitants* pushed out of the seigneuries along the lower St. Lawrence by population pressure; a few were merchants from New England. In Petite-Nation, they encountered an edge of the Canadian Shield and commercial capital in the form of the timber trade. The land was harsh, labour was oversupplied, and most of the habitants brought little more than the clothes on their backs – a recipe for struggle, poverty, and, eventually, the departure of most of the young.

Mono Township in Upper Canada was settled in the early to mid-nineteenth century, largely by immigrants from Ulster who, with industrialization, could no longer make a living from a tiny plot of land and a hand loom. They were Protestants of various Calvinist persuasions who took on the unremitting and often killing work of turning a forest into a farm. Eventually, farms were made, the land was overcleared, and beliefs were reinforced.

Part 3 looks more generally at the structure – the architecture – of settler colonialism. The introduction to a talk given at a conference on seventeenth-century New England is included because it sets out what, for me, is the point of departure for any generalized consideration of social change in settler colonies overseas. The chapter on "simplification" is an attempt to deal comparatively with social change in three seventeenth- and early eighteenth-century European colonies: French Canada, English New England, and Dutch South Africa. It posits that major elements of their European background were pared away in these colonial settings and that for a time, until new elements of complexity were introduced, social formations tended to simplify. The chapter on "Creating Place" is the most recent and perhaps the most comprehensive of several of mine on what I call the pattern of early Canada. It is here that I discuss the generic places of early Canada, their arrangement in bounded space, and some of the implications that follow therefrom.

The focus shifts in Part 4 to British Columbia and to the ways that an incoming settler society imposed itself on Indigenous peoples and lands. I deal first with the Lower Mainland – the region centred on the lower Fraser River, including the present city of Vancouver – during its early settler colonial years. There, with the establishment of the Crown colony of British Columbia in 1858, an introduced regime of property spread across the land, and Indigenous peoples, allocated tiny reserves, found their movements monitored by a decentred system of surveillance based on property owners who, backed by the law and the full arsenal of colonial power, watched and excluded. I then discuss the power embedded in systems of transportation and communication to open up land for capital and settlers and to confine Indigenous peoples. Superimposed on land thought empty and without a past, introduced systems of transportation and communication created the stark economic geography that situated and supported immigrant lives and undermined traditional livelihoods. Moreover, trains, steamboats, and the like, suddenly introduced and experienced, were hugely intrusive cultural artefacts. Finally, I show that the assault on custom in British Columbia (the assault on Indigenous ways of life) had deep antecedents in Britain, where, in the face of long and bitter resistance, the rights of private property and market economies had gradually overturned local customary rights. In Britain, however, this had been a confrontation within a known society; in British Columbia, it was a deeply racialized confrontation between "civilization" and "savagery."

In Part 5, I put together what are probably my most intricate writings on British Columbia. In an essay that asks the same questions that I asked about Acadia, I tried to establish the main contours of the immigrant society that had come to dominate British Columbia. What had come from afar, what had been left behind, and how was society being recomposed? Early modern British Columbia was far more variegated than Acadia in the seventeenth and early eighteenth centuries, and the questions I asked about it can have no definitive answers. In such circumstances, this probe is what I could manage. Set beside it is an article dealing with the means by which an incoming settler colonial society dispossessed Indigenous peoples of almost all the land. I had written a book on the reserve system, felt I had some understanding of the workings and interconnections of various forms of colonial power, and was uneasy with colonial discourse theory, less because I thought it wrong than partial and, because preoccupied with texts, unable to assess its own relative significance. Hence this article, which attempts to set out the array of powers bearing on the dispossession of Indigenous peoples and to consider their interconnections and relative weight.

Finally, and with all selections in this book in hand, there seemed another piece to write – about where, now, those who have come relatively recently and those who, judging by their stories, have always been here are with each other. I have no particular wisdom, and no specialized knowledge either of Indigenous societies or of contemporary Canada, and yet I have felt a need to say something about the matter that, more than any other, gnaws at the heart of a settler colonial society.

EXCEPT FOR THE LAST, none of these writings was undertaken with a collection like this in mind. As originally published, some were heavily noted, others were unnoted and followed by bibliographic essays. Some were written for academic readers, others for an educated public. They were written over a span of years when vocabularies of gender and race have considerably changed. Yet, with the following exceptions, I have republished them here as they were written: large parts of articles or book chapters are often pared away to expose the nub of an argument, footnote numbers are adjusted as necessary, and, very occasionally, I have tweaked the text.

PART 1
Early Encounters

The Fraser Canyon
Encountered

As Europeans reached into North America, radically different worldviews abruptly encountered each other, a meeting that, the Norse apart, began in the western hemisphere late in the fifteenth century and was repeated over and over again during the next four centuries as the newcomers pushed ever farther into the spaces of those who had always lived there. Little or no evidence survives of most of these encounters, but here and there they can be somewhat reconstructed. The example that follows is of such a meeting in a deep, isolated valley in what is now British Columbia. There, following the crest of the spring flood in 1808, a party of Montreal-based explorers from a fur-trading post far upriver encountered the Nlaka'pamux, the people living along that reach of the river. Neither had seen or, except perhaps vaguely in rumours, heard of the other. Simon Fraser, the leader of

From *The Resettlement of British Columbia* (Vancouver: UBC Press, 1997), 103–4.

the explorers, described the meeting in his journal, and the Nlaka'pamux told stories about it, one of which, a century later, an ethnographer recorded.

In my book *The Resettlement of British Columbia,* I used these two accounts to introduce a chapter on the Fraser Canyon (the river Fraser descended was named after him) as it lost most of its Nlaka'pamux ways and was absorbed into the world Fraser's coming anticipated. Here, I use them more generally to represent the innumerable first encounters that introduced the achievements and the tragedies of settler colonialism.

O N JUNE 19, 1808, Simon Fraser, explorer-trader for the Montreal-based North West Company, noted in his journal that he and his men had reached the Indigenous village of Nhomin on the west bank of what he thought was the Columbia River, just above its confluence with a large, clear tributary that Fraser named the Thompson.[1] At Nhomin, Fraser met some four hundred people who, he thought, ate well and seemed long-lived. From there, he was taken across the river to a camp where he found "people ... sitting in rows to the number of twelve hundred." He shook hands with all of them. The "Great Chief" made a "long harangue," pointing to the sun, the four-quarters of the world, and the explorer. An old, blind man, apparently the Chief's father, was brought to Fraser to touch. Next day, the dash to the sea resumed but had not made many miles when a canoe capsized and broke up. Most of the men got ashore quickly, but one, D'Alaire, was carried three miles downstream, where, exhausted and barely able to speak after dragging himself out of the river and up a cliff, Fraser found him. The precarious descent of one of the rawest rivers in North America by twenty-two experienced employees of the North West

Company and two Indigenous translator-guides had lost only a few hours.

Some Nlaka'pamux, the people along this part of the Fraser River, described these events very differently. Long after Coyote had finished arranging things on earth, he reappeared on the river with Sun, Moon, Morning Star, Diver, Arrow-Armed Person, and Kokwe'la.[2] They came down from the Shuswap country, landed at the junction of the two rivers, and many people saw them. Shortly after they left, Moon, who steered the canoe, disappeared with it under the water. The others came out of the river and sat on a rock. Arrow-Armed Person fired lightning arrows, and Diver dived. Sun sat still and smoked. Coyote and the others danced. "Coyote said, "Moon will never come up again with the canoe"; but Sun said, "Yes, in the evening he will appear." Just after sunset, Moon appeared holding the canoe, and came ashore. All of them embarked, and going down the river were never seen again."[3] This was Coyote's only appearance since the mythological age.

Here are two remarkably different accounts of the same event, both told not very long ago. Time seems telescoped in British Columbia; the place appears to rest on a vast ellipsis. In Europe, the equivalent of Coyote and his band are too far back to have any reality, and so, invented and abstracted, they appear as "noble savages" (Rousseau) or as members of traditional lifeworlds (Habermas). But in this new corner of the Europeans' New World, abstractions become realities, and the long story of emerging modernity, extending back through European millennia, is compressed into a hundred years or so. The ethnographers who, at the end of the nineteenth century, began to study the Indigenous societies of British Columbia, assumed this. Since then, most of our scholarship has become more local; British Columbia tends to be studied for its own sake or in relation to the development of Canada. But to do so, as the best of the ethnographers knew, is to diminish the monumental and relatively accessible encounter – here, not long ago – of European culture with Coyote, Sun, Moon, Morning Star, and the others, an encounter that underlies the world we live in.

Imagining and Claiming
the Land

As Europeans touched and began to penetrate land that, previously, had been entirely outside their experience, they began to name and map it, and in so doing to reconceptualize it in European terms. They replaced complex, finely worked-out Indigenous understandings of place and land with their own geographical general-izations – powerful simplifications that enabled them to explore, claim, and often colonize land they knew next to nothing about. In North America, the transfer of the un-European into a register Europeans could understand began with the first European comings and would long continue. Its sixteenth- and early seventeenth-century progress is considered here.

From *The Reluctant Land* (Vancouver: UBC Press, 2008), 20–29.

BEFORE MANY EUROPEANS could operate along the northeastern fringe of North America, the European imagination had to make some sense of it, less, perhaps, to establish "what was there" than to arrange and order the land in terms that Europeans could understand. Otherwise, it was bewildering and profoundly disorienting. The process of ordering New World space, and thereby of making it knowable, continues to the present, but for some time after initial contact, explorers' reports and maps were the principal means of bringing this space into some preliminary focus. Reports, based on fleeting observation and self-serving promotions, were usually tantalizing exaggerations. The maps that explorers and cartographers produced were egregious abstractions that represented endless complexities by a few lines. Yet these words and lines enabled Europeans to know and think in certain ways – ways embedded in systems of power that allowed them to begin to possess spaces they hardly knew.

Explorers' reports and the maps they and European cartographers produced were means of translation and simplification. They rendered the myriad voices of new lands in an accessible European language. Once translated into this language, the land could be communicated, and then could be argued and strategized over from afar. Moreover, to the extent that this language enabled Europeans to orient themselves in a space about which they knew little, it allowed them to ignore Indigenous voices situated in intricate but, from a European perspective, essentially alien systems of knowledge. A few lines on a map served to eviscerate the land of its Indigenous knowledge, thus presenting it as empty, untrammelled space available for whatever the European imagination wished to do.

The process of translation and simplification began as soon as Europeans came into regular contact with the northeastern corner of North America. Its modern European discovery began, as far as we know, in July 1497, when the Genoese explorer-merchant John Cabot, sailing with the financial backing of merchants in Bristol and the permission of the English Tudor king Henry VII, reached coastal Newfoundland or Nova Scotia. He found a bleak coast, waters teeming with fish, and some prospect of a sea route to China, for which he received ten pounds from Henry VII and support from his backers to outfit five ships for a voyage the next year. One of these ships soon returned, storm-damaged, but the other four never did. In 1499, a Portuguese, João Fernandes, reached at least Greenland (which he named Tiera de Lavrador, a name that would migrate west); a year later, another Portuguese, Gaspar Corte-Real, also authorized by King Manuel of Portugal, sailed as far as Greenland. He was back in 1501 and continued to Newfoundland but then was lost at sea, as was his brother Miguel who sailed to look for him. These precarious probes into the northwestern Atlantic had found and reported land, but what land? Cabot, along with his backers, thought he had reached a northeastern peninsula of China, an assumption represented on several early sixteenth-century maps. Fernandes and Gaspar Corte-Real thought they had found an island. The conceptual discovery of North America apparently had not been made, although a remarkable map by the Spaniard Juan de la Cosa and variously dated from 1500 to 1508 suggests that it might have been. La Cosa's map shows a continuous coastline between the Spanish discoveries in the Gulf of Mexico and English discoveries, marked with flags, far to the north. It is the first representation of the east coast of North America. Some hold that La Cosa, who was in the Caribbean in 1499, could have got this information only from John Cabot, who, according to this interpretation, charted the coast and somehow communicated his findings to La Cosa before he and his ships disappeared.

Whatever the case, most European cartographers did not accept anything like the continental outline on the La Cosa map until the late 1520s. By this time, the Florentine Giovanni Verrazano, sailing for France, and the Portuguese Estévan Gomez, sailing for Spain, had charted the east coast of North America between Newfoundland and Florida. With a fairly continuous land mass established, the eastern edge of North America was coming into focus, and exploration turned to other questions: how to get around or through this obstruction on the route to China and whether profit might be derived from it. Verrazano had reported what he took to be open ocean beyond an offshore bar along the coast of the Carolinas. In the north, the Gulf of St. Lawrence was not yet known, nor was Newfoundland again understood as an island.

By the 1530s, bullion from the Spanish conquests of the Aztecs in Mexico, the Maya in Guatemala, and the Inca in Peru was flowing to Spain, and the prospect of finding and looting other empires became as enticing as a short route to China. In this climate of speculative imperialism, Francis I, king of France, commissioned Jacques Cartier, a Breton master mariner from Saint-Malo, to enter a reported strait beyond the Baye des Chasteaulx (the Strait of Belle Isle, between Newfoundland and Labrador). Cartier sailed in April 1534 and before his return in early September had explored most of the Gulf of St. Lawrence, taken possession of the land in the name of the French king, and captured two St. Lawrence Iroquoians, whom he took to the French court. These achievements earned him a second commission, and he was back the next year with three ships and 112 men. Directed by his two captives, Cartier sailed up the St. Lawrence River as far as his larger ships could navigate. From there, he explored west to Montreal Island, where he found a large well-palisaded village (Hochelaga) comprising, he reported, some fifty houses, each about fifty paces long and twelve to fifteen wide. Returning to his ships, he spent a harrowing winter of unanticipated cold, scurvy (a quarter of his men died), and increasing Indigenous hostility before capturing ten villagers, including the local Chief (Donnacona) and getting away to France. But he had found, as he reported to the king, "the largest river that is known to have ever been seen," flowing through well-inhabited "lands of yours" of great fertility and richness. He also brought reports of a kingdom of the Saguenay, one moon's journey beyond Hochelaga, where he had been told "there are many towns and ... great store of gold and copper." Such reports, embellished by Donnacona in France, drew an expedition in 1541 of some five hundred men. Headed by a French nobleman, Jean-François de la Roque, sieur de Roberval, this was intended less to find a route to China (which now seemed unlikely via the St. Lawrence) than to establish a colony and exploit the riches of the Kingdom of Saguenay. Almost everything went wrong. Cartier and Roberval were at odds, diamonds and gold sent back to France turned out to be quartz crystals and iron pyrites, the Kingdom of Saguenay was not found, and scurvy and Indigenous attacks decimated the colonists. Roberval and the last of the survivors left in July 1543. The French would not be back on the St. Lawrence for almost forty years.

Cartier's explorations – and particularly the colonization venture with Roberval – had much in common with those of the Spaniards Coronado (with three hundred men) and De Soto (with six hundred), who at approximately the same time were drawn by tales of kingdoms and treasure into lands far north of the Gulf of Mexico. None of them found what they sought while traversing huge territories that Europeans had never seen before. In fact, Cartier had accomplished a great deal, although his politics had antagonized the St. Lawrence Iroquoians, the principal reason, probably, for the French withdrawal from the river. He had brought the Gulf of St. Lawrence and the St. Lawrence Valley into a European field of vision, had taken possession of them in the name of the king of France, and had transformed the cartography of northeastern North America.

Cartier's own maps have not survived, but cartographers in Dieppe drew on his discoveries to produce several magnificent maps. Part of one of them, drafted by Pierre Desceliers in 1550, is reproduced in Figure 1. Newfoundland is shown detached from the mainland, the islands in the Gulf of St. Lawrence are approximately in place, and the St. Lawrence River is drawn to and somewhat beyond its confluence with the Ottawa.

Wherever Europeans had been, the map is strewn with names. Along the Atlantic coast, it includes but a few of the many names associated with the inshore fishery. Figure 2 shows more of them: the place names on sixteenth-century maps that can be located precisely on modern maps of Newfoundland's Avalon Peninsula, a small fraction of the names that, undoubtedly, were then current in the largely oral world of the inshore fishery. Even within R de sam Joham (St. John's Harbour), there must have been dozens of place names in several European languages. Further west on Desceliers' map, the place names are either Gallicized renderings of Amerindian words or French names given by Cartier. All these names, superimposed on older namings in languages Europeans did not know and could not pronounce, served to make the land accessible to Europeans. It was acquiring an outline they could visualize and names they could recognize. Place names were a means of erasure: the name "Terre des Bretons," for example, obscured the Mi'kmaq and other Indigenous peoples who lived there and other European fishers

FIGURE 1
Eastern North America, 1550. The map is oriented with south at the top;
the peninsula at upper right is Florida. | Cartographer, Pierre Desceliers. For a large
colour reproduction, see Derek Hayes, *Historical Atlas of Canada: Canada's History
Illustrated with Original Maps* (Vancouver: Douglas and McIntyre, 2002), 29.

who came there. A few of them suggest a tentative hybridity as some
Indigenous words were rendered in European phonologies.

Desceliers' 1550 map, like other small-scale maps of the day, was
not for general distribution. He intended it primarily for Henry II, then
the king of France, and not simply for the king's pleasure. It showed
the territory discovered and claimed for France by a French explorer
commissioned by the king, and situated this territory in a continental
geography, as then understood. Such maps were statements of possession and geopolitical tools. In effect, they were a means to transfer a few
bits of information, real or fanciful, about a distant place to what the
French sociologist Bruno Latour calls a centre of calculation where this
spare information could be put to work. In this case, it entered the

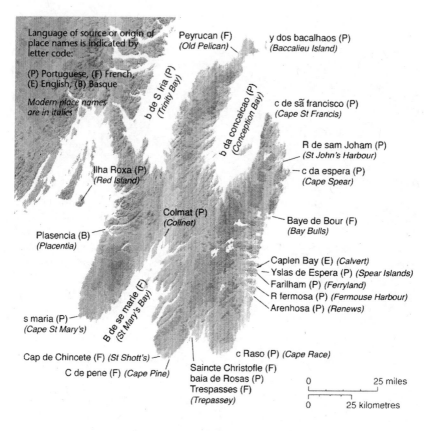

Language of source or origin of place names is indicated by letter code:

(P) Portuguese, (F) French, (E) English, (B) Basque

Modern place names are in italics

Peyrucan (F) *(Old Pelican)*

y dos bacalhaos (P) *(Baccalieu Island)*

b de S Iria (P) *(Trinity Bay)*

b da conceicao (P) *(Conception Bay)*

c de sã francisco (P) *(Cape St Francis)*

R de sam Joham (P) *(St John's Harbour)*

c da espera (P) *(Cape Spear)*

Ilha Roxa (P) *(Red Island)*

Colmat (P) *(Colinet)*

Baye de Bour (F) *(Bay Bulls)*

Plasencia (B) *(Placentia)*

Caplen Bay (E) *(Calvert)*
Yslas de Espera (P) *(Spear Islands)*
Farilham (P) *(Ferryland)*
R fermosa (P) *(Fermouse Harbour)*
Arenhosa (P) *(Renews)*

B de se marie (F) *(St Mary's Bay)*

s maria (P) *(Cape St Mary's)*

Cap de Chincete (F) *(St Shott's)*

C de pene (F) *(Cape Pine)*

c Raso (P) *(Cape Race)*

Saincte Christofle (F)
baia de Rosas (P)
Trespasses (F)
(Trepassey)

0   25 miles

0   25 kilometres

FIGURE 2

Sixteenth-century European place names, Avalon Peninsula | After S. Barkham, in R. Cole Harris, ed., Geoffrey J. Matthews, cart., *Historical Atlas of Canada*, vol. 1, *From the Beginning to 1800* (Toronto: University of Toronto Press, 1987), plate 22

diplomatic channels of French geopolitics. So recontextualized, bits of information from maps or reports could be transformed into territorial claims that, from the perspective of the peoples inhabiting the territory, seemed to have dropped from the blue. When, in 1569, Gerard Mercator first engraved and printed a map of the world in the projection for which he became famous, he identified the lands on either side of the St. Lawrence River as "Nova Francia."

The reports and maps generated by Cartier's voyages and the French claims to the St. Lawrence had the effect of shifting northward the search for a passage to China. Magellan had found a southern passage; surely

God, in his wisdom, had also created a northern one. Most of the effort to find it was English. Beginning in the 1570s with three expeditions led by Martin Frobisher, continuing in the 1580s with John Davis, and ending in 1616 with William Baffin and Robert Bylot, the search between Greenland and Baffin Island reached the extraordinary latitude of 77° 45' N. It produced several ceremonial possession takings of land, fighting with the Inuit, black gold ore mined in Frobisher Bay (it turned out to be highly metamorphosed igneous rock), and harrowing reports of ice – on which Coleridge probably drew for "The Rime of the Ancient Mariner" – but no passage. South of Baffin Island, Henry Hudson followed a strait into a huge chamber of the sea that became known as Hudson Bay, where he and his men overwintered in 1610–11. After the ice finally broke up the following June, most of his crew mutinied and abandoned him.

Other explorers followed: William Button in 1612–13; the Dane Jens Munk in 1619–20; Luke Foxe, backed by London merchants, in the early 1630s; and Thomas James, backed by a rival group in Bristol, also in the 1630s. With the technology of the day, the passage they sought did not exist to be found. But these voyages into Hudson Bay as well as those into Davis Strait and Baffin Bay transformed the cartography of far northeastern North America. Luke Foxe's map, published in 1635 (Figure 3), shows what was accomplished. There were still a few holes in the cartographic coastline that might lead to passages, but after so much negative information, investors were no longer willing to assume the cost of probing them. Although they had no return to show for investments spread over fifty years, the English had acquired experience with Arctic navigation and knowledge of Hudson Bay, and both would be drawn on when an English fur trade began later in the century.

By this time, there had been French settlements on the St. Lawrence for more than two decades, and the fur trade was well in train. In 1632, near the end of his life, Samuel de Champlain, the explorer-trader-cartographer who had established the French on the St. Lawrence, published his final cartographic synthesis of the regions in which he had spent most of his adult years. This remarkable map (Figure 4) shows the Atlantic coast with fair precision, identifies three of the Great Lakes –

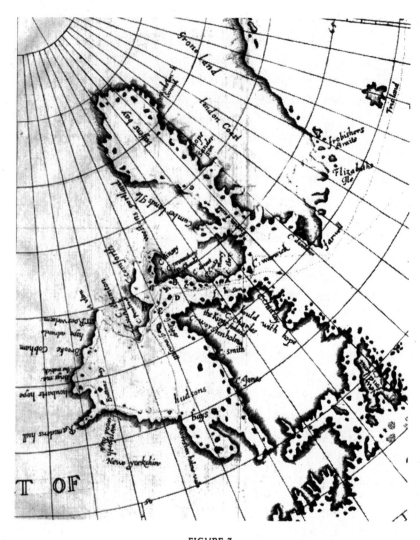

FIGURE 3
Luke Foxe, Part of America, 1635 | Royal BC Museum and Archives, 1–61569

Lac St. Louis (Lake Ontario), Mer Douce (Lake Huron), and Grand Lac (Lake Superior or Lake Michigan) – and suggests Lake Erie. Champlain's cartography had reached with some accuracy far into the continental interior, well beyond territory that any European had seen.

The map suggests just how far the venture on the St. Lawrence had drawn the French towards the continental interior and into contact with

FIGURE 4

Samuel de Champlain, New France, 1632 |
Library and Archives Canada, NMC, 51970

Indigenous peoples. To a considerable extent, Champlain had reproduced Indigenous geographical knowledge while, like other European cartographers, simplifying and decontextualizing it. He could not reproduce the intricate textures of Indigenous environmental knowledge, and the edges of that understanding that he did reproduce were detached from their cultural context. The pictorial representations of Indigenous settlements on Champlain's map include elements of Indigenous architecture while resembling European peasant villages. Much of the map simply creates blank space. At the same time, it produced a type of information that, at the scale of northeastern North America, Indigenous knowledge could not match. It had shifted the land into a different category of information, one that Indigenous peoples did not need but that Europeans did, for it allowed them to visualize space and, however approximately, to get their bearings. Ironically, the Indigenous information that Champlain incorporated in his map became a means of enabling Europeans to reconceptualize Indigenous space in European terms. Like Desceliers' before it, Champlain's map enabled the French Crown to claim territory and in so doing to ignore Indigenous possession while asserting its own interests. A rudimentary knowledge of the land, made available in Europe, became a considerable source of European power – a cartographic equation of power and knowledge that would be repeated across the continent.

Voices of Smallpox
around the
Strait of Georgia

Europeans carried diseases wherever they went in the western hemisphere. According to current estimates, Indigenous populations in the western hemisphere probably declined by some 90 percent in the century or so after their first contact with Europeans. For all the tyrannies of conquerors and colonists, diseases apparently had far more telling demographic effects. There is no good evidence, one way or the other, about epidemic diseases in northeastern North America in the sixteenth century. However, the Jesuit father Biard, writing in 1616, had this to say about the Mi'kmaq, the Indigenous peoples of Nova Scotia: "They are astonished and often complain that since the French mingle with and carry on trade with them they are dying fast and the population is thinning out. They assert that ... all their countries

From "Voices of Disaster: Smallpox around the Strait of Georgia in 1782," *Ethnohistory* 41, 4 (1994): 591–626.

were very populous, and they tell how one by one different coasts, according as they have begun to traffic with us, have been reduced by disease."[1] Scholars variously interpret Biard; there is no doubt, however, that the Iroquoian peoples around the lower Great Lakes were devastated by smallpox in the 1630s. Contagious Old World diseases had become established in northern North America and would eventually spread everywhere, even to the High Arctic. What follows deals with the coming of smallpox in the early 1780s to what is now the southwestern corner of British Columbia, a relatively visible edge of a ubiquitous catastrophe. There, as elsewhere, disease and depopulation would transform the terms of the settler-colonial engagement with Indigenous peoples and their lands.

Well, it's a good thing to study these things back, you know. Like the way the people died off.

– JIMMY PETERS, 1986[2]

The old Indians grow quite pathetic sometimes when they touch upon this subject. They believe their race is doomed to die out and disappear. They point to the sites of their once populous villages, and then to the handful of people that constitute the tribe of today, and shake their heads and sigh.

– CHARLES HILL-TOUT, 1904[3]

I T IS NOW CLEAR that Europeans carried diseases wherever they went in the western hemisphere and that among genetically similar peoples with no immunity to introduced viruses and bacteria the results were catastrophic.[4] In the century or so after Columbus, the population of the western hemisphere fell by some 90 percent according to current estimates.[5] For all the tyrannies of conquerors and colonists, diseases apparently had far more telling demographic effects.

In British Columbia little is known about contact-related disease and depopulation. Whites have told other stories, ethnographers have encouraged Indigenous informants to describe "traditional" ways, and the few recorded Indigenous accounts of disease usually have been treated as myths. Today, as political debates about Indigenous government and land claims intensify and appeals proceed through the courts, questions of disease and depopulation are being explicitly repoliticized – which does not make listening easier. For a society preoccupied with numbers, scale, and progress, more people imply fuller, more controlled occupation of land. Thus, it has been in the interest of non-Indigenous people to suggest small pre- or early contact Indigenous populations and in the interest of Indigenous peoples to suggest much larger ones. A disinterested position may not exist. Yet there are Indigenous accounts of disease, many of them long predating current political and legal calculations, as well as numerous references to disease by white explorers and traders.

Surviving Indigenous accounts of the arrival of smallpox are scattered and fragmentary. The great late nineteenth- and early twentieth-century ethnographers of Northwest Coast cultures did not work among the Coast Salish; the major ethnographic story collections do not come from these peoples. Nor did the ethnographers have pre- and early contact diseases in mind and, therefore, ask questions that would have elicited information about them. Generation after generation the elderly died, cultures changed, and, eventually, oral traditions thinned. What is left are short references and, condensed and often rephrased, a few whole accounts. All the material cited here has been written down, and it is impossible to reconstruct the circumstances of the stories or the intentions of the tellers. Often an account has been translated by one person and then recorded in summary form by another. In Jan Vansina's phrase, they are "mutilated messages" that present every opportunity for misunderstanding.[6] And yet these surviving fragments are powerful and generally consistent with each other.

Erna Gunther, writing on the Klallam (south coast of the Strait of Juan de Fuca), and Homer Barnett, writing on the Coast Salish of British Columbia, either heard no stories about early epidemics or did not record them.[7] Wilson Duff, writing on the Stó:lō (along the lower Fraser, well above its mouth) considered that early epidemics probably had reached the Stó:lō but had no information about them.[8] On the other hand, W.W. Elmendorf, ethnographer of the Twana (Hood Canal in Puget Sound) learned that his informants' grandparents had "lived at times of disastrous epidemics." The most severe, he was told, was very early, "perhaps about 1800," and came from the south via the Lower Chehalis; "from the Twana it passed north to the Klallam and peoples on southern Vancouver Island."[9] Wayne Suttles, writing on the Lummi (southeastern Strait of Georgia), reported that according to "native tradition" smallpox arrived before George Vancouver in 1792; "several villages were completely wiped out, while all suffered losses."[10]

Other accounts are fuller though somewhat filtered by white constructions. In the mid-1890s a Vancouver woman, Ellen Webber, asked the Kwantlen about a large unoccupied midden approximately a quarter of a mile long, one hundred feet wide and, at its centre, some twenty feet deep along the north bank of the Fraser River forty kilometres from its mouth. She published her findings "as they were given to me" (but largely in her own words) in *The American Antiquarian*. Apparently, the village was more than six hundred years old and had contained six hundred prosperous people. Attacks from the north had always been fended off, usually with stones piled in cairns along the riverbank in front of the village.[11] But, one year, the raiders came in such numbers that their canoes blackened the river. Even so, the Kwantlen defended their village ferociously. The river ran red with blood. Then, as a Kwantlen victory seemed assured, some of their enemy attacked from the rear.

> Now all was confusion. Many were killed, and many women were taken slaves. A few escaped to the woods, where they remained in

hiding two or three days. Then, with the children, they came out, and with sad hearts they laid away their dead ... But misfortune followed the little band of survivors. In the swamp, near the village lived a fearful dragon with saucer-like eyes of fire and breath of steam. The village was apparently regaining its former strength when this dragon awoke and breathed upon the children. Where his breath touched them sores broke out and they burned with the heat, and they died to feed this monster. And so the village was deserted, and never again would the Indians live on that spot.[12]

Until almost Webber's day, people "remembered and respected the dragon" and when passing the swamp crossed to the other side of the river and paddled softly and silently so as not to waken it. "Accursed is the one who awakens the dragon, he and all his people; for the sore-sickness will surely be their punishment."[13]

In 1896, Charles Hill-Tout, former theology student at Oxford and then master of an Anglican college in Vancouver, visited the Squamish "through the kindness of the Roman Catholic bishop" to record their history and cosmology.[14] The Chiefs produced "the old historian of the tribe," Mulks, decrepit, blind, and "about 100 years old." He spoke only archaic Squamish, which Hill-Tout could not understand and which Mulks uttered "in a loud, high-pitched key" that his Squamish listeners followed with rapt attention. Every ten minutes or so, the translator offered a précis not a fifth, Hill-Tout estimated, of what the old man had said. The story began with the creation of the world out of the water and continued with accounts of a flood from which only one couple survived and of a winter that did not end and during which all but two, a man and his daughter, died of starvation. In each case the land was re-peopled, and "the people learned to forget the terrible punishment the Great Spirit had sent upon their forefathers." Then,

one salmon season the fish were found to be covered with running sores and blotches, which rendered them unfit for food. But as the people depended very largely upon these salmon for their winter's food supply, they were obliged to catch and cure them as best they could, and store them away for food. They put off eating them till no other food was available, and then began a terrible time of sickness and distress. A dreadful skin disease, loathsome to look upon, broke out upon all alike. None were spared. Men, women and children sickened, took the disease and died in agony by hundreds, so that when the spring arrived and fresh food was procurable, there was scarcely a person left of all their numbers to get it. Camp after camp, village after village, was left desolate. The remains of which, said the old man, in answer to my queries on this head, are found today in the old camp sites or midden-heaps over which the forest has been growing for so many generations. Little by little the remnant left by the disease grew into a nation once more, and when the first white men sailed up the Squamish in their big boats, the tribe was strong and numerous again.[15]

In 1936, Old Pierre, then about seventy-five years old, told the ethnographer Diamond Jenness a similar story (although one more influenced by the missionaries).[16] Old Pierre, a Katzie, lived along the Pitt River, a tributary of the lower Fraser two days' paddle from the Squamish. The time came, he said, when the land was "overcrowded." When people "gathered at the Fraser River to fish, the smoke from their morning fires covered the country with a pall of smoke." Then the "Lord Above" sent rain that fell until most of the mountains were covered and most people had drowned. After the flood, the population multiplied again and "the Lord Above ... saw that once more they were too numerous in the land." "Then in the third month (October) of a certain year snow began to fall." Soon, every house was buried. Nine months passed "before the snow melted completely from the house-tops." Half the people died of starvation. A third time the population grew, and then came smallpox. Old Pierre's account is the most explicit surviving precontact description of the disease around the Strait of Georgia.

After many generations the people again multiplied until for the third time the smoke of their fires floated over the valley like a dense fog. Then news reached them from the east that a great sickness was travelling over the land, a sickness that no medicine could cure, and no person escape. Terrified, they held council with one another and decided to send their wives, with half the children, to their parents' homes, so that every adult might die in the place where he or she was raised. Then the wind carried the smallpox sickness among them. Some crawled away into the woods to die; many died in their homes. Altogether about three-quarters of the Indians perished.

My great-grandfather happened to be roaming in the mountains at this period, for his wife had recently given birth to twins, and, according to custom, both parents and children had to remain in isolation for several months. The children were just beginning to walk when he returned to his village at the entrance to Pitt Lake, knowing nothing of the calamity that had overtaken its inhabitants. All his kinsmen and relatives lay dead inside their homes; only in one house did there survive a baby boy, who was vainly sucking at its dead mother's breast. They rescued the child, burned all the houses, together with the corpses that lay inside them, and built a new home for themselves several miles away.

If you dig today on the site of any of the old villages you will uncover countless bones, the remains of the Indians who perished during this epidemic of smallpox. Not many years later Europeans appeared on the Fraser, and their coming ushered in a new era.[17]

The European record of the lands and peoples around the Strait of Georgia begins in 1790, when the Spaniard Manuel Quimper sailed through the Strait of Juan de Fuca as far as the San Juan Islands. Encountering small numbers of Indigenous peoples almost wherever he went, he estimated that there were five hundred people in the strait and a thousand at its southwestern entrance near Nunez Gaona (Neah Bay). Some of these people, he thought, had been drawn from the outer coast by the great quantities of "seeds" (camas?) available in the strait.[18] The next year, the commander at Nootka, Francisco Eliza, continued the Spanish survey through most of El Gran Canal de Nuestra Señora del Rosario (the Strait of Georgia). Again, he saw many people at the entrance to the Strait of Juan de Fuca and mentioned Indigenous settlements here and there around the Gran Canal del Rosario. Along the south shore of the Strait of Juan de Fuca, Indigenous peoples "from outside" came from time to time "to trade boys"; at the edge of all the beaches were "skeletons fastened to poles."[19] The next year, both British (Vancouver) and Spanish (Galiano, Valdes) expeditions circumnavigated Vancouver Island, surveying and mapping as they went. The Spanish wrote appreciatively about the Indigenous peoples but offered few comments on Indigenous settlements or numbers. They found deserted and inhabited villages in the Gulf Islands and inhabited villages near rivers at the head of some inlets and at several other places. Beyond Johnstone Strait, on the northeast coast of Vancouver Island, the Nuchaimuses ('Namgis) were a "populous tribe."[20]

The British, who had more officers and a little more time than the Spaniards and were more inclined to treat Indigenous peoples as objects for investigation, provided a good deal more information. Reaching the southeastern end of the Strait of Juan de Fuca, Vancouver began to find deserted villages and human skeletons "promiscuously scattered about the beach, in great numbers." After local surveys in the ships' boats, his officers made similar reports; it seemed, Vancouver wrote, as if "the environs of Port Discovery were a general cemetery for the whole of the surrounding country." In some of the deserted villages, "the habitations had now fallen into decay; their inside, as well as a small surrounding space that appeared to have been formerly occupied, were overrun with weeds." There were also "lawns" on eminences fronting the sea, which Vancouver thought might have been sites of former villages; in a few of them, the framework of houses remained. In Vancouver's mind, "each of the deserted villages was nearly, if not quite, equal to contain all the scattered inhabitants we saw."[21] As the expedition continued into Puget Sound, it found more of the same.

> During this Expedition we saw a great many deserted Villages, some of them of very great extent and capable of holding many human Inhabitants – the Planks were taken away, but the Rafters stood perfect, the size of many a good deal surprised us, being much larger in girth than the Discovery's Main mast. A Human

face was cut on most of them, and some were carved to resemble the head of a Bear or Wolf – The largest of the Villages I should imagine had not been inhabited for five or six years, as brambles and bushes were growing up a considerable height.[22]

In a "favoured" land that was "most grateful to the eye" there were not many people.[23] "We saw only the few natives which are mentioned, silence prevailed everywhere, the feathered race, as if unable to endure the absence of man, had also utterly deserted this place."[24]

The expedition continued north and found more deserted villages along the eastern shore of the Strait of Georgia. At Birch Bay, there was "a very large Village now overgrown with a thick crop of Nettles and bushes."[25] There were deserted villages in Burrard Inlet, Howe Sound, and Jervis Inlet and only occasional "small parties of Indians either hunting or fishing [that] avoided us as much as possible."[26] Farther north, Toba Inlet "was nearly destitute of inhabitants," although there was a deserted but well-fortified village that "seemed so skillfully contrived and so firmly and well executed as rendered it difficult to consider the work of the untutored tribes we had been accustomed to meet."[27] Only as the expedition travelled into and through Johnstone Strait did it encounter a country that was "infinitely more populous than the shores of the gulf of Georgia."[28]

The next Europeans in the region were the American overland explorers, Lewis and Clark. Near the mouth of the Willamette, a few miles from the present day city of Portland, they found the remains of "a very large village."

> I endeavored to obtain from these people the situation of their nation, if scattered or what had become of the natives who must have peopled this great town. An old man who appeared of some note among them and father to my guide brought forward a woman who was badly marked with the Small Pox and made signs that they all died with the disorder that marked her face, and which she was very near dieing with when a girl. From the age of his woman this Destructive disorder I judge must have been about 28

or 30 years past, and about the time the Clatsops inform us that this disorder raged in their towns and destroyed their nation.[29]

A year later, David Thompson wrote from Kootenay House in the Rocky Mountain Trench: "These people the Kootenays were once numerous, but being continually at war with Nations more powerful and far better armed than themselves, they diminished continually, 'till at length the Small Pox almost entirely rooted them out, leaving only about 40 families, and now they may count about 50 Families of 6 & 7 to a Family."[30]

On the lower Columbia three years later, he was asked: "Is it true that the white men ... have brought with them the Small Pox to destroy us ... is this true and are we all soon to die."[31] Descending the Fraser River in 1808, Simon Fraser mentioned smallpox once: "The small pox was in the camp [an Indigenous village some two hundred kilometres from the mouth of the Fraser River] and several Natives were marked with it."[32] The fur trader Ross Cox, who spent two months at the mouth of the Columbia in 1814, said that the Indigenous peoples remembered smallpox with "a superstitious dread."[33] John Work, a member of a Hudson's Bay Company (HBC) expedition sent from the Columbia in 1824 to explore the lower Fraser, noted that an old chief near the mouth of the Fraser River seemed to be marked with smallpox.[34] The next year a Scottish botanist, John Scouler, visited the Strait of Georgia in an HBC ship and saw an elderly, pockmarked native in the retinue of the Cowichan chief Chapea at Point Roberts, just south of the mouth of the Fraser. He had seen no other direct evidence of smallpox on the Northwest Coast.

> The rarity of such an occurrence at once indicated the fatality of the disease and the dread they entertain of it. This epidemic broke out among them in 17— and soon depopulated the eastern coast of America, and those on the Columbia were not secure behind the Rocky Mountains, and the ravages of the disease were only bounded by the Pacific Ocean. The Cheenooks to the present time speak of it with horror, and are exceedingly anxious to obtain that medicine which protects the whites meaning vaccination. Such is

the dread of this disease that when about to plunder the tribes of the interior, they have been deterred by the threat of disseminating smallpox among them.[35]

Three years later, the HB established Fort Langley on the lower Fraser. In the fort journal (1827–30) and in the correspondence associated with the fort's early years, physical evidence of smallpox is not mentioned.

Indigenous oral traditions and the texts of European explorers and traders provide largely independent records of late eighteenth-century disease and depopulation around the Strait of Georgia. Besides their distinct cultural contexts, the two accounts are differently positioned in relation to the events they describe. The one grows out of the curiosity and ignorance of outsiders and the durability of writing; the other, out of the intimacy of experience and the shifting nature of oral tradition. Yet the contents of one seem to be broadly reproduced in that of the other. The two sets are mutually reinforcing and undoubtedly address the same horrendous event: late precontact depopulation around the Strait of Georgia and Puget Sound caused principally by smallpox.

The outbreak of smallpox was part of a pandemic that broke out in central Mexico in 1779 and quickly spread.[36] In 1780–81, it devastated the Guatemalan Highlands and a decade later reached southern Chile, enabling the Spaniards to expand into an area they had been unable to conquer for 250 years.[37] The New Mexican pueblos were hit in 1780; from there, transported indirectly by horse, smallpox diffused rapidly northward to affect all groups on the northern plains and, by early 1782, the forest Cree north and west of Lake Manitoba.[38] From there, it soon reached the Denesuliné (Chipewyan). According to David Thompson, who was on the plains a few years later, "From the Chipeways it extended over all the Indians of the forest to its northward extremity and by the [Dakota] Sioux over all the Indians of the Plains and crossed the Rocky Mountains."[39] The same epidemic affected groups around the Great Lakes. Thompson, who estimated that half to three-fifths of the people on the northern plains had died, talked with an Orcadian employee (from Orkney) of the Hudson's Bay Company who had witnessed the devastation: stinking tents in which all were dead, bodies eaten by wolves and dogs, "survivors in such a state of despair and despondence that they could hardly converse with us." "The countries were in a manner depopulated."[40] Twenty-three years later, when Lewis and Clark reached the middle Missouri, they found the "fallen down earth of the houses" and the scattered bones of men and animals in empty villages.[41]

An elderly man at Fort Cumberland on the North Saskatchewan River told Thompson that a war party of "Nahathaway" (upper Churchill and Saskatchewan River Cree) had contracted the disease from the Snake (Shoshone).[42] William Tomison, the trader at Cumberland House on the North Saskatchewan River, understood that the disease had reached the Shoshone from the Spaniards.[43] Certainly, smallpox was among the Shoshone in 1781. From a major rendezvous in southwestern Wyoming, the Shoshone traded with the Bitterroot Salish (Flathead), Nez Perce (Nimiipuu), Walla Walla, and various peoples along the Snake River.[44] Any of these trading connections could have brought smallpox to the lower Columbia. So could parties of Sallish, Kalispel (Pend d'Oreille), Nez Perce, and others that crossed the Rockies to hunt and raid along the upper Missouri.[45] In 1840, Asa Smith, a Congregational missionary, reported that sixty or seventy years before smallpox had reached the Nez Perce this way, "very few surviving the attack of the disease."[46] In 1829 the Hudson's Bay Company trader John Work reported "a dreadful visitation of smallpox" on the Columbia Plateau near Fort Colvile that, he estimated, had occurred fifty or sixty years before. The Jesuit missionary Gregory Mengarini reported smallpox among the Bitterroot Salish at about the same time.[47]

[...]

In southern British Columbia, the process of disease-related depopulation probably began with the smallpox epidemic of 1782 (Figure 5).[48] Eventually, in recurring epidemics over approximately a century, smallpox visited all Indigenous groups in the province, some several times. However, it was only the most spectacular of a complex of European infectious diseases that together were far more devastating than any one alone. The eventual result, everywhere, was severe depopulation at precisely the time that changing technologies of transportation and communication were bringing more and more of the resources of the

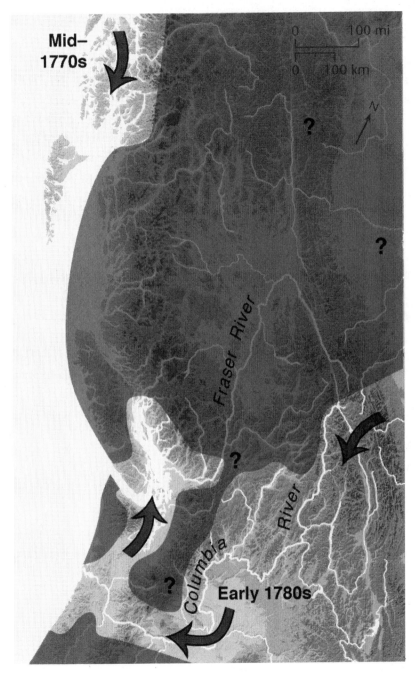

FIGURE 5
Approximate distribution of smallpox, 1770s and 1780s

northwestern corner of North America within reach of the capitalist world economy. Here was an almost empty land, so it seemed, for the taking, and the means of developing and transporting many of its resources. Such was the underlying geographical basis of the bonanza that awaited immigrants to British Columbia.

Passing through the province by train just before the First World War, Rupert Brooke, a poet as English as the ancient village of Grantchester where he lived, missed the dead and "the friendly presence of ghosts." Mountain breezes, he said, "have nothing to remember and everything to promise."[49] This was a stranger's conceit. Jimmy Peters, who poked as a lad in the graves of his ancestors, knew otherwise. So did Charles Hill-Tout, who listened to Mulks, the old Squamish historian, and the Scowlitz Elders, who believed "their race is doomed to die out and disappear."[50] Rupert Brooke was travelling through a profound settlement discontinuity, measured not, as it would have been in Europe, by decaying cities, wasted fields, and overgrown orchards but by the abandonment of countless seasonal settlement sites, the unnaming and renaming of the land, and the belief of some that their world was coming to an end and of others that it was opening towards a prosperous future.

PART 2
Early Settlements

Acadia:
Settling the Marshlands

Acadia (the French colony centred on the Bay of
Fundy) and Canada (the French colony centred on the
St. Lawrence River) were the first settler colonies in the
country eventually known as Canada. Acadia never
attracted many immigrant settlers and was never very
securely governed. Beginning in 1755, at the start of the
Seven Years War, the British rounded up and dispersed
most of its French-speaking population, then more
than ten thousand people. This small, fragile colony is a
fascinating early window on social and cultural change
in a settler colonial society. Virtually all the immigrants
to it were from France, and it is broadly accurate to
describe Acadia as a French peasant society. But no
French peasantry was quite like the Acadian peasantry.
The complex hierarchy of French power was not at hand.
Although many details of French peasant life crossed

From *The Reluctant Land* (Vancouver: UBC Press, 2008), 52–65.

the Atlantic to Acadia, no French peasants quite lived as did the Acadians, or spoke the same French. In a different place, lives were working themselves out in different ways. A distinctive people was coming into being.

ARLY IN THE SEVENTEENTH century, the French crown began to attach the responsibility for colonization to the monopolies it granted to fur traders. French settler colonies began to appear and with them farms and towns, new forms of European settlement in northeastern North America. At first, these were proprietary colonies chartered by the Crown and administered privately. Canada, the colony along the lower St. Lawrence River, was Crown-granted to the Company of One Hundred Associates (the Company of New France) in 1627 and obligated by its charter to bring four thousand colonists in fifteen years. In Acadia, the colony around the Bay of Fundy (La Baie Française), trading privileges were also coupled with the responsibility to colonize. However, colonization and fur trading were not complementary activities; trading companies never met their charter responsibilities; and, in 1663, a young Louis XIV and his ministers revoked the charter of the Company of One Hundred Associates. Canada then became a Crown colony administered by government officials. At this date, the English held Acadia, but when France got it back in 1670, it too became a Crown colony.

With the creation of colonies, women began to cross the Atlantic in some number; as they did, French settlement in northeastern North America became permanent. Unlike the migratory workforce of the fishery, some of the immigrants to Canada and Acadia stayed. They were not numerous. In Canada perhaps a thousand immigrants, many in families, arrived and settled during the tenure of the Company of One Hundred Associates; another eight or nine thousand came and left descendants during the years of royal government from 1663 to

1759 (many more came and left or died in the colony without issue). Acadia drew only a trickle of immigrants who settled and left descendants, probably not many more than three hundred. A few families had come before 1654, when the English captured the colony, and hardly a hundred immigrants, almost all of them men, came after 1670. Most of the men were soldiers, indentured servants (*engagés*), or fishermen who had managed to quit the fishery for a marshland farm and an Acadian woman.

In both colonies after the early years, most immigrants were single, young, and from urban backgrounds. These immigrants reached places associated with fur trade economies that depended on Indigenous labour. For most of them, farming at the edge of a mixed coniferous-deciduous forest and near the northern climatic limit of agriculture was their only possible livelihood. Plantation crops were out of the question. Only the hardier crops and livestock of northwestern France could be raised and then only after farms had been hewed out of the forest or made by diking and draining marshes. Markets for farm produce were few and hard to reach. In these circumstances, family farms began to spread along the St. Lawrence River and on the marshes around the Bay of Fundy. In Canada, the small town of Quebec had emerged by the 1680s and Montreal shortly thereafter, each in a countryside stretched along the river. Port Royal, the largest centre in Acadia, was never more than a village – a small garrisoned fort, a warehouse, a couple of stores, a church, and a scatter of houses and barns.

Tucked away in the continental interior some twelve hundred kilometres from the open ocean, Canada was not easily taken, especially after its towns were walled and garrisoned, a military alliance was in place with Indigenous groups around the Great Lakes, and the Canadian militia emerged as a mobile, forest-experienced fighting force. The colony was in French hands from 1632 to 1759, and during these years the French state often administered it more closely than any province in France. Open to the North Atlantic and situated in the borderland between the French and English positions in North America, Acadia was administered much more irregularly. The colony fell to the English in 1613, 1628, and 1654 and was not restored to France until 1670. Twenty years later, during another French-English war (the War of the League of Augsburg, 1689–97), an expedition from Massachusetts again captured Port Royal; Acadia would not be fully recognized as a French possession until 1697. In 1710, Port Royal fell yet again, this time to a force of two thousand English marines and New England militiamen. Three years later the Treaty of Utrecht (ending the War of the Spanish Succession, 1701–13) confirmed the loss; the Acadians, French-speaking and Roman Catholic, found themselves in an English colony that did not know quite what to do with them. More often than not in these fluctuating circumstances, they were hardly governed.

Settled by similar people, largely dependent on mixed family farming, and very differently served by the state, these early French colonies raise fundamental questions about the transferability of society and culture from one place to another. Their settlers were no longer in a country of 20 million people living on scarce, unevenly distributed land and within a mosaic of local cultures and steep hierarchies of social and political power. *That* France was an ocean away and, for the illiterate majority of immigrants, soon out of reach. At hand were a forest, a few Indigenous peoples, and elements – more here, less there – of French power. Migration had left a great deal behind, subjected immigrants to new experiences, and, overall, changed the context of their lives.

But what were the leading edges of change, and how substantial and how influential were they? Is it possible to generalize about the nature of social and cultural change in European settler colonies overseas? Over the years, a large and contentious literature has emerged around these questions. It has been possible to argue – as in their very different ways did early nineteenth-century political economists, Karl Marx, and the American frontier historian Frederick Jackson Turner – that the changing relative cost of land and labour reorganized settler societies overseas. Others have suggested that settler colonies became, in a sense, refugia where particular clusters of European ideas flourished and extended their lifespans. Among these scholars are the English historian Arnold Toynbee, who held that European religions tended to fossilize in colonies overseas, and the American political scientist Louis Hartz, who posited that only fragments of European cultures emigrated overseas, where, no longer checked by competing interests, they reproduced and expanded. Early Canada and Acadia, two small colonies settled in somewhat different circumstances by immigrants of the same national background, most of whom became family farmers, pose these larger analytical questions with particular clarity.

Partly because the Acadian settlements around the Bay of Fundy were shattered by deportations that began in 1755 and systematically depopulated the region over the next several years, a huge literature has accumulated about them. For the French historian and Christian moralist Rameau de Saint-Père, writing in Paris in the 1870s, Acadia was a feudal colony in which seigneurs provided leadership for a Catholic people of simple wants, high moral purpose, and the French, Catholic instincts of civility and progress. For Francis Parkman, prominent nineteenth-century American historian, the Acadians were a poverty-stricken Catholic people living in a rough, poverty-induced equality. For Émile Lauvrière, a French historian writing in the 1920s, Acadian society was "une sorte de communisme spontané," made possible by the abundance of land and selfless moral virtues. For Andrew Clark, an American historical geographer writing in the 1960s, the Acadians were sharp traders – as shrewd as the Yankee merchants with whom they dealt – linked to the North Atlantic trading system. Myth succeeds myth, and Acadia has become, in effect, a moral and social primal variously constructed by those who have written about the colony.

That said, much about Acadian life is known, especially since the publication of historian Naomi Griffiths's monumental book *From Migrant to Acadian* (2005). For example, it is known that, from its small beginning, the Acadian population grew rapidly, largely by natural increase, and that the Acadians found niches for a mixed crop-livestock agriculture, derived from northwestern France, on the marshes created by the great tidal range of the Bay of Fundy. By the 1650s, if not before, the Acadians were diking these marshes, fitting the dikes with sluice gates (*aboîteaux*) and clapper valves to allow fresh water to drain and exclude the sea. Land so diked and left for a few years to freshen made excellent arable (plowland) and pasture. It is known that there was no agricultural export staple and very little local market beyond the garrison, whether French or English, at Port Royal, and also that Acadians traded with New England and, after 1717, with Louisbourg. English officials at Port Royal in the 1730s worried that as many as six to seven hundred cattle and two thousand sheep were exported to Louisbourg each year, although the Louisbourg records show few such imports, and it is far from clear how large this trade actually was. The volume of Acadian trade with New England, which was illegal when the French controlled Acadia, cannot be established precisely but certainly was larger than that with Louisbourg. From time to time, merchants from Boston operated stores at Port Royal or sent trading ships to the Acadian settlements farther up the bay (primarily to obtain furs). For their part, small Acadian-built ships traded in Boston, occasionally even in the Caribbean.

It is also clear that colonial state administrations, whether French or British, impinged weakly on Acadian lives. In the 1630s and 1640s, at the beginning of continuous Acadian settlement, feuds between the holders of different royal commissions left the few Acadian settlers largely to their own devices. Between 1654 and 1670, when Acadia was in English hands, English control was confined to the forts; the Acadians fended for themselves on their marshland farms. In 1670, when the French regained control of Acadia, it became a royal colony defended by French troops and administered by a governor sent from France and an intendant in Canada (an Acadian governor complained that it was easier to communicate with France than with Canada). At this point, the official regulation of Acadian life increased. Titles to large undeveloped seigneuries were rescinded, and smaller seigneuries were conceded. Attempts may have been made to organize local militias. Corvée labour probably was demanded for public projects, and troops probably were billeted in peasant households. A royal warehouse was built at Port Royal, and, in principle, trade was more regulated. But by this time settlement was dispersed on marshes around the Bay of Fundy, and just how far such organization reached into the countryside is impossible to say. Probably not very far. With eleven different governors or deputy governors between 1670 and 1710, there was little administrative stability, and there was never enough money to create an efficient bureaucracy. Officials complained that the Acadians were independent and ungovernable. An illegal trade with New England continued. In any event, Acadia was a royal French colony for only forty years, during eight of which an

English force occupied Port Royal. After 1710 the British again controlled the forts but struggled to administer a countryside inhabited by unfamiliar French-speaking people whom, as Catholics, English law excluded from public office and jury duty. Acadians cooperated with the new colonial administration in various ways – repairing the fortification at Port Royal (renamed Annapolis Royal), piloting British ships in the Bay of Fundy, selling foodstuffs for the garrison, and providing some liaison with the Mi'kmaq, the Indigenous peoples of the area. Elected Acadian deputies served on a council appointed by the governor; the minutes of the council at Annapolis Royal suggest that they acted as channels of communication for council orders and proclamations, as some approximation of a rural police force, and as adjudicators (drawing on jumbled elements of French civil and English common law) of civil and, more rarely, criminal disputes. The deputies were also expected to oversee the maintenance of roads and to collect quit rents (a small charge intended less as a source of revenue than as a measure of the authority of the British Crown). The Acadians cooperated with a British colonial administration in these ways, but the British state was hardly a burden on them: it neither maintained local militias nor recruited troops; nor (apart from the nominal quit rent), did it tax this countryside. For the most part, the Acadians looked after their own lives and maintained their neutrality in the face of confrontations between Britain and France. When, in 1730, most of them swore an oath of allegiance to Britain, they did so with qualifications: as long as they remained British subjects on British soil, they would not take up arms with the French.

It was in the context of rapid population growth, available marshland that could be turned to a northwestern European crop-livestock combination, limited markets, uncertain geopolitical control, and weak or erratic interference from above that the Acadians took up land around and eventually beyond the Bay of Fundy. From a base on the marshlands at Port Royal, their settlement spread to all major marshes around the bay (Figure 6). By the 1730s, as marshland became scarce, more families turned to the uplands, principally by moving to Île Saint-Jean (Prince Edward Island). In 1750 there were at least ten thousand Acadians, virtually all living on family farms and descended from a small number of immigrants. The family farm was the basic unit of production and the primary locus of sociability. At the intersection of strikingly different ecologies, it provided subsistence for a family and, eventually, some modest surplus for sale, basic peasant goals everywhere. Acadian farmers principally raised wheat, peas, and hay on the diked marshland (also some oats, rye, barley, and flax) and pastured their cattle there. In kitchen gardens or fields on higher ground near the farmhouse at the edge of the marshland, they grew the hardy vegetables of western France, particularly cabbages and turnips, and also a few fruit trees, apples primarily but pears and cherries as well. Most farmers kept a few hogs, sheep, and poultry; by the early eighteenth century, many of them had a horse or

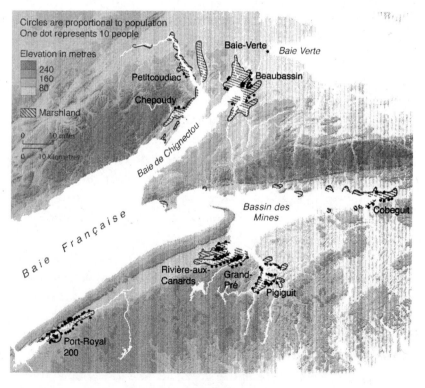

FIGURE 6
Acadian marshland settlement, 1707 |
After J. Daigle, in R. Cole Harris, ed., Geoffrey J. Matthews, cart., *Historical Atlas of Canada,*
vol. 1, *From the Beginning to 1800* (Toronto: University of Toronto Press, 1987), plate 29

two. With the forest (and therefore wood, berries, and game) and the Bay of Fundy (and therefore fish) as well as diked marshland and a kitchen garden all at hand (Figure 7), the Acadian farm provided the large portion of a family's domestic needs in return for the consumption of virtually all of its labour.

Groups of such farms constituted a countryside that depended on broad grass-covered dikes some two to six metres high. Behind the dikes were fields of wheat, peas, and hay; behind these diked fields at the edge of the upland were farmhouses, gardens, some upland fields, and small farm buildings. In some places the farmhouses were considerably isolated from each other, in others grouped in hamlets (usually of close kin), in yet others scattered in irregular lines above the marsh. These buildings were wooden (often on stone sills), of various forms of log or post-and-beam construction, and usually whitewashed. Roofing consisted of thatch, bark, or board. Beyond the dikes at low tide were tidal mud flats, at high tide the sea. Behind the upland buildings and gardens was a dark, predominantly coniferous forest. It was a strikingly distinctive landscape, like no other anywhere. Within it were the local services required by a peasant society: small grist- and sawmills, a blacksmith, a wheelwright, a cooper, occasionally a merchant (most tradesmen were also farmers). There were also small churches, which at least one French observer likened to barns. This was a reproducible countryside that first emerged along the Rivière au Dauphin at Port Royal and then spread, with some variation, as Acadian settlement expanded. It became the local context of Acadian life.

That context provided relatively well for the ordinary peasant family, as the rapid growth of the Acadian population, virtually entirely by natural increase, attests. For all the work of building and maintaining dikes, farmland was far more accessible than in France, and, as a result, the subsistence needs of farm families were more easily met. As long as land was available, the means of social reproduction was at hand. In these circumstances, Acadian women married at an earlier age, on average, than French peasant women; their children, better fed than their equivalents in France, were much more likely to reach adulthood. Families with ten or twelve surviving children were common. Close relatives often lived on adjacent farms (perhaps on divided parental

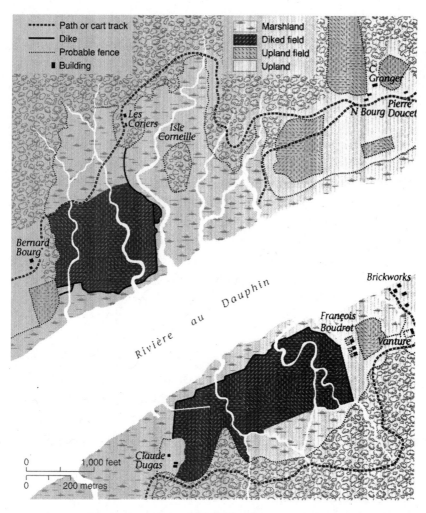

FIGURE 7
Acadian farms near Port Royal, 1710 (cartographer, Delabat) |
After J. Daigle, in Harris and Matthews, *Historical Atlas of Canada*, vol. 1, plate 29

land), and hamlets of close kin seem to have been a common form of Acadian settlement. The work of building and maintaining the dikes was probably shared among such relatives. Beyond these local kin groups were more extensive ties of consanguinity. After a time, most people in each settlement were related to each other, and blood ties linked all the Acadian settlements – as would be expected given a small founding population and few incoming marriage partners. In this sense, the Acadians were soon a people constructed around nuclear farm families and their myriad genealogical extensions.

The question, then, is what lay on top of these peasant families? The answer, apparently, is not very much. Of the powers that bore directly on the French peasantry, the church appears to have survived best. The Acadians were erratically served by resident or itinerant priests responsible to the bishop in Quebec. The priests were supported either by an annual "pension" or by a tithe introduced, with some resistance, in the 1680s and fixed, on instructions from Quebec, at one twenty-sixth of the grain harvest. When Acadia became a British colony, the priests remained and were supported by the Acadians but viewed suspiciously by a colonial administration convinced, not without cause in some cases, that they conspired with the French. Besides performing their religious functions, priests often arbitrated civil disputes. A few itinerant or parish priests and a distant bishop were, however, a very lean slice of the hierarchy of the Catholic Church in France.

A feudal regime seems to have fared even less well. In France almost all land was held from the Crown in seigneuries, and seigneurs were expected to subgrant it through a descending hierarchy that eventually reached the peasant landholding (the *roture* in French legal terminology), for which annual rents were due and that required tenants to use, and pay for, a variety of seigneurial services. A few seigneuries were granted in Acadia, most of them by the Crown after 1670, but the extent to which seigneurial rights were ever exercised is very unclear. Early Acadian seigneurs were usually fur traders for whom a seigneurie was a means of acquiring a trading monopoly. One or two may have organized the initial settlement of their seigneurie (dikes, land allocation), and probably the basic seigneurial charges were collected for a time here and there. A few seigneurs drew up notarized deeds for the land they conceded to tenants (*en roture*). A notary established for a time at Port Royal followed the Coutume de Paris, the codification of French customary law used in much of northern France. One surviving deed, issued in 1679 for land near Port Royal that the tenant had already farmed for some years, describes the holding in a system of metes and bounds (an irregular survey sensitive to local physical features).

Metes and bounds were probably the rule, but most farmers probably never held a notarized deed from a seigneur for their land or paid any seigneurial dues. Acadian settlement was not far from squatting, with some leaven – more or less in different places – of seigneurial control. After 1713 the legal status of seigneurial tenure was as much in doubt as its practice had always been. Occasionally, British colonial officials did report that seigneurial dues as well as quit rents were being collected here and there. Whatever the law, from the seigneur's perspective the management of a seigneurie in a sparsely populated colony without an export staple was hardly a paying proposition.

Acadia was, overwhelmingly, a peasant society. Its land, more available than land in France, had provided the opportunity for a few people to create farms and reproduce peasant families through several generations. The economy, never strong except during the early years of the fur trade, had deflected capital. The smallness of the population, the low return from rent, and the legal confusion following conquest had deterred seigneurial management. France and England both claimed sovereignty over Acadia, and the Acadians could not avoid some effects of the wars between these powers, but they were largely free of the annual state exactions that, in France, were another heavy burden on the peasantry. A few settlers were not worth the expense of close administration. One might think of Acadia as a peasant "fragment" of France, but not (as Louis Hartz would have had it) because peasants had settled there. The majority of immigrants to Acadia came from urban backgrounds. Acadia was a peasant society because land that provided fairly generously for peasant households did not provide much support for the hierarchy of power that, in France, sat upon the peasantry. There was little inducement for these elements of French rural society to come to Acadia; if they did come, there was little to sustain them.

What, then, can be said about social power and culture within this peasant society? The records are exceedingly thin. It was not an egalitarian society. There was no wealth, but some of the farmer-merchants who operated small ships out of the Bay of Fundy must have been comfortably off and probably provided much of the Acadians' political leadership. A favourable inheritance, an advantageous marriage, and perhaps a particular shrewdness allowed a few farmers to own as many as forty to fifty head of cattle and to plant almost fifty *arpents* (one arpent equals five-sixths of an acre) of field crops each year. The largest holdings at Beaubassin and Chignecto, settlements at the foot of the bay, were on this scale and may have belonged to farmer-merchants. Near Port Royal, a French immigrant who arrived some time before 1715 and married into a well-established Acadian family owned a good deal of land, two gristmills, a sawmill, and two small trading vessels – a fortune by Acadian standards. Most families had far less but seem to have had enough to get by. Excavations of an Acadian house near Port Royal reveal imported iron tools and kitchen crockery, purchases that sales of farm produce allowed. There was no reason for healthy young people to be landless, although the dikeable marshlands were taken up by the 1730s, and some young families had to move to Île Saint-Jean. Overall, the social range in the Acadian countryside was slight compared to that of French peasant societies, but presumably in Acadia, as in other societies where the social range was narrow, fine differences were particularly remarked within intricate, closely read, local hierarchies. Most of such detail cannot now be recovered, although it is known that, caught as the Acadians were between French and British spheres of influence, allegiances even within families to one or the other were often sharply divided.

Acadia did not reproduce any of the many French peasant cultures. Acadian culture merged the various local ways that immigrants carried in their minds across the Atlantic with the common experience of marshland life around the Bay of Fundy. People from different regional backgrounds in western France mixed and married in Acadia. Their progeny further mixed the brew. Not all the remembered French ways survived; even in the immigrant generation, a selection was being made based on the relevance of particular memories to the circumstances of marshland life and, to some extent, on the number of people sharing them. French pasts were being recomposed and recontextualized in a different setting on the other side of an ocean. To this was added the experience of the marshlands and some contact with the Mi'kmaq – in at least five of the seventy-odd households at Port Royal in 1671, the wife was Mi'kmaq – contacts that were close in the early years and then increasingly distant as the needs of settler and of hunter-fisher-gatherer societies diverged. After a time, a way of life emerged that, though French in most details, did not correspond to any particular French rural culture. The Acadians spoke, for example, a distinctive dialect of French; indeed, the whole Acadian way of life might be thought of as a distinctive dialect of French peasant culture that reflected more of its particular New World context and less of its diverse French inheritance with each generation. The regional cultural variety within this way of life cannot now be recaptured, but given the small number of immigrants to Acadia, the blood relations that ran through its society, the common marshland experience, and fairly easy travel by water and eventually by trail between settlements, there is reason to surmise that Acadian culture was fairly homogeneous.

The marshlands and the family farms made from them, the keys to the Acadian world, were far more attractive to some elements of French society than to others. Essentially, they provided a type of access to land that rewarded the labour of the peasant household. In terms of political economy, the entry costs of land were too low to allow for the reproduction of the social hierarchy of the European countryside. Moreover, the mixing of peoples of different French regional backgrounds, the selective retention of former ways, and the ongoing experience with the marshlands prevented the replication of any particular French peasant culture. The distinctive French peasant society that emerged in Acadia was the product, essentially, of these circumstances. In this reading (as mythic as many others?), the terms of access to land were as critical as, in their very different ways, the political economists, Marx, and Turner held. If it is useful to think of Acadia as a refugium of a variant of French peasant culture, this was not so much because a few French peasants had settled there as because, within the technologies and possibilities of the day, the Bay of Fundy context in which settlers found themselves had largely eliminated any other option.

A few Acadians, more of them women than men, moved to Louisbourg, the French fortress town on Île Royale built to protect the entrance to the Gulf of St. Lawrence after the loss of Acadia and Newfoundland

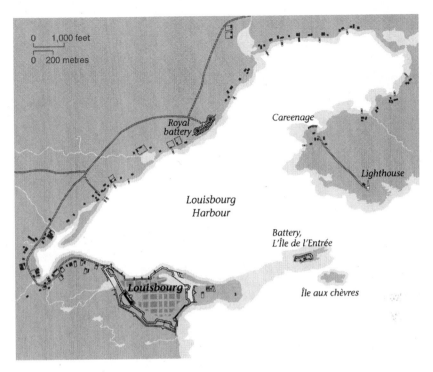

FIGURE 8

Plan of Louisbourg Harbour, 1742 | After K. Donovan, cart. unknown, in Harris and Matthews, *Historical Atlas of Canada*, vol. 1, plate 24

under the terms of the Treaty of Utrecht (1713). In so doing they entered a drastically different society. Fishing installations lined Louisbourg Harbour (Figure 8), but the rocky, often fogbound land behind barely permitted gardening. An opportunity for the generational reproduction of farm families did not exist. Rather, the town of Louisbourg was the largest military fortification of its day in North America, a centre of the French cod fishery, and a major North Atlantic port. Its massive walls enclosed a grid of streets and a society dominated by rank in the colonial administration or the military, merchant power, and wage relationships. The town provided the trades and services of a military base and a port; manufactured goods were imported. Its population was exceedingly diverse, the women usually born in the New World, the men coming from all French provinces and a few from elsewhere in Europe. Its society was stratified and hierarchical. A French garrison town and port perched at a western edge of the North Atlantic, yet connected administratively, commercially, and personally to France, Louisbourg was, in many ways, the diametric opposite of the peasant farming societies the Acadians had created on the marshes around the Bay of Fundy.

Of Poverty and Helplessness
in Petite-Nation

In the early nineteenth century, most of the settlers in the Ottawa Valley seigneurie of Petite-Nation had come out of a well-established Canadian population that had developed along the St. Lawrence River over several generations. Like the Acadians, they were no longer quite French. Like many others at this time, they had left the lower St. Lawrence because land and employment had become scarce. The relative opportunity available to their ancestors when land was at hand and labour was scarce was not available to them. Most of them went south, into the United States. Those who went north encountered a margin of the Canadian Shield, commercial capital in the form of the timber trade, and an overstocked labour market

I wrote this article almost fifty years ago, and am still pleased with it. I would caution readers, however, on two counts. First, Petite-Nation was situated within a body of

From "Of Poverty and Helplessness in Petite-Nation," *Canadian Historical Review* 52, 1 (1971): 23–50.

French customary law of feudal origin and a related vocabulary. A *seigneurie* was a grant of land that could be subgranted and that was held in principle from the king in return for an oath of fealty. The holder of such a grant was a *seigneur.* A *roture* was a concession of land that could not be subgranted and that was held from a seigneur. The *cens* was a token payment that identified this type of concession. Legally, a *censistaire* was anyone who paid a cens; more generally, the term was broadly synonymous with "peasant" or, in Canada, with "habitant." A *rente* was a substantial annual charge levied by a seigneur on the holder of a roture. A seigneur's *droit de retrait,* was the right to acquire a roture offered for sale by paying the sale price less any accumulated debts, and the *lods et ventes* was a tax, imposed by the seigneur, of one-twelfth of a roture's sale price. Not a legal term, a *côte* was a short line of rotures and settlement along a river or road.

Second, I was shocked by the poverty and lack of institutional support for struggling lives that I found in Petite-Nation, and this led me to say in conclusion, as I would not now, that the rural heart of French Canada was hollow. Nor did I know, as I know now, that wherever across the span of Canada, from the highlands of Cape Breton to many odd corners of British Columbia, people without means tried to farm where farming was hardly possible, the results were much the same. Moreover, be somewhat wary of my closing picture of the boisterous independence of habitant life along the lower St. Lawrence during the French regime. The state billeted troops in that countryside; local militias drilled there. The largest and most populated seigneuries, usually held by religious orders, were carefully managed.

URING THE CENTURIES of white settlement along the lower
St. Lawrence River, there have been three major migrations
of French-speaking people: the first bringing some ten thousand French immigrants across the Atlantic before 1760; the second, beginning shortly before 1820, taking French Canadians to the Eastern Townships, to New England, or to the Canadian Shield; and the third, following closely on the second, gradually urbanizing French Canadian society. Each of these migrations was predominantly a movement of poor people, and each characteristically involved individuals or nuclear families rather than groups or communities. Their results, however, have been vastly different. The first created a modestly prosperous base of agricultural settlement along the lower St. Lawrence. The third brought French Canadians into the technological orbit of the modern world. But the second, especially when it turned north to the Canadian Shield, led to poverty as acute as that of any sharecropper in the American South and then, often within a generation or two, to land abandonment and migration to the cities. The magnitude of the third migration was partly a product of the failure of the second, and this failure still echoes through contemporary Quebec.

Here, the focus is on the French Canadian migration to and settlement in the seigneurie of Petite-Nation, a small segment of the Quebec rim of the Canadian Shield some forty miles east of Ottawa. I describe the coming of French Canadians to Petite-Nation and the ways of life there before approximately 1860; I then considers the reasons for the extreme poverty and the institutional weakness, which were, perhaps, the dominant characteristics of French Canadian life in the seigneurie. Although in most general respects the habitant economy and society of Petite-Nation were reproduced throughout the Shield fringe of southern Quebec, there is some justification for a close look at this particular place. It belonged to Louis-Joseph Papineau, the leading French Canadian nationalist of his day and a man who believed, at least in his later years, that the seigneurial system and a rural life were central to the cultural survival of French Canada; and it can be studied in detail in the voluminous Papineau Papers in the Bibliothèque et Archives nationales du Québec.

The Occupation of Petite-Nation

Although the penetration of the Shield for agricultural purposes had begun as early as the 1730s,[1] it gained little momentum until well into the nineteenth century. By 1820 a great many rotures in the older seigneuries had been subdivided until they produced a minimum subsistence living. French Canadian agriculture – inflexible, uncompetitive, and largely subsistent – was incapable of supporting a growing population. Some of the young French Canadians whom the land could no longer support moved to the local village, finding there a way point, a time, and a place of transition between the closely knit society of kin and côte and a new life among strangers. Others moved directly from the parental roture to a destination outside the St. Lawrence lowland. Whether from farm or village, French Canadians left the parish of their birth as individuals or in nuclear families. Those who settled in Petite-Nation before 1820 had come from the Island of Montreal, Île Jésus, and the surrounding mainland seigneuries. Most later settlers came from a scattering of parishes in the lower Ottawa Valley (see Figure 9).[2] A few of the earliest settlers had been brought to Petite-Nation by the seigneur,[3] a few others had scouted out the land and brought some capital to their destination[4] but the great majority came unassisted and penniless. They had heard that there were jobs and land up the Ottawa Valley; they had set out with no specific place in mind, had perhaps worked here and there, and arrived, almost by chance, in Petite-Nation.[5]

Petite-Nation was a tract of land approximately fifteen miles a side and bounded on the south by the Ottawa River. Barely a tenth of the seigneurie lay in the Ottawa River plain; the rest, in the hilly southern fringe of the Canadian Shield.[6] Only approximately a third of the land was at all suited to agriculture, the rest being too rough, too swampy, or its soils too thin and acidic. The best soils, although they were hardly good even by the standard of those in Quebec, had developed on the marine clays of the lowland or on alluvial material in the north-south valleys in the Shield that once had been glacial spillways. The forest cover of this abrupt, knobby land was a typical segment of the mixed Laurentian

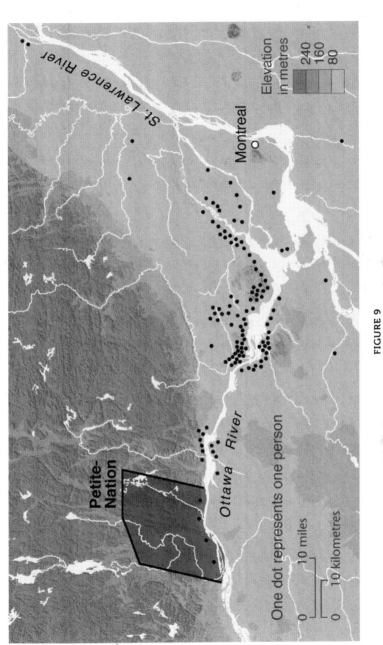

FIGURE 9

Place of birth of adults in the parish of Saint-André Avellin, Petite-Nation, 1861

forest:[7] white, red, and jack pine, fir, and white spruce predominated in rocky, excessively drained areas; black spruce, cedar, and larch dominated the bogs; and a beech-maple-birch association that included white ash, red oak, poplar, and a few coniferous species was common on more moderate sites. The climate was considerably more severe than at Montreal. Along the Ottawa River, the average frost-free period was 125 days and was less than 115 days along the northern border of the seigneurie. The climatic limit of wheat cultivation crossed Petite-Nation along the boundary between the Shield and the lowland.

The white settlement of this tract of land began in 1807 or 1808, when Joseph Papineau, then seigneur of Petite-Nation, contracted to cut a small quantity of squared timber[8] and brought some twenty French Canadian woodcutters to the seigneurie.[9] Early in 1809 he sold two-fifths of his seigneurie for £7,220 to a Boston timber merchant, Robert Fletcher,[10] who in March of that year arrived in Petite-Nation with 160 well-provisioned New Englanders.[11] Within a year, Fletcher had defaulted on payments, committed suicide,[12] and his portion of the seigneurie reverted to Joseph Papineau. In 1817, when Joseph Papineau sold the entire seigneurie – mills, domain, back *cens et rentes*, and unconceded land – to Louis-Joseph Papineau,[13] his eldest surviving son, there were perhaps three hundred people there, a third of them the remnants of Fletcher's New Englanders, and almost all the rest French Canadians. One of the latter was Denis-Benjamin Papineau, younger brother of Louis-Joseph, a resident of Petite-Nation since 1808 and seigneurial agent for his brother until the late 1840s. For some twenty years after Louis-Joseph purchased the seigneurie, only a few settlers trickled into Petite-Nation each year: in 1828 there were 517 people, in 1842 only 1,368.[14] In the 1840s the rate of immigration increased sharply as population pressure in the older settlements dislodged a steadily larger number of French Canadians and declined again in the 1850s when almost all the cultivable land in Petite-Nation had been taken up. Over 3,000 people lived in the seigneurie in 1851, and some 4,000 a decade later.[15] By this date, five-sixths of the population was French Canadian.

Settlers in Petite-Nation, as in all other Canadian seigneuries, acquired a roture (a farm lot or, legally, the final form of land concession

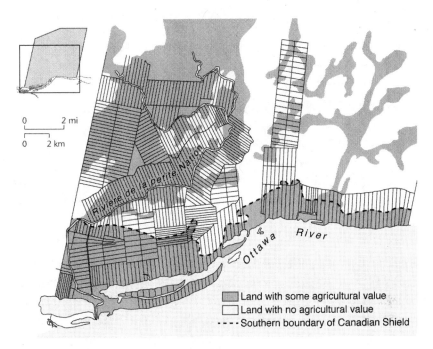

FIGURE 10
Rotures in Petite-Nation, 1855

within the seigneurial system), which they held from the seigneur. Joseph Papineau had made forty such concessions before 1817,[16] and by the mid-1850s the rotures shown in Figure 10 had been conceded, most of them by Denis-Benjamin Papineau. The Papineaus adopted without modification the cadastral system of the St. Lawrence lowland, conceding land in long lots laid out, as far as the interrupted terrain of Petite-Nation permitted, in côtes (or *rangs*) along the Ottawa River and its tributaries.[17] They charged surveying to the censitaires, which meant that it was usually inadequately done,[18] and they expected the censitaires to build their own roads.[19]

There is no evidence that the Papineaus withheld rotures from prospective censitaires while Petite-Nation was still a sparsely settled seigneurie. They were well aware, however, that some rotures were better than others and that it was advantageous to establish responsible settlers in new areas. From time to time Louis-Joseph wrote from Montreal to his brother in the seigneurie with instructions about the settlement of specific rotures.[20] By the late 1840s rotures were becoming scarce – almost invariably there were several applications for each new lot available[21] – and Louis-Joseph, who had returned from exile in France and spent much of his time in the seigneurie, granted land more cautiously. His prejudices ran strongly against English-speaking applicants – "foreign squatters ... infinitely less satisfactory than our Canadians"[22] – partly because they were wont to cut his timber. In 1848 he began withholding formal title to any new roture until the settler had cleared six *arpents* (one arpent equals approximately five-sixths of an acre). Each applicant was informed that, until that time, he was a tenant, not a censitaire,[23] a procedure that was unheard of during the French regime, when seigneurs were required to grant unconceded rotures to any applicant for them.[24] One habitant, wrote Louis-Joseph, "had the insolence to tell me that I was obliged to grant him land."[25] He also required anyone taking an abandoned roture to pay all the back cens et rentes.[26] As the back dues frequently equalled the value of the land, this was, in effect, a sale.

In Petite-Nation, as in most other seigneuries in the nineteenth century, roture contracts were standardized, printed forms with blanks left for the addition in longhand of information about the particular censitaire and roture. Joseph Papineau had prepared the original contract, and when these forms ran out, Louis-Joseph ordered a second and almost identical printing.[27] Apart from their printed form and much greater consistency, these contracts differed in two principal respects from any drawn up during the French regime: they increased the seigneur's access to timber, and they stipulated a higher cens et rente. To achieve the former purpose, roture contracts in Petite-Nation permitted the seigneur to cut oak and pine for profit on the roture and forbade the censitaire to do so. They allowed the seigneur to confiscate up to six arpents for the construction of a mill and prevented the censitaire from building either a saw or a grist mill without the seigneur's written consent. Before 1760 many seigneurs had the right to cut timber on their censitaires' rotures for the construction of the banal mill or the seigneurial manor, but they never had the right to cut oak and pine there commercially.[28] Some contracts had given the seigneur power to confiscate an arpent or two, but not more, for a mill. Although the seigneur always had first claim to the grist mill banality, roture contracts had never forbidden the censitaires to build grist mills.[29] Sawmilling had not been a banal right, and during the French regime any censitaire had been allowed to build a sawmill provided that, in so doing, he did not interfere with the operation of the seigneur's grist mill. In Petite-Nation all of this had been changed, with the result that rights to all important forests on conceded as well as on unconceded land, and to the milling of timber, rested entirely with the seigneur.

The rotures granted by Joseph Papineau before 1817 and by his son thereafter paid an annual cens et rente of one *minot* of wheat (1 minot equals 1.07 bushels) and two *livres tournois* for each thirty arpents, a rate that was a third higher than the highest rate consistently charged during the French regime.[30] For a roture in Petite-Nation, the annual charge was six and two-thirds minots of wheat plus thirteen livres, six sols, eight deniers (approximately $2.50 Halifax).[31] The Papineaus charged in wheat rather than in capons because the price of wheat was more tuned to inflation.[32] In Montreal in the first half of the nineteenth century, the average price of wheat was between five and six livres a minot, twice the average price a century earlier.[33] In 1813 wheat sold in Petite-Nation at fourteen livres ($2.58) a minot, and the cens et rentes for that year were calculated on this basis. These prices could almost quadruple a cens et rente: at two and a half livres a minot, a roture of two hundred arpents paid 30 livres ($5.50) a year; at 6 livres a minot, it paid just over 53 livres ($9.70); and at 14 livres a minot, it paid more than 106 livres ($19.40). Because wheat rarely ripened on Shield lots in Petite-Nation, and was a subsistence crop on lowland farms, cens et rentes were usually paid in the cash equivalent of the minots of wheat owed.[34]

After acquiring land on these terms, a settler usually built a tiny log cabin and cleared a little land. Most of the first cabins were shanties of perhaps ten to twelve feet long, with a one slope roof, a dirt floor, and a chimney, usually made of short green rounds heavily chinked with clay. In a few years a settler might build another, larger cabin, some fourteen to eighteen feet long, with gable ends, a stone chimney, and a plank floor. Most of these buildings were of *pièce-sur-pièce* construction (squared logs laid horizontally and pegged to vertical timbers at the corners and at intervals along the walls), but some were made of round logs cross-notched at the corners,[35] and a few were frame. By the 1840s a cabin was typically in a clearing of some ten arpents.[36]

The Habitant Economy

The occupations of working men and boys in Petite-Nation in 1851 are given in Table 1. At this date more than 90 percent of the working French Canadian men in Petite-Nation gave their occupation to the census enumerator as farmer, labourer, or river man. Most of the remainder described themselves as artisans or tradesmen, and only sixteen, some of them members of the Papineau family, as merchants, clerks, or professionals. Of those describing themselves as farmers, the great majority were heads of households, married men with several offspring. The labourers and river men were largely youths, some of them only twelve or thirteen years of age, who still lived on the parental roture, and many of the tradesmen listed in the first column were boys working with their fathers. Some men gave two occupations – "cultivateur et menuisier," "negociant et cultivateur" – and many of those describing themselves only as farmers must also have worked intermittently in the logging camps.

Although the nominal census indicates that farming was the dominant occupation in Petite-Nation in 1851, agriculture had developed slowly in a rocky seigneurie that had been first settled for its timber. In the first years, both Joseph Papineau and Louis-Joseph had sent biscuit and pork from Montreal,[37] and Denis-Benjamin, who doubted that agriculture was climatically possible in Petite-Nation, had imported wheat.[38] Only by the 1820s were the logging camps supplied locally and most settlers self-sufficient in basic foods. Even in 1842, when the first agricultural census was taken in Petite-Nation, virtually all habitant farms were subsistence operations on a few arpents of cleared land. The habitants were not selling produce to the lumber camps, which were supplied almost entirely by a handful of large farms. Table 2 gives examples of both subsistence and commercial farm types.

TABLE 1

Occupations of working males in Petite-Nation, 1851

Occupation	All male residents[1]		All heads of households[2]	
	French Canadian	Others	French Canadian	Others
Farmer	384	67	344	52
Labourer[3]	287	30	46	1
River man[4]	40	7	2	
Carpenter or joiner	22	2	14	2
Blacksmith	12	4	6	1
Woodcutter	1			
Fisherman	2		2	
Baker	1	1	1	
Mason	4		3	
Sawyer		1		1
Tanner	4		1	
Cooper	6	1	4	1
Tinsmith	1		1	
Painter	1		1	
Carter	1		1	
Saddler	2	1	1	
Miller	2		1	
Shake maker	3		2	
Sextant	2		2	
Bourgeois		1		1
Innkeeper		2		1
Merchant	7	8	7	6
Doctor	1	1		1
Clerk	5	6	4	1
Priest or minister		2[5]		1
Bailiff		1		1
Clerk of the JP		1		1
Clerk of the court	1		1	
Notary	1		1	
Surveyor	1		1	

1 This column includes all male residents of Petite-Nation under seventy years of age for whom an occupation is listed in the census.

2 This column includes all married men and widowers under seventy years of age for whom an occupation is listed in the census.

3 Includes *journaliers* and *engagés*.

4 In French, "voyageurs." Some of this group may have been hired on the river boats, but most must have had some connection with the timber drives.

5 Comprising a Belgian priest as well as a Methodist minister.

Source: Based on Nominal Census Petite-Nation, 1851, reels C-1131 and C-1132.

TABLE 2

Farm types in Petite-Nation, 1842

	Subsistence farms (number of arpents)		Commercial farms (number of arpents)	
	(1)	(2)	(3)	(4)
held	100	120	1,229	90
cleared	7	7	320	40
in wheat	2	1	1	1
barley	1	¼		
rye		1		
oats	2	2½	10	
peas		1	3	
potatoes	1	1	1	2
meadow and pasture			300	37
other	1		5	
cattle	1	2	36	36
horses			7	2
sheep	1		57	18
pigs	3	2	12	5

Source: Derived from examples in Nominal Census, Petite-Nation, 1842, reel C-729.

In 1842 there were six large commercial farms in Petite-Nation. One of them (farm 3 in the table) belonged to Denis-Benjamin Papineau, the other five to English-speaking settlers, among them Alanson Cooke, the sawmill operator, and Stephen Tucker, the timber merchant. Between the commercial and subsistence farm types illustrated in Table 2, there were a few semicommercial operations, and of these three belonged to French Canadians.

By 1861 there were twenty-five commercial farms in Petite-Nation, a quarter of them held by French Canadians. Examples 1 and 2 in Table 2 still describe characteristic habitant farms except that by 1861 there were likely to be fifteen to twenty cleared arpents and corresponding increases in crop acreage and livestock. Without manuring or adequate crop rotation, seed-yield ratios on the thin soils of Petite-Nation were extremely low, probably not higher than 1:6 for wheat or 1:12 for oats.[39] Livestock were scrub animals that browsed or grazed in the bush for most of the year. Such a farm rarely produced a marketable surplus.

With clearing proceeding at an average rate per farm of well under one arpent a year, and with women and children doing much of the farm work, it required no more than a man's part-time attention.

The farmers and farmers' sons who sought off-the-farm employment usually worked in the sawmills or logging camps, thereby providing most of the labour for the Papineaus or the English-speaking timber merchants who controlled the forests. Joseph Papineau and his son Denis-Benjamin had managed the earliest sawmills, but when Louis-Joseph acquired the seigneurie, he leased the mill rights in the western half of it to Thomas Mears, a timber merchant from Hawkesbury.[40] Peter McGill, nephew and heir of the director of the Bank of Montreal, took over the lease in 1834, but the mills were managed by Alanson Cooke, son of one of the early settlers from New England.[41] In 1854 Louis-Joseph sold the mills and timber rights for ten years in the western half of the seigneurie to Gilmour and Company, a firm of Scottish origin then based in Liverpool, and with British North American operations on the St. John and Mirimichi Rivers as well as the Ottawa. Besides these mills, Asa Cooke, father of Alanson, operated a small mill in the first range,[42] and in the eastern part of the seigneurie another New Englander, Stephen Tucker, held a concession to cut and square timber.[43] A few habitants cut firewood for the steamers on the Ottawa River,[44] and others made potash. There were fourteen asheries in Petite-Nation in 1842, eight of them belonging to French Canadians. In 1851 there were thirty-nine asheries, two-thirds of them in the hands of habitants. These were part-time, family operations, each producing three to five barrels of ash a year.[45]

The number and the aggregate income of the men employed in the forests and mills of Petite-Nation cannot be determined exactly.[46] Although most of the labourers and some of the farmers listed in Table 1 worked intermittently in forest industries, the census enumerator noted that only thirty to forty men were employed in Alanson Cooke's mill and another ten at his father's in 1851 and did not list the number of men cutting or squaring timber.[47] In 1861 Gilmour and Company employed 147 men in Petite-Nation, and Stephen Tucker employed sixty.[48] Certainly, during the 1850s there were sawmill jobs for perhaps half the year for not more than 50 to 60 men, jobs in the lumber camps for four or five winter months for not more than another 150 to 200, and jobs in the spring timber drives for perhaps 50.[49] Seeking these jobs were the great majority of able-bodied French Canadians in Petite-Nation. At any given time most of them were unemployed or were engaged in work around the farm that brought almost no cash return. In these conditions, wages were extremely low. Mill hands earned $12 to $14 dollars a month in 1861, and wages had been even lower.[50] While some French Canadians earned as much as $100 a year in the forest industries, a great many more earned far less. In the 1850s, sawmill and forest jobs could not have brought more than $20,000 in cash or credit into the seigneurie each year.[51]

Among the approximately 1,300 people in Petite-Nation in 1842, there were only twelve artisans and tradesmen, nine of them French Canadians.[52] The two merchants then in the seigneurie were English-speaking. In the next decade the population almost trebled, and the number of artisans and tradesmen increased to the point shown in Table 1. As along the lower St. Lawrence at the same time, the number of tradesmen was essentially a reflection of poverty. With not enough work available in the forests, and little good farm land, several men would turn to carpentry, for example, when there was opportunity for one. Of the handful of French Canadian merchants and professionals in Petite-Nation in 1851, the doctor was a Papineau; the notary, Francis Samuel MacKay, was the son of an immigrant Scot and a French Canadian; the clerk of the lower court was another Papineau; and the eight French Canadian merchants were small shopkeepers.

Essentially, then, the habitants in Petite-Nation were farmers, loggers, or sawmill hands. Farming was a subsistence activity that attracted few young men who competed for scarce jobs in the forests or mills. When the family depended entirely on farming, as frequently was the case, its annual cash income can rarely have exceeded $25, and often must have been virtually nothing. When the father worked on his roture and one or two unmarried sons had some work in the lumber camps, the family income would likely have been between $50 and $150 a year. In a few cases, as when the father was employed in the sawmill or had a trade, and two or three unmarried sons worked through the winter in the forests, the family income would have exceeded $200. Almost certainly, however, the gross annual income of most habitant families in Petite-Nation was between $50 and $150 a year.

Arriving without capital in Petite-Nation, taking out a roture that only slowly became a subsistence farm, finding intermittent and poorly paid work in the sawmills or logging camps, and facing payments for basic supplies and for land, almost all habitants in Petite-Nation quickly found themselves in debt. By 1822 the holders of forty-eight rotures in Petite-Nation owed Louis-Joseph over 11,000 livres ($2,017).[53] In 1832 only ten lots, several of them belonging to the Papineaus, were free of debt, fifty-one lots each owed more than 500 livres ($92), and five owed over 1,000 livres.[54] Indebtedness had become a chronic condition, most of the habitants owing their seigneur a sum that was approximately equivalent to the value of a man's labour for six months in the sawmill. Many habitants had tried to reduce their debt by subdividing their rotures – as early as 1822 a third of the sixty-six rotures along the river had been broken up[55] – but after a few years even these fractions were likely to owe several hundred livres. Others attempted to escape from debt by selling their rotures, but the seigneur could exercise his *droit de retrait* in these sales, taking over the roture by paying his former censitaire the difference, if any, between the sale price and the debt.[56]

In the twelve years from 1825 to 1836, Denis-Benjamin Papineau collected just over 19,000 livres ($3,480) from the censitaires in Petite-Nation.[57] As the cens et rentes accumulating during this period amounted to 55,000 livres ($10,080), and the *lods et ventes* to some 20,000 livres ($3,670), he collected each year about a quarter of the annual dues. At least 20,000 livres were also owing for the years before 1825. Louis-Joseph had made several short visits to the seigneurie, partly with the hope of collecting more of his debts, but found his censitaires no more able to pay him than his brother. He could sue his debtors but, although he blustered and threatened, in these years he rarely did so. Restraining him was the high cost and inconvenience of court action,[58] the advice of his brother Denis-Benjamin,[59] and undoubtedly, also, Papineau's recognition of the plight of his censitaires.[60] When Louis-Joseph returned to Canada in 1845 after eight years in exile, he began to manage his seigneurie much more rigorously. He was no longer as involved in politics and had more time for his own affairs; he was more cantankerous, more concerned about his own rights; and he was planning to build an expensive manor house, a project that depended entirely on the collection of debts.[61] In letter after letter, Louis-Joseph railed against his brother for allowing "ces animaux" (the censitaires) to fall so heavily into debt,[62] against the high cost of justice, and against the sheriff ("maudite invention anglais comme tant d'autres") for pocketing a commission on the sale of rotures. He could also write:

> We will threaten court action and we will sue a few people, but in such a new area there is really so much poverty that I feel more repugnance in suing than they do in paying. Lack of foresight, ignorance, the tendency to become indebted to the merchants are the common failings of all the habitants without exception, but a few have acted out of ill will ... which it is certainly necessary to rectify.[63]

When a censitaire lost his roture after court action, it was sold by public auction, usually to the seigneur. As Louis-Joseph pointed out to his brother, "The certainty that the creditor is owed as much as the land is worth and that the debtor has not and never will have other means to pay means that the creditor is in reality the proprietor."[64]

Most habitants in Petite-Nation were also indebted to at least one merchant. At first Denis-Benjamin had acted as merchant, but he was neither particularly astute nor demanding, which may explain why, around 1830, the New Englander Stephen Tucker became the principal, and for a time the only, merchant in Petite-Nation. Tucker was a Baptist, a man, according to Denis-Benjamin, "so filled with the missionary spirit that he has promised up to $40.00 to any of our poor Canadians who will agree to join his sect."[65] Some years later he was still described as the most fanatical Protestant in Petite-Nation; nevertheless, the Papineaus and a great many habitants bought from him. Of 145 *obligations* (statements of indebtedness) drawn up between 1837 and 1845 in Petite-Nation by the notary Andre-Benjamin Papineau, ninety-one recorded debts to the seigneur, and forty-nine debts to Stephen Tucker.[66] By the mid-1850s, Tucker owned forty-four rotures,[67] almost all of them confiscated from his debtors.

Stephen Tucker and Louis-Joseph Papineau disliked each other intensely, and in the late 1840s and 1850s, when Louis-Joseph lived in the seigneurie, disputes between them were frequent. On one occasion, when the value of many rotures would not cover the debts owed to the two creditors and Tucker complained bitterly about prospective losses, Louis-Joseph who, as seigneur, had prior claim, replied icily: "You forget the high credit prices of goods; the interest charges on back accounts, and what you have received from many when I had the right of being paid before you. If you advanced too much with too many, it was your choice."[68] From the habitants' point of view, both men were creditors to whom their farms were vulnerable, but Tucker, who combined economic and religious coercion and was usually the more insistent, must have been the more feared.

The Habitant Society

By the 1820s, French Canadian society in most of the older parishes and seigneuries of the St. Lawrence lowland had sealed itself from outsiders; not only were there few if any non-French Canadians in many parishes, but as time went on there were fewer French Canadians who had not been born in the immediate vicinity. These areas exported many of their young while, with almost no immigration, the people who remained formed an increasingly consanguineous population. Petite-Nation, in contrast, was being settled, and it attracted different people: French Canadians from many parishes and seigneuries, New Englanders, Englishmen, Irishmen, and some English-speaking people of Canadian birth. In several cases Catholic Irishmen and French Canadian girls married in Petite-Nation, and the progeny of these matches were assimilated quickly into French Canadian society.[69] At least three Protestants in Petite-Nation had also married French Canadians.[70] For the most part, however, the two groups kept to themselves socially. In 1842, 47 of the 53 English-speaking families in Petite-Nation had such a family in an adjacent lot while 205 of 208 French Canadian families lived next to a French Canadian household.[71] In 1861 the interior parish in Petite-Nation was overwhelmingly French Canadian (with only four Irish by birth and 1,489 Catholics against 45 Protestants), and most

English-speaking people lived on the Ottawa Valley plain towards the western corner of the seigneurie (in the parish of Ste-Angelique, with 1,007 French Canadians against 545 others). By this date there were three tiny villages in the seigneurie, and only in one of them, Papineau-ville in the parish of Ste-Angelique, were French- and English-speaking people in Petite-Nation likely to live close together. The habitants encountered the English-speaking settlers as employers, as merchants, as creditors, occasionally as co-workers, but rarely in the ordinary social round of their lives.

The social importance of nuclear family, nearest neighbour, and côte in habitant life in Petite-Nation was not different, as far as can be ascertained, from that in the older settlements of the St. Lawrence lowland. However, migration into the Shield had weakened drastically the importance of kin group and parish. Not only had settlers in Petite-Nation come as individuals, but they had come recently and in relatively large numbers. At mid-century, most adults were still immigrants and, because of the speed of settlement, many of their sons had not found land close to the parental roture. Table 3, which compares the kin affiliations in Petite-Nation with those in Lotbinière, a long-settled seigneurie on the south shore of the St. Lawrence some forty miles east of Quebec City, illustrates the effect of migration on the kin groups. The French Canadians who straggled up the Ottawa Valley had left a web of blood, ties which they could not quickly re-create. Habitants in Petite-Nation were far less likely to have a relative as nearest neighbour, or even a relative in the same côte than were habitants in the older seigneuries. Where kin groups existed in Petite-Nation, they rarely extended beyond sibling and parent-child relationships.

In many ways the parish in Petite-Nation resembled the parishes along the lower St. Lawrence in the late seventeenth and early eighteenth centuries.[72] For many years the seigneurie was visited briefly twice a year by a missionary priest who arrived in January on snowshoes and in June by canoe.[73] The first resident priest, an Irishman, was appointed in 1828 and stayed three years, his successor stayed for two years, and in 1833 the parish reverted to the missionary system.[74] In 1835 the bishop appointed another priest who, in turn, soon begged to be relieved. When in 1838 the bishop acquiesced, Petite-Nation was

TABLE 3

Surnames in the seigneuries of Petite-Nation and Lotbinière, 1842

	Petite-Nation	Lotbinière
Number of families	267	458
Number of different surnames	143	126
Percent of families with the most common surname	3	12
Percent of families with one of the ten most common surnames	9	43
Percent of families with unique surname	33	14

Source: Nominal Censuses, Petite-Nation and Lotbinière, reels C-729 and C-730.

left without a resident priest for another four years. In this interval, missionaries continued to visit the parish twice a year, but these were short visits, their essential purposes to baptize babies and to say mass for the dead. For the most part, Catholics in Petite-Nation were left alone, and exposed, as one missionary priest put it, "to fatal communications with methodists and baptists."[75] In 1841 the bishop established yet another priest, and this man stayed until 1849, when, amidst bitter factional quarrels over the school tax and the location of a new church, he left for a newly constructed chapel and presbytery in the interior of the seigneurie.[76] The bishop attempted to placate the feuding parties by dividing Petite-Nation into three parishes,[77] but for several more years the two parishes along the river were visited irregularly by their former *curé* or by the curé from l'Orignal, a seigneurie twenty miles away.

Priests did not stay in Petite-Nation because their financial support was inadequate. They could not have lived on the tithe (in Canada, one twenty-sixth of the grain harvest) had it been paid regularly and agreed to come only after the habitants had subscribed a sum for their maintenance. Yet, whatever the financial arrangements, priests in Petite-Nation were rarely paid. The first complained that he had been reduced to "scratching among the stumps"[78] for a living, another that he had paid out twice what he had received from the habitants and was indebted to the merchant.[79] On one occasion, the habitants agreed to tithe in potatoes,[80] but when the new priest arrived in a buggy pulled by two horses, the habitants decided that he was rich and refused to pay either tithe or subscription. The priest explained to his bishop that the buggy was old and had cost only a few dollars. "The mistake," he wrote, "is that I had it varnished, and that gives an appearance of luxury."[81] There were some who doubted that the habitants wanted a priest. One priest noted bitterly that the habitants could support several taverns,[82] and in 1833 the bishop informed Denis-Benjamin that "experience has proved that the habitants could not *or would not* pay even half of what they owed without being forced by law."[83] The priests had attempted to curtail the heavy drinking[84] and some adulterous behaviour in Petite-Nation, and this may have led to a reaction against them; but in the light of many meetings to petition for a priest, the number of times that funds were subscribed for his support, and the bitter rows over the location of a church, it is clear that most habitants wanted to have a resident priest, but that he was a luxury they could hardly afford.

After 1840 a number of civil functions, notably the assessment and collection of taxes and the maintenance of roads and schools, were organized within the parish.[85] These civil functions were open to all parish residents, whatever their religious affiliations (the parish corresponding in this sense to the township in Ontario), and in Petite-Nation most responsible parish positions were held either by members of the Papineau family or by New Englanders. Illiteracy alone disqualified almost all the habitants. New Englanders had established a school in Petite-Nation in 1820, but only two French Canadians (one of them Denis-Benjamin) sent their children to it. The habitants saw no need for formal education, and most of the effort to create schools had to come from outside the seigneurie.[86] The first major initiative in this direction came with the Common School Act of 1841,[87] which provided for the election of five school commissioners in each parish, for the division of parishes into school districts, for an assessment of fifty pounds ($200) on the inhabitants of each district for the building of a school, and for a monthly fee of one shilling and three pence for each child at school. These were heavy charges on a poverty-stricken people who attached no value to formal schooling.[88] Then, when three of the first five school commissioners were English-speaking (elected because the New Englanders had attended the organizational meeting in greater number), the priest began preaching that the three English-speaking school commissioners were agents of religious and cultural assimilation.[89] In these circumstances, schools were slowly built and then were often closed for want of pupils. The School Act was modified in 1846 to provide more operating revenue from property taxes whether or not parents sent their children to school.[90] Even so, Denis-Benjamin estimated in 1851 that not one French Canadian in thirty in Petite-Nation was literate.[91] The habitants usually became viewers of ditches and fences, the New Englanders the tax assessors and collectors.[92] Although the seigneur or his agent was a powerful presence in Petite Nation, the seigneurie itself was not a social unit. All censitaires had acquired land from the Papineaus; all paid, or were supposed to pay, annual charges for their land; almost all were in debt to the seigneur. This, coupled with Louis-Joseph's fame, his sense of himself as a leader, his excellent education and meticulous knowledge of Canadian civil law and, after 1849, his mansion at Montebello, which was by far the finest residence that most habitants in Petite-Nation had ever seen, made him an awe-inspiring figure in the seigneurie. Louis-Joseph liked to think of himself as the leader of a flock,[93] but the habitants undoubtedly viewed him with fear. He was a force in rural life, as seigneurs had not been during the French regime, but not the focus of a rural society. As during the French regime, seigneurial boundaries were irrelevant to social patterns.

Until Louis-Joseph settled at Montebello, Denis-Benjamin Papineau, Stephen Tucker, and the two Cookes had been the most powerful men in the seigneurie. At one time or another, each was a justice of the peace. In 1840 Denis-Benjamin was elected unanimously to represent Petite-Nation in the newly formed District Council; four years later, he was succeeded by Alanson Cooke. In 1842 Denis-Benjamin was elected to the Legislative Assembly. His son was parish clerk and, at times, surveyor of roads in Petite-Nation, and for several years Stephen Tucker was the tax collector. Several prosperous farmers and merchants, all of them English-speaking, were fringe members of the elite.[94] The position of all this group rested, finally, on economic power. Denis-Benjamin's authority depended on his position as seigneurial agent, Tucker's on his role as employer and creditor, the Cookes' on the many jobs they controlled in the sawmills. The habitants elected these men to the District Council, the Legislative Assembly, or to a local parish office because their livelihood, however meagre, was controlled by them. Moreover, the elite were the only men in the seigneurie who met the property qualification of $300 (1,500 livres) for such public offices as district councillor or justice of the peace.

Petite-Nation in 1860

By 1860 parts of Petite-Nation had been settled for more than fifty years. The Ottawa Valley plain was cleared, long lots were conceded across it, and much of the land was farmed. Farmhouses stretched in côtes along the river, and two small villages, Montebello and Papineauville, had taken shape towards opposite ends of this line. In the Shield, the patterns of clearing and settlement were much more irregular, but most of the fertile pockets in the valleys were farmed. In the largest of these valleys, the village of St-Andre Avellin contained a church, a number of stores, and even a few streets laid out but still largely unoccupied at right angles to the main road. North and west from St-Andre Avellin, where côtes had been settled in the previous two decades, there were still many shanties in tiny clearings amid the bush that was the aftermath of logging. Still farther north, pine and spruce were being cut and floated down the Petite-Nation River to Gilmour and Company's sawmill. In all, some four thousand people lived in Petite-Nation. Rough as in many respects it was, with stumps in many fields and the slash of recent logging almost everywhere, a settled place had emerged where just over fifty years before there had been only forest.

In this place there were three principal groups of people and three landscapes associated with their different lives. In the manor he had built in 1848 and 1849 at Montebello lived Louis-Joseph Papineau and as many of his immediate family as he could entice away from Montreal.[95] His was one of the finest country houses in Lower Canada, its main unit forty by sixty feet and twenty-four feet high,[96] and its architectural inspiration an amalgam of ideas that Louis-Joseph had brought back from France. The house was sheltered by a row of towering pines and overlooked a spacious garden to the river. In the village of Montebello just outside the gate to his domain, Louis-Joseph had considerably widened the through road from Montreal to Hull and had lined the streets with trees, naming each street after its particular tree: Rue des cèdres, Rue des érables, Rue des pins, Rue des ormes, Rue des sapins.[97] Several miles to the west in the village of Papineauville and its surrounding farms lived Denis-Benjamin Papineau and a group of prosperous New Englanders. Most of their houses were white clapboard in the New England style, or the brick or frame buildings with Italianate trim that were becoming common in Ontario. Their large, well-managed farms produced oats, potatoes, hay, oxen, and meat for the logging camps, and their stores in Papineauville supplied settlers in much of the seigneurie. Throughout most of the rest of the coastal plain and in the cultivable valleys of the Shield were the tiny log houses, the barns, the fields, and the côtes of the French Canadian habitant. However imperfectly, three traditions had emerged in the human landscape of Petite-Nation: that of the aristocrat,[98] that of the Yankee trader, and that of the habitant community of the lower St. Lawrence.

Underlying and shaping the habitant landscape in Petite-Nation were the two essential characteristics of French Canadian life in Petite-Nation, its poverty and its weak institutions. The habitants faced the world individually or in nuclear families feebly supported by nearest neighbour or côte. The seigneur was a creditor not a leader, the parish priest was more often absent than not, the kin group was barely forming, and the local government was dominated by those who controlled the habitants' livelihood. Paradoxically, the New Englanders, who valued self-reliance, created more institutional support in Petite-Nation for their way of life than did the habitants, who tended to value community. To conclude, it is necessary to consider why this was so.

An explanation for the character of French Canadian settlement in the Shield lies only partly in nineteenth-century Quebec, and even less in the physical character of the Canadian Shield or the commercial ascendancy of the English. The same soils on which French Canadians scratched out a living also supported large and prosperous farms. The forests in which the habitants worked for a pittance made the fortunes of others. English-speaking timber merchants exploited the habitants.

So did Louis-Joseph Papineau. The Papineau manor at Montebello, Stephen Tucker's forty-four rotures confiscated from debtors, and the profits of the Mears, the McGills, and the Gilmours who built and operated the sawmills in Petite-Nation all rested on a poor habitant population. Seigneur and lumberman profited from the situation in Petite-Nation, but neither had created it. Rather, to understand the habitant landscape and society in Petite-Nation is to understand the evolving character of French Canadian rural society over the previous century and a half.

What apparently had happened was this.[99] The few immigrants who crossed the Atlantic to the lower St. Lawrence in the seventeenth and early eighteenth centuries were, for the most part, poor and dispossessed people who had had only a toehold in French society before they crossed the Atlantic. Among them were approximately 1,000 girls from Paris poorhouses, 2,000 petty criminals (mostly salt smugglers), over 3,000 ordinary soldiers most of whom had been pressed into service, and perhaps 4,000 engagés who came largely from the same group of landless labourers and unemployed as the soldiers. Many of the engagés were young, merely boys according to the intendants, and not very robust. These people came as individuals or within the type of temporary social structure – that of a poor house, a prison, or an army – in which they had never intended to spend their lives, and which was irrelevant to the settlement of Canada. Along the lower St. Lawrence they found an abundance of land that, when cleared, yielded a higher standard of living than that of most French peasants. They found an opportunity to settle along the river, away from official eyes, and in a setting where their lives could not be controlled. And they found in the untrammelled life of the fur trade contact with largely nomadic Algonquin, whose rhetoric, courage, and apparent lack of regime they admired and emulated.

Out of this emerged a habitant population characterized by bravado, insouciance, and a considerable disdain for authority. The habitants lived boisterously, spending their income, enjoying the independence and modest prosperity of their lives in the côtes, and perhaps, too, the Indigenous girls along the upper Ottawa; a style of life that grew partly out of their French background but probably more out of the opportunities of a new land. They had brought few institutions with them and needed few in Canada. The Canadian seigneurie was neither a social nor an economic unit; the parish was only slowly emerging as a social unit at the end of the French regime. The village was almost absent; collective open-field agriculture never appeared. The côte did become a loose rural neighbourhood; as time went on neighbours were frequently kin; and, after perhaps the earliest years, the nuclear family was always important. In the background was the colonial government, eager to promote the settlement of the colony, paternalistic, tending to side with the habitants in disputes with the seigneurs. The government could not impose itself on the habitants, but it could offer certain services – inexpensive regional courts, for example, or the right of free appeal to the intendant. In operating hospitals, orphanages, and poorhouses, the religious orders did the same. Such support only increased the independence of the habitants, who were not forced to compensate for an oppressive officialdom by a tighter social organization at the local level.

In the century after the Conquest, this way of life slowly changed. Habitant mobility was constrained by the declining relative importance of the fur trade and, after 1821, by its loss to Hudson Bay; by English-speaking settlement in Upper Canada; and by growing population pressure along the St. Lawrence lowland. Farm land became scarce as the seigneurial lands filled up, the value of land rose, and that of labour gradually fell. Seigneurs found their revenues rising and close seigneurial management a paying proposition. They kept accounts regularly, insisted on payment of debts, and began to build sizable manors throughout the lower St. Lawrence. Without an intendant to interfere, they often increased their cens et rentes[100] (indeed, they interpreted the seigneurial system to the English), and as alternative land became scarcer, the habitants had no alternative but to accept these charges. A situation that once had favoured the censitaire had turned to favour the seigneur.

At the same time, French Canadians were losing control of commerce to more single-minded and better-connected Englishmen, Scots, and

New Englanders. A government that had never controlled but had often supported the habitants during the French regime was taken over by an alien people with a different language, religion, and values. This was no longer a government to turn to as the habitants had turned to the courts and the intendant during the French regime. For a time the Conquest connected French Canada to a larger market for its agricultural products, but not to the larger world of social and intellectual change. It shielded French Canadians from the full impact of the French Revolution, for which most of them were thankful, and it filtered the late eighteenth- and nineteenth-century world through the eyes of the English-speaking merchant, the colonial administrator, or, especially in the nineteenth century, the parish priest. The fragment of France that had crossed the Atlantic to settle the côtes of the lower St. Lawrence and become the habitant population of the French regime, had been poorly connected before 1760 to contending French values and ideologies, and the long-term effect of the Conquest had been to prolong its isolation.

In this situation, French Canadian life had become increasingly rural. Before 1760, 20 to 25 percent of the people along the lower St. Lawrence lived in towns, but by 1815 only 5 percent of the French Canadians did so. The central business districts and the upper-class residential areas of Montreal and Quebec were overwhelmingly English-speaking. French Canadian seigneurs who once had lived in the towns now lived in their seigneuries. In this rural introversion there were two deep ironies. French Canadians were turning to a rural life at a time when, for the ordinary habitant on the ordinary roture, such a life meant subsistence farming, poverty, debt, and, eventually, the departure of most of his children. Then, too, many of them gloried in an image of the French regime, of a rural way of life before the coming of the English built around seigneurie, parish, and Coutume de Paris,[101] without understanding that in the vastly different conditions of the French regime these institutions had been extremely weak. Economically and institutionally, the rural core around which French Canada had folded was hollow.

All that could be done was to make the most of what they had. The parish, which slowly had been gaining strength after the decision taken in 1722 to establish resident priests, gradually became more vital after the Conquest and would have developed more rapidly had there not been a serious shortage of priests.[102] The extended family or kin group enlarged and probably strengthened and, with less rural mobility within its seigneurial lowlands, the côte and nuclear family may have strengthened as well. The Coutume de Paris – with its emphasis on family rather than on individual rights and its protective view of landholding, which became more relevant to the lower St. Lawrence as the population increased – became an essential prop, in many nationalist minds, of French Canadian life. The seigneurial system, although neither a social nor an economic unit of habitant life, had become profitable for the seigneurs, most of whom insisted that the survival of French Canada depended on the survival of the system. These institutions, particularly the kin group and the côte, provided a measure of stability, but they did not provide an institutional framework for change, especially as parish priest and seigneur usually defended the status quo. French Canadian society had achieved some strength in rural isolation; in closely knit, interrelated communities; and in a retrospective outlook but had not the ability to cope with change, least of all with the internal problem of population pressure.

When young French Canadians were pushed out of the St. Lawrence lowland, they left in much the condition in which their forebears, a century and a half before, had crossed the Atlantic. They were young, illiterate, often destitute and, in the sense that they were not part of groups bound by ties of blood and tradition, alone. Immigrants in the late seventeenth century had found an abundance of agricultural land and a heady outlet in the fur trade. The many more French Canadians who settled in the Shield found a far more meagre agricultural land and lumber camps and sawmills operated by another people. In this setting, they had no defence against what they became, subsistence farmers and underpaid labourers. When their children or grandchildren left for the cities, they too left as their predecessors had come to the Shield. The years in the Shield had availed French Canadians nothing but poverty and some lag in the adjustment to changed conditions.

Finally, the tragedy of French Canadian settlement in Petite-Nation lay perhaps less in poverty than in the habitants' inability to maintain a distinctive way of life. The values of the closely knit, rural communities of the lower St. Lawrence were neither those of an aristocrat such as Louis Joseph Papineau nor of liberals such as Stephen Tucker or Alanson Cooke. The habitants' outlook was more collective than that of the New Englanders, more egalitarian than that of Louis-Joseph Papineau. But communities such as those along the lower St. Lawrence in the nineteenth century depended on isolation and internal stability. When either is removed, they are likely to be undermined, as they were for the habitants in Petite-Nation who stood almost alone to face a changing world.

The Settlement
of Mono Township

This article grew out of a wager with two fourth-year students at the University of Toronto, Pauline Roulston and Chris de Freitas, that we could choose any township in Ontario and write a solid academic paper about it. We chose Mono Township (monotonous township) because it seemed so nondescript. When we got there, we found ourselves in "Mona," pronounced with a broad "o." Most old gravestones identified a county in Ulster, and, in hilly terrain, there was a lot of damaged land. Our exploration of these ingredients led to a good deal of fieldwork, to various archives, and to the literature on early nineteenth-century Ulster.

Eventually, and with some presumption, we wrote a far more ambitious paper than we had ever intended. For immigrants from Ulster, the challenges of pioneering in the forests of Mono were altogether new, and their

From R. Cole Harris, Pauline Roulston, and Chris de Freitas, "The Settlement of Mono Township," *Canadian Geographer* 19, 1 (1975): 1–17.

lives were worked out differently there. Yet an axis of
ideological continuity seemed to connect the two. The
strong individualism of Protestant Ulster – underlain by
Calvinist assumptions about the individual's relationship
with God, the virtue of hard work, and the relationship
between prosperity and God's favour in this world and
the next – were transferred to Mono, as was a belief
in progress, measured in material terms. The whole
experience of pioneering in Mono – where the land was
being transformed and those who survived the rigours
of pioneering to create farms did so, in their eyes, by
the sweat of their own brows – reinforced these values.
To leave a small holding in Ulster for a British city was to
encounter the emerging collective defences of the working class; to leave it for Mono township was to perpetuate an ideology based on individual rights, the virtue of
work, and God's sanction of material achievement.

I N THE SECOND QUARTER of the nineteenth century, southern Ontario
became, to some extent, an industrial byproduct. Although not itself
industrial, the extension of its settlement during those years was
largely initiated by the demographic, social, economic, and technological changes of British industrialization. Particularly in the Midlands, in lowland Scotland, and in Ulster, traditional economies and
societies were being dislocated. People were moving, some to the new
industrial cities of the British Isles, others in unprecedented numbers
across the Atlantic to New World cities or farms. When this wave hit
southern Ontario in the 1820s, there were 150,000 Ontarians. When it
abated thirty years later, there were approximately 1 million. The influence of British industrialization on the forested land of southern Ontario
had been abrupt and massive – it obliterated the forest and established

the dominant landscape and society of rural Ontario, which only now are being undermined by spreading cities and exurbanites.

The shock waves from industrializing Britain that extended into southern Ontario in the second quarter of the nineteenth century transformed its landscape more totally than any event since deglaciation. The forest was cleared; roads, fields, and townsites were laid out; steamboats and railways were introduced. Social relationships, too, were in flux as a result of the dislocation of migration and the mobility of pioneer society. Immigrants lived within these changes, adjusting to and generally approving of them. By the 1850s and 1860s, Ontarians, in common with many people in the United States and the British Isles, believed theirs an age of outstanding progress. Yet we suggest in this essay that, in terms of the immigrants' basic goals and values, the settlement of southern Ontario had been conservative. Southern Ontario presented an opportunity to continue a way of life – or, at least, a frame of mind – that emphasized the social and economic independence of the small farmer on the land. Put another way, the settlement of southern Ontario, like the defence of the status quo in eighteenth-century Pennsylvania, constituted a conservative defence of liberal individualism.[1] Moreover, the work and isolation of pioneering, the round of material preoccupations inevitable in establishing a farm, and the constant exposure to physical change intensified this individualism while giving it a particularly materialistic cast. For land hungry, rural Ulstermen, the land of southern Ontario was a means of this conservative defence; that is why it was sought so eagerly, cleared so rapidly, often damaged so irreparably.

In a tentative, introductory way, our essay explores this argument in Mono Township – a hilly, sandy, unremarkable tract of land lying sixty miles northwest of Toronto (Figure 11). Of approximately 1,100 people in Mono Township in 1842 there were, excluding those born in Canada, 417 who had been born in Ireland, 52 in Scotland, and 14 in England.[2] In 1850 there were 2,300 people in Mono, some 80 percent of them of Ulster stock, and almost all of them Protestant.[3] Most of the Irish came from the counties of Armagh, Tyrone, and Monaghan, the most densely settled counties in prefamine Ireland. In 1841 the rural population density in Armagh exceeded five hundred people per square

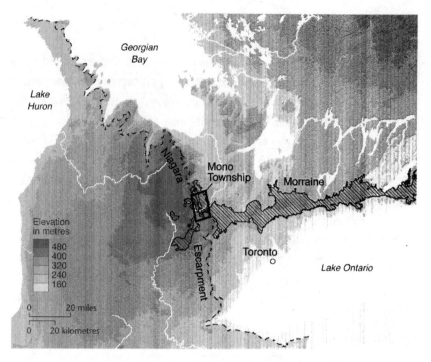

FIGURE 11
The location of Mono Township

mile of improved land, and in Monaghan half the farms were under six acres in size. In these counties, and particularly in Armagh, many small farmers participated in the domestic linen industry. Men wove, women and children spun. At the beginning of the nineteenth century, combined family earnings usually produced a sufficient living. But as cotton cloth competed with linen, as spinning-mills began producing linen yarn, and as the coarse linen industry shifted to Scotland and England, where spinning-mills had been established earlier than in Ulster, work that had brought a shilling a day in 1800 brought a penny or two in the 1830s. Domestic spinning and weaving continued in many cases only because there was nothing else to do. Without funds or land for a commercial agriculture that was becoming increasingly dependent on pasture, with no expectation for the improvement of the domestic linen industry, and with insufficient employment in the towns, many Ulster families that once had combined the work of field and loom to gain an adequate livelihood were being pushed towards a subsistence economy and the cottier (landless) class. For a century, Ulster Protestants had been immigrating to North America, and in the early nineteenth century many more sold their tenant right to obtain passage money and a little capital."[4]

Mono Township itself was forested, morainic, and rough. It was crossed by the Niagara escarpment and, at right angles to the escarpment, by a deep glacial spillway. Throughout the rest of the township the terrain was rolling or abrupt, with glacial drift or moraine, kames, and dunes formed out of periglacial sands and silts overlying limestone or shale. In parts of the township the land was swampy; on the eminences, it was dry. Almost everywhere, glacial sands or gravels lay close to the surface. Thick tangles of cedar or tamarack covered the swamps: the driest, sandiest areas along the edge of the glacial spillway were dominated by hemlock and a few pine trees. Deciduous broadleaf species predominated on sites between these edaphic extremes. On drier, steeper land, a maple-beech association included some hemlock and a scattering of hardwood species. On slightly moister sites there was more basswood, elm, red and white oak, and ironwood, and less hemlock. The organic mucks in the swamps and the light, sandy soils under the hemlocks were unsuited for pioneer farming, whereas the grey-brown podzolic soils under the deciduous forest were cultivable. In sum, the steep slopes, relatively high elevation, and thin soils of Mono Township presented a meagre physical base for agricultural pioneering. Here in Mono, then, converged the basic ingredients of Ontario settlement in the second quarter of the nineteenth century: a land-hungry people moving away from a rural way of life that the spread of the factory system was rendering untenable, and land available for settlement. To understand what happened is to understand what people from Ulster brought to Mono Township and how they were affected by the experience of pioneering. The next section of this essay sketches aspects of the Ulster legacy, a further section considers the pioneer experience, and the conclusion returns to the thesis outlined above.

The Ulster Background

Ulster contributed inflections, expressions, and superstitions to Mono Township: the Loyal Orange Lodge and anti-Catholicism; some would say a drab architecture; and, for a short time, many distinctive agricultural practices, tools, household appointments, and items of clothing. Perhaps more basically, it contributed social and economic individualism, a fervent individual attachment to land, and a belief in hard, individual work to achieve prosperity.[5]

Most immigrants who colonized Ulster in the seventeenth century had been granted individual leases, lived on their leaseholds, enclosed their land, and made their own agricultural decisions.[6] Eventually, some of these Protestant settlers formed partnership groups, but the Irish *clachan* (an informal cluster of farm houses and associated buildings) was a settlement form characteristic of the native Irish rather than the British sector of the population. These two settlement patterns and associated agricultural traditions – one collective and the other individualistic – both survived in early nineteenth-century Ulster, although in many areas the clachan had become rare. Hill society, largely native Irish and Roman Catholic, was essentially egalitarian and depended on an elaborate system of mutual aid (swapping or neighbouring) in which groups of men built, planted, tilled, harvested, and performed many other tasks together. Lowland society, more commonly Protestant and British than native Irish, was socially much more individualistic and stratified. Living on their own farms and working them independently, a farmer and his family were masters of their own destinies, and lowland people ranged in social categories from cottiers to gentry. The cottiers worked for a pittance for a few months each year and begged for the rest. Above them, and comprising the bulk of the rural population of Ulster, were small farmers with perhaps five to fifteen acres of leased land. More prosperous were those few – perhaps 4 percent of the rural population – who worked as much as thirty acres of land. Beyond them, and usually totally removed from the local, rural society, were the gentry. Unlike the upland clachans, where interfamily relations were informal and close, in the individualistic and stratified lowland society personal relations were more formal, and visiting more of an affair.[7]

Made up less of kin groups and communities than of individuals and nuclear families who settled on individual leaseholds, the British migrations to seventeenth-century Ulster, like those to North America in the same century, had weakened the bonds of community. There were Protestant settlements in Ulster in which kin and community relationships resembled those among the native Irish but, on the whole, kin and community traditions were relatively weak in the British plantations. Native Irish inheritance, for example, was usually partible among males; among Protestants, money was often divided equally or on the basis of esteem; but capital goods, particularly land, were commonly left to the eldest or a preferred son.[8] If a man died without male issue, it was important to "keep the name on the land," and preference was often given to one of his brother's sons or to a cousin who bore the family name. Living on his land and working it individually, a man viewed his land as his support and his achievement; thus, inheritance often emphasized the continuity of property and name rather than family group. Although many native Irish farmers in the lowlands lived as did their Protestant counterparts, in sum, there was a shift in Protestant Ulster from the community towards the nuclear family and the individual, and from shared to personal property.

Contributing to what Estyn Evans considers the "bellicose independence" of the Ulster farmer was a system of tenancy known as tenant right.[9] In much of Ireland, leases were given for a short term (often for a year with six months' notice), and with such a lease the tenant who improved the property would soon pay a higher rent or face eviction. To avoid the abuses of rack renting, the tenant let the land deteriorate until it produced only a subsistence living for his family and a slight surplus for the landlord. On the other hand, the system of tenant right, which was widespread in Ulster and occurred here and there in the south, gave a tenant security of tenure, a moderate and fixed rent, and compensation for improvements.[10] The term of lease might be as long as several lives, and if a man sold his interest, or tenant right, in the holding, the incoming tenant paid a sum, often as much as forty years' rent, for improvement of it.[11] Sales of tenant rights, which could be worth as much as twenty pounds per acre,[12] paid for many transatlantic crossings; the existence of tenant right made the individual Ulster farmer the virtual master of a property.

Even in the poorest areas, Ulster farmers participated in a monetary economy. There was always the rent to pay and a few items to purchase.[13] Families who lived essentially on potatoes often sold a little wheat or oats, and perhaps some eggs, chickens, and butter; the pig, it was said, paid the rent.[14] Those who participated in the domestic linen industry purchased flax or grew it on their leasehold and sold cloth, much as agricultural produce was sold, in one of the open-air markets for brown (unbleached) linen. In the nineteenth century, the domestic weaver commonly worked for a master weaver who supplied him with yarn and sold his product to one of the large Quaker bleaching firms that by then were sending buyers directly to the brown-linen markets.[15] In effect, the combination of a little farming to meet the needs of subsistence, pay the rent, and perhaps grow some flax, together with paltry earnings, enabled the impoverished Irish weaver to undersell the machine, and the power loom made slight headway in Ulster until after 1850, when wages rose with population decline.

However poor the Ulster farmer-weaver, he appears to have been relatively well off by Irish standards. Travellers in Ireland frequently remarked on the economic difference between north and south;[16] most thought that the people, too, were more enterprising and industrious. "The middle and upper classes are not loungers and men of pleasure. Pleasure in Belfast is a very secondary consideration. Business is life here – and life is business ... It is impossible that Cork, Limerick, or Waterford should ever become altogether like Belfast, because the Character of the Scotch and the Irish is essentially different ... The people of Belfast count the cost of every thing."[17] Modern analysis of nineteenth-century census data confirms that per capita incomes were higher in the Protestant north.[18] Yet it is not at all clear how travellers' accounts, often written by Englishmen who were biased against the native Irish, or even data on per capita income drawn from the census, are to be interpreted. Certainly, there were wealthy businessmen (mostly Quakers) in Belfast; certainly, early in the nineteenth century, areas

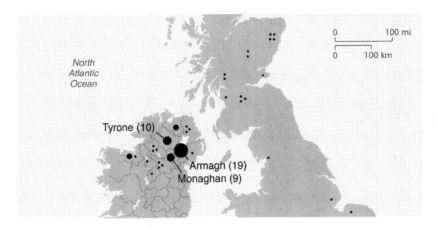

FIGURE 12
The Ulster origin of immigrants to Mono | Data from Mono tombstones

where the domestic linen industry coexisted with farming were islands of relative prosperity; but the cottier class was numerous in both Protestant and Catholic Ulster. Many small Ulster farmers, like farmers everywhere in Ireland, lived very close to the margin. It does appear that in early nineteenth-century Ulster many rural people of lower-middle-class status – small farmers and farmer-weavers – were prepared to work exceedingly hard to maintain or improve their economic positions. These people were predominantly Protestant, and they, rather than the cottiers or the few prosperous farmers, were the people who immigrated to Mono Township (Figure 12).[19]

The relative industriousness of these people is perhaps best explained in class terms. When times were relatively good, small farmers aspired to the success and standing of the few prosperous farmers; when times were bad, they struggled to maintain a position above the cottier class. The fact that most of them were Protestant may be associated with tenant right, with special privileges for Protestants, and ultimately, perhaps, with the dislocation and individualization associated with the seventeenth-century migration to Ulster. The influence of a Protestant ethic is difficult to assess. Three centuries after the Reformation, religious, social, and economic attitudes in nineteenth-century Ulster were not sufficiently separate to permit the drawing of clear lines of causation.

It can be said that Ulster Protestantism, overwhelmingly Presbyterian or low church Anglican and thoroughly conservative, combined a strong this-worldliness with a belief in the awesome majesty of God; emphasized individual activity and responsibility; and, especially among the Presbyterians, insisted on the relationship of the individual to God and to the sacred tradition. These beliefs, depending on and reinforcing individual autonomy and self-sufficiency, apparently were incorporated in the fabric of social and economic individualism. However one argues this convergence of belief, self-interest, and action, it is clear that in nineteenth-century Protestant Ulster, religious belief and economic enterprise were mutually reinforcing, that in an increasingly individualistic society, consistent enterprise, frugality, honesty, sobriety, and success were virtues equally in church and marketplace. The God-fearing Protestants who arrived in Mono Township believed that in working hard to achieve prosperity they fulfilled God's will and might secure his favour. Ulster Catholics of similar socioeconomic status may have held similar beliefs.

The Pioneer Experience

In Mono, Ulstermen perpetuated their social and economic individualism, centred it as in Ulster on the family farm, and buttressed it as before by hard work and a supportive theology. Immigrants took up land that had been surveyed into rectangular 100 or 200 acre lots. Some had received land scrip for military service, perhaps acquiring location tickets in Toronto for land they had never seen. Others purchased land from the Crown at public auction, from the Canada Company, from an absentee speculator, or from an earlier settler. In the 1840s, uncleared land in Mono brought from five to ten shillings an acre.[20] In comparison with Ulster, the size of individual holdings had increased many times,[21] the per-acre cost of land had fallen precipitously, and freehold had replaced leasehold, but the principle of independent, individual control of land was unaltered.

In Mono, where settlers lived on their own land and farmed it independently, the basic social unit was the nuclear family. Beyond the nuclear family, there were social connections at the local church; before its establishment, the visits of itinerant ministers and the occasional revival meeting served social as well as religious functions. The many taverns in Mono were gathering points for the men. The Loyal Orange Lodge and temperance societies made their early appearance. Different families came together at bees of various kinds, and loose rural neighbourhoods must have formed along some of the roads. But in common with most of lowland Ulster, the social primacy of the nuclear family in its own house, on its own land, was clear. When a horse had to be harnessed and considerable distances covered, travel off the farm was an event. Diaries often recorded little else. A week in January 1871 is described as follows in the oldest surviving diary in Mono:

Jan. 15   Sun. – the sacrament in our church

Jan. 16   Mon. – went to Miss Bingham's wood bee with horses

Jan. 18   Wed. – met J. McBrien at Camilla [a hamlet three miles away]

Jan. 19   Thur. – drew 2 cords of wood from J. Stills in the afternoon

Jan. 20   Fri. – was at Camilla this morning, drew one saw log to Turnbull's mill in evening ... went over to Camilla at night

Jan. 21   Sat. – went to Orangeville [a village 8 miles south] to pay bills

Jan. 23   Mon. – was over at D. Johnstons ... called at the old man's ... went down to Mrs. Parks after night with our girls.[22]

Even social visiting was inclined to be formal: "Mar. 8 Wed. – Drove Mrs. Phoenix [the diarist's wife] over to see Mrs. Doherty."

Settlers in Mono as in Ulster participated in a commercial economy. Here and there in Ontario half-pay officers and other Englishmen of means and education built substantial houses, landscaped their grounds, and practised a type of agriculture that depended more on their conception of what was fit and proper for a gentleman than on the economic realities of Ontario. There were none such in Mono. There, agriculture was pared to the essentials. Fields were sown down as quickly as possible into a rotation of wheat-fallow-wheat or wheat-fallow-oats[23] that enabled a farmer to produce a cash crop quickly with a minimum of labour and to combat the recolonization of his fields by weeds.[24] For many years, wheat was almost the only marketable crop. "People here," wrote a settler, "are all interested in the high price of wheat, which is the staple production, and the most welcome news any steamer brings from Britain is news of a rise in the grain market."[25] By the 1850s some storekeepers began accepting butter and eggs, and produce speculators were buying limited amounts of pork, oats, peas, and barley as well as wheat.[26] Mortgage money was more readily available, and in the region as a whole the supply of seeds and quality stock was diversifying. Farmers who were no longer forced to give much of their labour to clearing and who had surmounted the problem of weeds usually began to replace some of their wheat acreage with oats, peas, barley, and hay and to increase their number of livestock. In 1862 one settler intended "to sow less wheat and more peas, oats, and perhaps barley. I find wheat is no sure crop as these."[27] Always tied to the market, farmers began to move towards mixed farming as the market diversified and as the means became available to practise a more heavily capitalized agriculture.

The creation of a farm in Mono's forested hills depended on hard work. Bees distributed some of the work, and a little clearing and plowing was done by hired hands, but farms were created, essentially, by long days and years of family work. "It is wonderful," wrote one settler, "the amount of labour a person has to do before they get things as they would like."[28] Substituted for the capital settlers did not have, labour was the means to some comfort and security; it was a necessity, but, in Mono, also a virtue. None of the sermons preached in early Mono have survived, but the Orangeville *Sun,* which began publishing in the early 1860s, offered its readers regular homilies on the subject of work. "Let *Enterprise* and her handmaiden *Industry* be the ruling features in the agricultural community" stated an editorial on agriculture in the *Sun;*[29] a settler writing to a brother in Scotland thought that if the Glasgow poor "could be transplanted in this space [unsettled lots] and possessed of habits of temperance, industry, and economy, how much better they would certainly be."[30] "The true art of life," reported another editorial in the *Sun,* "consists in working your way."[31] Labour had made the world, cleared its forest, cut its canals. "It is labour that has done it all, and the knowledge of this fact should act as an incentive, urging us to toil with ceaseless activity. This is the principle on which we retain whatever talents God has lent us." Labour could bring success, first on earth, and afterward in heaven.[32] Such ideas, which turned the inevitable round of back-breaking pioneer work into a fulfillment of God's purpose and a promise of the world to come, drew on a theology that was not foreign to Ulster.

But Mono was not Ulster, and the experience of pioneering was new in several important ways. Mono made both success (in the form of a sizable cleared farm) and failure accessible to the ordinary immigrant. After a lifetime of work, some settlers created substantial farms. Others died or gave up. Mono held out the possibility of success as Ulster had not, but between the possibility and the reality lay years of work and the spectre of failure. Then, too, Mono intensified individual isolation, especially in the early pioneer years as pioneers carved tiny, remote clearings in the forest and as new settlers came and went. Finally, Mono forced pioneers to adjust to physical change in a place without a past.

Today, the oldest inhabitants of Mono remember "the early days," which for them are the 1890s, as a time of abundance, but life was bitterly hard in the first decades of pioneering. Forests in nineteenth-century Ulster were protected on estates; most immigrants had never used an axe and knew nothing of land clearing. Bears, wolves, and the Mississaugas were equally unfamiliar, all threatening ingredients of an alien setting. The handful of Indigenous peoples in or near Mono were soon found to be peaceful; the only incident widely attributed to them was the theft of two children. Bears and wolves were found to "prowl about mostly at night"[33] and rarely attacked anyone. The forest was a more implacable threat. It surrounded and isolated farmsteads and could lose anyone who wandered into it. "Being lost in the forest," reported one newcomer, "was equivalent to losing your life,"[34] and many would-be settlers recoiled at the prospect of living there. The following matter-of-fact account describes a common reaction:

> The bearer of this is a discharged soldier named George Hopkins lately of the Second battalion rifle brigade – having served under his Grace the Duke of Wellington through the whole of the continental war in Portugal and lastly at Waterloo.

> Having arrived in this country last summer with a wife and
> family of Small Children and being disappointed in not having his
> pension forwarded to him was under the necessity of repairing to
> this back township in the neighbourhood of which he had drawn
> 100 acres as his servitude land not being acquainted with chopping
> and his land being in a remote situation surrounded by an extensive
> cedar swamp and inhabited only by beasts of prey – was advised
> to buy an acre in the immediate neighbourhood of a mill and
> inhabitants.[35]

Later, as clearing proceeded, the settlers' perception of the forest
changed. A school teacher wrote of "these glorious woods";[36] most
farmers hunted and kept a deer log (a chopped tree impregnated with
salt); and at least one maintained that it was easier to settle in the
"shelter" of the forest than on the open plains of the American west.[37]
These appraisals emerged when the prospect of a farm seemed assured;
initially, the forest – unfamiliar, implacable, and terrifying – was a
massive barrier between the settler and his farm.

When cleared, much of Mono's rolling, morainic land could not
produce a living. Lots that an inspector in the mid-1830s had declared
"hilly and swampy and not fit for settlement" were occupied a few years
later.[38] In 1866 another inspector reported:

> The said half lot w ½ lot 27, 4th concession has been occupied for
> a number of years past by George Frines. That he has a dwelling
> house, barn and other buildings erected thereon and Some fifteen
> acres cleared and improved. That no other improvements have
> been made on said half lot by any other person or persons whom-
> soever, but all that is made thereon has been made for and by the
> Said G. Frines That he has a wife and Some eight children, the
> eldest only about 16 years of age, and that he is a very ... Sickly man
> himself. That the land is of an exceptionally bad quality Hilly, Stony
> and Sandy, Scarcely worth living upon.[39]

Settlers had avoided swamps but had accepted all other land. Guide
books warned against the light soils of the beech-maple upland, but

some 40 percent of the settlers in Mono were illiterate,[40] and probably few others ever read a guide. Although established settlers had advice for newcomers, poor immigrants who had acquired lots sight unseen often struggled to make the best of what they had. Even on good land, the task of establishing a farm could be overpowering. Some men gave up, deserting their families. "I lived with my Father and Mother on the said Lot," wrote an immigrant's daughter, "and helped them to work upon it in the year 1834 my Father went to Toronto for his Pension he never returned nor any account of him."[41] Many died, usually of what settlers called swamp fever (probably malaria). "I am now informed by the Heir at Law that the Locattee Michael Killeen settled upon the grant shortly after he obtained it, and that he Cleared about Ten acres and Built a house upon one of the lots, and then took Sick and died, and his family being young they were obliged to move from the land."[42] Although the frequency of failures is now almost impossible to determine,[43] references such as these in the Crown Land papers as well as frequent notices of sheriffs' sales and of the transfer of land to mortgagees leave no doubt that they were common.

There were also successes. By the 1860s, advertisements in the Orangeville *Sun* described the farms some immigrants had created.

> To be sold on easy terms that Excellent Farm of Land being the West half of Lot No. 15, 6th concession, East Hurontario Street, Mono, containing 100 acres, 60 of which are well cleared, fenced and in a good state of cultivation. There are on the premises a Log Dwelling and Barn in good condition, also a frame Barn, a thriving young orchard and other improvements on premises.[44]

By the 1870s there were descriptions of more elaborate farms:

> The subscriber offers for sale that desirable farm property, 10 miles from Orangeville ... in the township of Mono, containing 100 acres more or less, 75 acres cleared, nearly free from stumps, well fenced with cedar, the soil is good, and in a high state of cultivation, the balance being good hardwood with some cedar and hemlock – on the premises are a good enough cast frame dwelling house 32 × 23

feet containing seven rooms with stone cellar ... there is also a
frame barn 48 × 60 feet. These buildings are nearly new. Also a
Log Barn and Stable capable of holding 20 tons of hay, also two
well of water.[45]

Such farms represented a level of material achievement unknown to
any of the immigrants in Ulster, a level equivalent to, or better than,
that of the few prosperous Ulster farmers. However high the failure rate,
Mono's knobby terrain held out the opportunity for Ulster farmer-
weavers to improve their lot in the world.

For many years settlers were isolated from their immediate neighbours.[46] The story is still told in Mono that two of its first pioneers, the
Turnbulls and the Henrys, lived within two miles for more than a year
without knowledge of each other until one day a strange cow appeared
in the Turnbull clearing. Followed back through the forest, it led to the
Henrys.[47] The tale is credible, for the two families apparently had entered Mono from opposite directions, and within the forest the smoke
of pioneer burning could not be seen from a distance. In 1843, clearings
were still tiny patches in the forest (Figure 13); in the northern two-
thirds of Mono, clearings on adjacent lots began to coalesce only in
the 1850s. In 1857 one pioneer noted that there had been "considerable
difference in the appearance of this neighbourhood since we came
here, places which were then mere spots in the great forest begin to
assume the appearance of farms. Clearances are beginning to join each
other; roads are being opened up."[48] The joining of clearings brought
pioneer families out of the isolation of the forest, usually put a neighbour's farmhouse within sight, and must have appeared to mark the end
of the worst years of pioneering. Often, it had not come quickly. Many
Mono settlers had lived on their own, surrounded by the forest, for ten,
twenty, or more years. During all these years, they were connected to
markets and to supplies by sled in winter, but otherwise, before regular
church services and the establishment of schools, they did not often
travel off the farm. Some gathered on July 12 or when a preacher passed
through. Occasionally, there was a clearing bee or a barn-raising bee
in the vicinity,[49] and forest trails must have permitted some visiting, but
many settlers, particularly the women, must have gone for weeks or

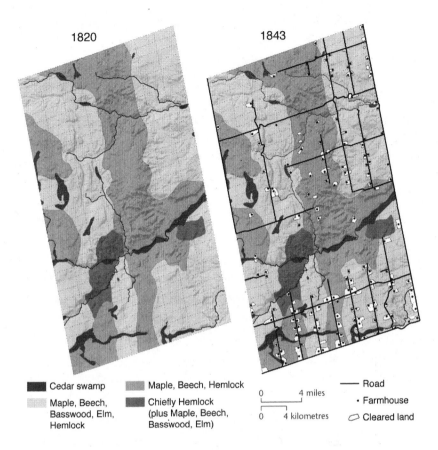

1820   1843

Cedar swamp   Maple, Beech, Hemlock   Road

Maple, Beech, Basswood, Elm, Hemlock   Chiefly Hemlock (plus Maple, Beech, Basswood, Elm)   Farmhouse   Cleared land

0   4 miles

0   4 kilometres

FIGURE 13

Mono Township, circa 1820 and in 1843 | Forest data from the surveyor's notes; settlement data primarily from the Crown Land Papers, Archives of Ontario

months at a time without human contacts beyond the immediate family. In 1855 a new arrival in a small settlement just north of Mono Township claimed: "There is no communication whatever from this [place] with any town or village, except when a farmer goes once or twice a year to market, and that is rarely unless when he can drive a sleigh, as the roads are so bad."[50] He exaggerated, but in so doing reveals something of the sense of isolation that emigrants from Ulster's densely settled countryside must have felt on their few cleared acres amid the forest of Mono.

The pioneers who settled amid the forests of Mono came as single men or as members of nuclear families. Often brothers followed each other to the township, and sometimes an uncle or a cousin settled close to his previously established relative, but the prevailing social unit of migration was always the nuclear rather than the extended family. Even in 1861, when many sons and grandsons of pioneers were farming in Mono, only eleven surnames were each represented by more than five families, and many nuclear families apparently had no relatives in the township.[51] Migration and settlement had exposed pioneers to strangers, an exposure that continued as neighbours came and went in the flux of the early pioneer years. Mono, then, isolated families physically much more than they had been in Ulster, and neighbours were not nearly so likely to be relatives or long-standing acquaintances. Later, as the local population and services increased and as roads improved, visiting became common (see the diary quoted above), and a loose rural community undoubtedly developed; even then, the Mono farmer appears to have been far more isolated than his Ulster counterpart.

Even more important, probably, in contributing to the distinctive experience of settlers in Mono was the lack, for them, of an authentic, local past. For its settlers, Mono was a future. Except for a handful of Indigenous people who were quickly pushed aside, there were no local pasts to impede change, no local reminders of alternative ways of living or of what the settlers themselves had been. Rather, there was the relentless work of pioneering that settlers with little capital could not avoid and the results of this work. Mono was a place where, by the sweat of their own brows, individuals might break out of poverty. Living without a local past, they tended to lose sight of the reasons why they had been forced into such a struggle, to lose touch with alternatives to it, and to define the acceptable in terms of their own experience of getting ahead in the world. Getting ahead depended on physical changes, many of which they themselves could work. Settlers sought, worked for, and lived within material change; and it was in this context that they received and assimilated the widespread mid-nineteenth-century belief in progress.

By the early 1860s, if not well before, the idea of progress was current in Mono Township. Inhabitants of Mono felt that things should be done "in a manner becoming the progress of the times."[52] Almost any candidate for election presented himself as "a friend of progress" or as "a commercial man who has a large stake in the prosperity of the Province."[53] Clearly, these were "times of progress in which it is our privilege to live." Tangible evidence of change, particularly the burgeoning industries and towns of Britain, the application of science to technology, and the rush of New World settlement, had popularized the idea of progress in the nineteenth century.[54] Immigrants to Mono Township came out of industrializing society, they depended on a changing technology, and they transformed a New World landscape. More than for most nineteenth-century people, their physical context was in flux. The striking changes in their world were material, and the exigencies of pioneering channelled their energies to bring them about. In the nineteenth century, the idea of progress became many things to many men,[55] but in Mono Township, a place without a past and a place settled by immigrants who had come to improve their lot in the world, it represented above all the real physical changes in which settlers themselves had participated.

THE KNOBBY TERRAIN OF Mono Township held out an opportunity for Ulster farmer-weavers to improve their lot in the world. Mono did not change essentially either their wants or their way of life. Most Ulster Protestants lived individually rather than collectively, farming individual leaseholds, living in dispersed settlements, and developing relatively formal social relationships. They reproduced all of this in Mono. Ulstermen were deeply attached to personal property, particularly land. Mono Township presented immigrants with the opportunity to own and improve land. Ulstermen worked hard for profit, and in Mono they could not survive without such work. In Ulster, individual economic drive was supported by religious belief, as it was in Mono. The racking experience of pioneering in Mono Township had left its considerable mark, but it did so by reinforcing certain Ulster traits. Pioneer families in Mono, settled on hundred-acre lots, enclosed by the forest and largely cut off from other people by poor roads and the lack of strong institutions, relied even more on their own initiative than did the independent farmer-weavers of Ulster. In Mono, neighbours were farther away, clachans absent, kin fewer. The physical isolation of pioneering, coupled with the social dislocation of migration, apparently had made Mono's the more individualistic society. Ulstermen worked hard for economic reward. In Mono, where there was no alternative to hard, protracted work, and where its rewards seemed tantalizingly great, the idea of work became even more enveloping. It was the difference between work without apparent prospects and work to create a farm. Those who survived the onslaught with the forest and the years of pioneer farming to create, by the late 1850s and 1860s, a moderately prosperous mixed farm felt a boundless satisfaction in their achievement. For them, at least, the gamble taken on leaving Ireland had paid off. They had brought their families out of poverty, they had succeeded where so many had failed, and they had done so, it seemed to them, on their own. Settled by a fragment of Ulster society, by poor people whose single-minded objective was to improve their lot, Mono encouraged their single-mindedness. Increasing the rewards for hard, individual work, it emphasized and acclaimed this activity.

Such energy quickly transformed Mono Township, and its evolving landscape lent material local support to the idea of progress. As a prescription for material change, the idea of progress was held conservatively. When progress could be achieved by changing the physical conditions of life, wrenching changes of society or self could be avoided. Progress became external to society and was associated with the physical environment.[56] Mono Township presented an opportunity for settlers to change their physical environment while leaving basic values and social structures intact; to transform a place while reinforcing an ideology. Ulster farmer-weavers who immigrated to a British city had no such opportunity. Most of them joined an industrial labour force, their independence controlled by factory whistle, foreman, and standard wages; their social philosophy eventually turning to those forms of collectivity associated with the working class in industrial society: unionism, socialism, and, for a few, Marxism. This was a radical change, unlike any that occurred in the settlement of Mono. Its settlers believed that they lived in an age of change and improvement; but Mono Township had provided a safety valve, and the material progress they lauded had enabled them to fortify what they were.

In this case, the safety valve was a hummocky, interlobate moraine in southern Ontario. That immigrants came to such a place is a measure of their economic plight in Ulster and of their attachment to a threatened way of life. Mono offered a chance to gain economic security without drastic social change, and it was in pursuit of that chance that Ulstermen sought out Mono and reworked its land. In so doing, they severely damaged a fragile physical environment. By the 1860s, alien weeds were common along roads and fence rows. Salmon no longer spawned in Mono's streams. As the forest was cleared, thin soils disappeared from sloping land. In many parts of the township, sheet erosion and gullying washed A and B horizons into hollows or streams, while exposed sands and silts began to blow as they had not since their consolidation under a postglacial forest.[57] Today, the denuded hills of Mono stand as by-products of British industrialization just as surely as the slums of Belfast, Glasgow, or Liverpool, while the social values those hills protected and enhanced still shape the mentality of Ontarians.

PART 3

The Architecture of Settlement

European Beginnings
in the Northwest Atlantic

There is no simple consensus about the extent to which settler colonies overseas reproduced metropolitan ways, or about the causes of such social and cultural change as there was. In my view, migration recontextualized people, and lives in different contexts could not come out quite the same. New contexts exerted selective pressures on former ways or introduced ingredients unknown in Europe, but perhaps the simplest and most powerful point to make about them is that they changed people's relationship with land. Compared to anywhere in Europe, land in these new settlements had lost most of its value; for that reason alone, social change was an inevitable result. In the early 1980s, I made this case in Boston at a conference on seventeenth-century New England, the centrepiece of which was a recent book

From "European Beginnings in the Northwest Atlantic: A Comparative View," in *Seventeenth-Century New England*, ed. David D. Hall and David Grayson Allen, Publications of the Colonial Society of Massachusetts, vol. 63 (Boston: Colonial Society of Massachusetts, 1984), 119–52.

on the transplanted, local Englishness of the early New England townships. Knowing far less about New England than anyone else in the room, I argued that details, but never the whole composition, of English life could be reproduced. The introduction to that paper suggests my approach to these matters.

MIGRATION IS A SPATIAL means of changing the relations of people and property that in situ change more or less rapidly with the passage of time. In medieval and early modern Europe, when changes in property relations were rapid, they were likely to have been unpremeditated and uncontrollable, as after war, plague, or accident; when they were slow, they were usually bound by rules of inheritance or by long-term adjustments in the relative costs of factors of production. Migration, on the other hand, could substitute new land – new property – for both chance and time, as it did, in a limited way, when people moved from the open-field lowlands of southeastern England to the more forested western uplands, or as it would do, more decisively, when they moved overseas. Transatlantic migration changed the relationship between people and property more drastically than the Black Death and more rapidly than any system of inheritance.[1] For many, this was North America's attraction: the opportunity to bypass both the confining grid of custom and power that dominated European property and the vagaries of chance that, at the personal level, usually turned on relatives' life spans. The opportunity could be seized individually (to improve one's lot in the world) or collectively (to impose, untrammelled, a European social vision on a new setting). Perceptions of opportunity were rooted in European custom and thought, but immigrants found themselves in new settings where people and property could not be recombined as in Europe. The change was quick and pervasive. Those of European descent in North America at the end of the seventeenth century spoke European languages and practised countless European ways while living in societies without precise European equivalents.

It was not only, or even primarily, that they had moved back into the forest, although of course they had. There is something of north-western France before the eleventh- and twelfth-century clearances, or of Anglo-Saxon England when beaver, bears, boars, and wolves were still in English forests and commoners hunted freely there, in the experience of seventeenth-century Europeans in North American middle latitudes. When William the Conqueror established royal forests and forbade hunting in them, "the rich," reported the Anglo-Saxon Chronicle, "complained and the poor lamented."[2] They also became poachers and over the centuries reached into dwindling forests for turf, wood, lops, faggots, berries, fish, and game and practised their innumerable evasions against the constables, rangers, foresters, woodwards, verderers, regarders, and gamekeepers – to use English names for offices that were European – who were there to protect trees and game: another's property.[3] In seventeenth-century North America, forests again were relatively open for gathering, chopping, and hunting but, of course, early modern rather than medieval Europe participated in this transatlantic reencounter. Commercial capital vigorously crossed the Atlantic, and with it came the technologies of resource exploitation, the labourers and settlers, and the trade that placed the early European settlements on the edge of North America within a seventeenth-century transatlantic web of prices, laws, institutions, and values.

Yet when seventeenth-century Europeans settled in eastern North America, their context was drastically altered. There was forest where there had been cleared land; sparse, isolated populations where there had been dense, continuous settlement; and beginnings in strange places where there had been continuity in familiar ones. There were unknown, neolithic people, missing European ways, and new relationships among the factors of production and with markets. Europeans were no longer in Europe. If European elements could be reestablished overseas, Europe could not – not even the fullness of any of its local regions. The context of life was different, and perhaps the most basic assertions that can be made about this pervasive change are that the relationships between people and property had changed and, following therefrom, the relationships between people as well.

The question then is raised of whether there was pattern in these changes and, if so, in what elements of European life overseas and at what scale? While the literature on European settlement in seventeenth-century North America frequently toys with the possibility of pattern,[4] it trusts local or regional studies that emphasize the variety of European experiences overseas. There is wisdom in such caution. Yet were a more vigorous comparative and interdisciplinary literature to develop, it would have to rest on the assumption that individual settlements were not entirely unique, and also on some tentative assessment of the nature of their common patterns and of the processes that created them. This is a daunting order, but ... perhaps an analytical framework for comparative study can be discerned. In any event, such presumption forms the basis of this essay.

Its essential premise is that the ideas implicit in European cultures were mobile, and that emigrants carried them far and wide to new settings that then exerted selective pressures. By "new settings" is meant the new relations among land, labour, and capital in which immigrants found themselves or, succinctly, their new relations with property. It is assumed to be in response to this nexus of New World relationships, rather than in response to the influence of the physical environment itself, that new settlements and societies emerged in the northwestern Atlantic area in the seventeenth century. Certainly, in the view presented here, the nature of New World societies cannot be deduced from an understanding of Old World ideas. If most of the details of seventeenth-century European settlements in northeastern North America were European, their compositions reflected selective pressures imposed in new settings.

The Overseas Simplification of Europe

Less bold than its title suggests, this essay treats the beginnings of three middle-latitude corners of European overseas expansion: early French Canada, early English New England, and early Dutch South Africa. Within these colonies, it leaves aside towns and work camps (fishing stations, trading posts) and considers only the agricultural settlements in which most people lived. These were settlements that, for the most part, reproduced northwestern European crop-livestock combinations on small farms dependent on family labour and that found limited markets for their produce. It is in relation to these circumstances that I consider the simplification of Europe overseas.

Were one to compare any substantial part of Europe today with any substantial part of the overseas places where Europeans have long been settled, it would be

From "The Simplification of Europe Overseas," *Annals of the Association of American Geographers* 67, 4 (1977): 469–83.

foolish to argue that one is simpler or more complex than the other. But if one goes back to the beginnings of European settlement overseas, it is possible, I think, to show that some aspects of European life did not transplant well and that, therefore, the European legacy was simplified in these settings. And it may be that until this weakened European legacy was filled in, as it were, by "New World" experience, relatively pared back societies had a considerable life. Such is the work this article attempted. Reading it now, more than forty years after I wrote it, I find my writing too strident, my case perhaps pushed too far. But the argument is clear, and I would still defend most of it.

I T IS A STRIKING INSIGHT that Europeans established overseas drastically simplified versions of European society.[1] For the political scientist Louis Hartz, the mechanism of simplification was the emigration of a fragment of the larger society and then its long isolation and independent development in a colonial setting.[2] In essence, according to Hartz, simplification of the rich pool of European ways occurred at the point of departure. In this essay I shall argue that the Hartzian mechanism is characteristically wrong and that a similar result can be explained more accurately by a model that emphasizes the nature of the European encounter with a new environment.[3] Customs, values, and ideas were mobile, and a remarkable range of them entered most colonial settings; there, they experienced strong selective pressures that emphasized some tendencies and atrophied others. The task is to identify the factors that exerted selective pressure and to describe the results of that selection with considerably more precision than emerged in Turner's tantalizing frontier vision.[4]

European society reflected its particular connection with the land. When emigrating Europeans suddenly transformed their access to land, social change was the inevitable result. Those who found their way to the countryside of middle-latitude colonies in the seventeenth and eighteenth centuries usually encountered cheap land and poor markets for agricultural products, conditions that were sufficient to pare away most of the social hierarchy of the European countryside, and to emphasize the family farm within a relatively homogeneous and egalitarian society. A measure of complexity would be reintroduced – but European rural society would not be reestablished – when these conditions no longer applied. A first part of this essay explores these general relationships. A second part assesses the relevance of the argument to early Canada, South Africa, and New England, areas settled by quite different groups of Europeans who, for a time at least, faced broadly similar conditions: uncertain markets, cheap land and, because of it, expensive white labour. Similar conditions would be expected to have elicited similar social and landscape responses, and I attempt to show that they do. A brief final part considers the wider relevance of the environmental model as I have used it. If my general proposition is sound, the social change induced in rural areas by cheap land and poor markets is but a particular instance of the pervasive social changes that ensued because Europeans overseas had access to land in ways that Europeans did not.

The General Argument

In those parts of northwestern Europe from which early in the seventeenth century emigrants began to trickle overseas, land was scarce and expensive and labour abundant and cheap. Agricultural land was still the primary source of wealth; peasants clung to the small holdings that stood between them and ruin, royal treasuries depended on taxes levied on those who worked the land, and gentry and nobility financed their comforts with rents from landed property. The rising bourgeoisie, who as creditors, managers, and owners controlled a large and growing percentage of the countryside, brought an aggressive conception of commercial opportunity to an old, land-based, socioeconomic system. Those who controlled a good deal of land were prosperous and, eventually, socially acceptable, but when labour was cheap and land was dear, few who did not have land had any means to acquire it. In such circumstances, wealth and status were distributed very unevenly. Within countless agricultural villages, there were farmers who had enough land to support a team of horses and many more day labourers who were virtually landless. Between them were artisans and small farmers with their bits of land and precise social standing. Outside the villages usually – a world away from the peasantry – were the abbeys and priories, the walled estates, the often elegant residences of the owners of village land and, at the top of this land-based social pyramid, the monarch.

Except in the Celtic fringe of western Europe, and in parts of central France, the nuclear family was the primary unit of social organization throughout this differentiated society.[5] A compact medieval society – in which the nuclear family often had been submerged in the family name of the nobility; in the households of gentry, merchants, and successful artisans; and in the village community of the peasantry; in short, in the intimate daily juxtaposition of people of different station – had been giving way over several centuries to another, more cellular society organized around the parent-child group. In the seventeenth century, this social transformation was far from complete. The children of the poor commonly left their parents at an early age, and noble inheritance still emphasized name and line, but most Europeans who emigrated overseas took with them the sentiment, if not always the experience, of the independent nuclear family. Usually, they came from the poorer peasantry or from the equally poor in the towns. Central to the lives of such people was an aspiration for family-centred independence in a trade or on enough land to pay taxes and rents, to provide some cushion when harvests were poor, and to avoid debt. The constraints on individual initiative embodied in the open-field system and in the use of common pasture served to give poor families some economic security rather than to embody a community.[6] Where living standards were higher, collective constraints relaxed and prosperous farmers often farmed individually; where living standards were lower, these constraints were vigorously defended. In all the peasant agitation that accompanied the gradual enclosure of the English countryside, the social importance of the village community was hardly mentioned for the perceived threat of enclosure was to the livelihood of poor families.[7] By the end of the eighteenth century, the doctrine of natural right would turn the craving for independence into a political ideology – many French peasants and labourers became Jacobins, and English labourers and artisans were deeply influenced by the liberal argument popularized in Thomas Paine's *The Rights of Man* – but most Europeans carried overseas a far older and far less explicitly ideological aspiration for family-centred independence.

Throughout northwestern Europe, rural society was still deeply local. Goods, people, and ideas moved slowly across a countryside where there were dense networks of local cart roads and paths but few rapid, safe routes of interregional travel. Few goods travelled more than fifteen miles overland, much production was of subsistent nature, and little reached beyond nearby regional markets. Unless they lived on navigable water, most people were cut off from outside goods and ideas. The few rich might travel a good deal; some of the landless poor wandered and begged. Population pressure in parts of seventeenth-century England was forcing many young adults out of the parishes of their birth, but very few of them moved much further than the neighbouring parish or two, hardly far enough to leave the local cultural regions of their birth.[8] Ordinary people lived within a web of inherited custom, some of it orally taught, much acquired unconsciously by example, little of it ever written down. Such societies were spatially confined and temporally extended. They had little capacity for overland movement but, in situ, a deep inertia.

As the centuries had worked innumerable local traditions into the land, the European countryside had become a carpet of different human landscapes. For a traveller, the look of the land would change after a day or two's slow traverse, as would the accents, superstitions, and material culture of its inhabitants. But almost everywhere land was nearly as densely settled as the prevailing agricultural system allowed. Almost everywhere there was evidence of protracted competition for the private control of scarce land, and of the uneven results of that competition. Here and there, more in some areas than in others, the land was enclosed and settlement was dispersed. This was sometimes the work of improving landlords but as often of individual peasant families who had acquired the means and confidence to move away from the agricultural routine of the village community. In general, ordinary people found more opportunity for independence where population pressure was less. In the century after the Black Death, when depopulation raised the price of labour and reduced the price of land, many peasants had achieved a considerable measure of independence, as in some areas of newer settlement and lower land prices they still did in the seventeenth century.[9]

The compact, dense, socially stratified, family-based, and regionally varied rural societies of northwestern Europe, rooted in a much tilled land and expressed in a mosaic of traditional landscapes, would not be reproduced in middle-latitude settings overseas. These settings were powerful filters that admitted some European elements, rejected others and, in sum, drastically simplified a complex European heritage. Their most influential characteristics, cheap land and poor markets for agricultural products, favoured the establishment of the independent nuclear household and pared away most of the socioeconomic hierarchy and local regional variety of European rural life.

Agricultural land in new colonies was not quite for the taking. Yet Indigenous peoples were relatively easily displaced by immigrants with a superior armament, and official entry fees and surveying charges were low, absent, or disregarded. Usually, the forest was the more implacable obstacle to agricultural settlement, and many pioneers gave their lives to clearing it. In spite of the high labour cost of clearing, arable and pasture were far cheaper than in the mother country, never more than a third, often no more than a tenth, of the price. For many years uncleared land was virtually free. White labour in these colonies was several times more expensive than in Europe. Usually there was not a pool of cheap Indigenous labour, and the cost of white labour was bid up by the accessible alternative of farming.[10] In these circumstances the immigrant, who in Europe would have worked out his life to stay alive and would never have purchased land, might eventually live in relative independence on his own.

Emigration placed thousands of miles between the colonist and Europe, enough to exclude the common European cereals and stock raised in middle-latitude colonies from the depressed agricultural markets of seventeenth-century Europe. In time, markets developed within the colonies, with the shipping that called at colonial ports and, in some cases, with other colonies, but they were largely supplied by a few well-situated farmers near the ports. Each move to new land in the interior took settlers farther from their markets at a time when overland transfer costs were high. With land but no export staple, falling prices, and chronic overproduction, seventeenth-century farmers in middle-latitude colonies faced an overriding problem of marketing. Their agriculture, in such circumstances, was primarily subsistent.

As long as land was accessible to the poor, each of the seventeenth-century extensions of Europe into middle-latitude environments overseas was a "poor man's country." In such conditions, the mass of desperately poor people in the European countryside would not be reproduced. The children of immigrants would achieve a living standard comparable to that of the average French *laboureur* or English yeoman, that is, within the top 10 percent of the northwestern European peasantry. They held more cleared land, kept more stock, ate better, married on average a little younger, had more children, and lived longer than most European peasants.[11] But in colonies where markets were poor and land values static, rough sufficiency could not be turned into ease. Farmers provided for their families and occasionally sold a few stock or a little grain, but the prosperity of the few most successful European peasants – the rich laboureurs, yeoman, and tenant farmers – eluded them. For the same reason, the socioeconomic superstructure that in Europe was built on the land and the labour of those who worked it, could not be reestablished. The rural penetration of the bourgeoisie was thwarted because for many years the countryside rewarded neither investment nor entrepreneurship; a landed aristocracy could hardly emerge where land was cheap and its products largely unmarketable; colonial officials could not dominate settings where harsh taxes would deflect immigrants and settlers could move to cheap land on a scarcely regulated frontier. In effect, colonial conditions quickly pared the rich and powerful as well as the destitute from the countryside.

At the same time, the European craving for family-centred independence had found territory for its abundant expression. Family homesteads and farms spread across the land. As long as land remained available and markets remained poor, the circumstances of one family were much like those of another. Socioeconomic differences among immigrants would be pared away quickly, while among relatively homogeneous groups of poor immigrants socioeconomic differentiation would not develop very far. When the father died, one son would take over the family farm; the others would move on to reproduce a similar unit of settlement. By European standards these were monotonously simple, egalitarian societies. The external spheres of influence that, in Europe, impinged on the independence of the ordinary family church, village, seigneurie or manor, town, province, and state – had weakened. Associations were less frequently imposed, more frequently voluntary. The social structure was dominated by individual nuclear households, each on a primarily subsistent farm that gave the family a large measure of autonomy but hardly the opportunity to dominate others.

European regional customs were thrown together in these societies, often within individual households. Immigrants brought a wealth of different local superstitions, accents, dialects, languages, social customs, and material cultures, but most of this would not survive when, suddenly, there was no longer a sustaining society of people steeped in the same traditions. The first colonial marriages were powerful cultural mixers; the marriages of their offspring stirred the brew further. Micro-regional differences in the settlers' collective heritage were quickly lost in a process of simplification and generalization. The many different house types that immigrants had known gave way to a few, accents converged, dress became more nearly common, and many local European demons and sprites must have disappeared from view. Elements of a complex European heritage that were dominant among immigrants or that were particularly suited to new conditions were emphasized. Other elements were eliminated as in each colony the many local cultures of the immigrants' backgrounds collapsed into one.

The human landscapes of these settlements were European in detail but not in composition. There had been little borrowing from Indigenous peoples, very little invention. Most of the elements of material life were

European, although the mix was not that of any particular European place. The rural landscapes had been enormously simplified. Gone were the extremes of wealth and squalor of the European countryside – the mansions, walled estates, and landscaped gardens; the hovels and minuscule garden plots. In their place rose farmhouse after farmhouse, most of them set amid their own fields, one house much like another, one farm much like the next. Where settlement was recent, clearings and buildings were small and rough, where it was a little older they were larger and more finished, different stages of a common process that culminated with the establishment of a family farm. Such landscapes were the monotonous, powerful compositions of settings that had released one current of European life while stifling the others.

In every colony the homogeneous and egalitarian rural societies that had emerged around the nuclear family in settings where land was cheap and markets were poor contained the seeds of their own destruction. Land would not remain cheap. Eventually, markets would improve. Sooner or later, population growth alone would fill the available territory and bid up the price of land. A larger population would improve the local market for agricultural products and, in time, colonies would establish regular channels for agricultural exports. In colonies where immigrants were few, the land base extensive, and the market chronically depressed, a simple society of subsistent farmers might be sustained for generations. Some of the young would stay on the parental farm amid an increasingly consanguineous population. Others would establish on new land replicas of the family farms of their childhoods, and in this way the life and landscape created near the coast by the first generation might be reproduced far in the interior four or even six generations later. Without the infusion of new immigrants from Europe such societies would have a striking capacity to spread a simple way of life over a huge territory. Yet eventually and ineluctably, population pressures would increase land prices, and when this happened the opportunity for every man to establish his family on a subsistent farm would no longer exist. In other colonies, population growth, territorial limitations, and improving markets might compress the same process into a few years.

As soon as land became expensive, socioeconomic differentiation increased. The poor could no longer afford land. Their labour became cheaply available. Those with land profited from its rising value and from the declining value of labour. There was now an opportunity, particularly if agricultural markets were also buoyant, for some to become rich and for inequality to be compounded generation by generation. Mansion and hovel would again coexist in the countryside. The autonomy and independence of the ordinary nuclear family would again be threatened. Many men would leave their families to seek seasonal wage labour. Many individuals and families would migrate to the cities or to cheap land far away, moves as momentous for them and for their descendants as the decision of their forebears to leave Europe, and moves that were powerful carriers of the recent experience and nostalgia of rural self-sufficiency.

Canada, South Africa, and New England

Early Canada, South Africa, and New England were distinctive physical environments settled for different reasons by different Europeans who had little or no contact with one another. Canada was French and Catholic, a colonial byproduct of the fur trade. South Africa was primarily Dutch and German, Calvinist, an inadvertent colonial offshoot of a refreshment station of the Dutch East India Company. New England, for some of its founders, was a haven from religious persecution, a place where, freed of the trammels of corrupt society, a Puritan utopian vision might become a reality. The prosperous, dissenting Hampshire yeoman, the regimental foot soldier from Saintonge, and the indigent Rhinelander employed by the Dutch East India Company apparently had little enough in common.

Throughout the French regime in Canada, and for some years thereafter, uncleared land could be obtained free in most seigneuries and held for an annual rent that was less than 10 percent of the gross product of the developing farm.[12] Cleared land brought a price, its value reflecting the labour cost of clearing. Early in the eighteenth century, a farm with fifteen cleared acres, a one-room cabin, a small farm building, and perhaps sixty acres still in forest was worth 1,000 to 1,500 *livres*, the price of two to four acres of good arable land in Normandy.[13] In this colony with few immigrants, abundant land for new farms, and a chronically depressed market for agricultural products, land values remained static for almost a century and a half. Near the Cape of Good Hope early in the eighteenth century, good arable land was worth a third as much as its Dutch counterpart, although its value would not increase until the 1770s, when more ships began to call at the Cape and the market for arable produce improved.[14] In the interior, grazing permits (*leeningsplaatsen*) for a minimum of six thousand acres could be obtained for an annual fee equivalent to the cost of two to four cows.[15] Leeningsplaatsen were virtually freeholds. Their holders could sell buildings and improvements (the *opstal*), and land use was officially constrained only by rules preventing subdivision and subleasing. When the holder of a leeningsplaats died, his children often sold the opstal, using the divided money to purchase stock for a new leeningsplaats that, on application, could be obtained farther in the interior. In New England, an early commentator advised immigrants: "If any man doubt the goodness of the ground let him comfort himself with the cheapness of it."[16] Applicants who supported the social order obtained free land grants in the early townships, the most important individuals usually receiving four or five times as much land as the least important. Before the end of the eighteenth century, land was usually acquired by purchase. On the eve of the revolution, wild land brought one-half to fifteen shillings an acre depending on location.[17] There were steep gradients in land prices around the ports, and in many older townships rising land prices and a tight oligarchy of important early settlers restricted access to land, excluding newcomers and forcing the emigration of many of the young. The poor could still find cheap land on the frontier, although in the eighteenth century, as the population rose rapidly and as commercial connections improved, land values in some frontier townships would increase tenfold within a generation.[18]

In Canada, South Africa, and New England, most farmers made some sales every year, but overproduction was chronic and prices were low. Canada was isolated by its inland location from the commercial world of the North Atlantic, and its towns were small markets for agricultural products. The price of wheat, the colony's principal agricultural product, declined irregularly from 1650 to 1720 and then rose sluggishly when, for a time, there was some sale to Louisbourg, the French fortress on Cape Breton Island, and to the French islands in the Caribbean.[19] There was a small market for the Cape colony's agricultural products in Cape Town and a somewhat larger but limited export market with Dutch East India Company shipping and occasional other ships that happened to call. Before 1685 the colony was an importer of food; by 1700, there were regular problems of overproduction. At subsidized company prices, South African wheat brought seven and a half to eight guilders the muid (3.1 bushels) throughout the eighteenth century, but on the open market the price of wheat fluctuated as much as a third below the subsidized price. Although mutton was the Cape's principal meat export, sheep prices were low and falling through much of the eighteenth century; the price of draft oxen followed a similar if less extreme curve.[20] Commercial opportunities in New England were much more diverse. More immigrants and a far larger population stimulated local markets, while New England merchants were soon trading food-stuffs from Newfoundland to the Caribbean. Yet only farmers who lived close to navigable water participated in this coasting trade, and their participation was limited by the high cost of labour.[21] There were patches of commercial agriculture along the coast, but most farms were primarily subsistent, a characteristic of New England's agriculture that changed only slowly in the eighteenth century as population and prices rose and labour costs declined. In rural Canada and South Africa, the social and landscape responses to these conditions were simple, durable, and almost identical. Town and countryside became different social worlds. The nuclear family acquired a striking autonomy and independence on a long-lot farm stretching back from river or road, or on a vast leening-splaats on the South African veld. Rural life exhibited a remarkable sameness: the socioeconomic range of the European countryside was severely compressed, and in each colony the many local regional cultures of the immigrants' backgrounds fused into one. As long as there were few employment alternatives to agriculture and cheap land remained available, relatively undifferentiated white, rural societies were perpetuated by territorial expansion. When, after many generations, cheap land was no longer available, such rural societies were no longer viable.

For most immigrants who stayed in Canada, there were no vocational alternatives to farming. The fur trade required little manpower; there were not many opportunities for artisans and labourers in the towns. An engagé would work out his years of indenture, perhaps farm for a few years on rented land, and sometime during these years he would apply for and receive a forested riverfront lot on one or other seigneurie nearby. Had he amassed a little capital, he might hire a man to clear a few acres while he lived on the rented farm. Perhaps after several moves he would settle down on a lot, build a tiny house of *pièce sur pièce,* raise a family, apply for lots nearby for his sons and, when he died, leave his property to all his offspring. One son would stay on the family farm, gradually paying off his brothers and sisters for their equal shares in the inheritance, and the other children would move off to establish their own farms and families. When riverfront land was taken, interior *rangs* would open, and in this way the opportunity of the first generation would be reproduced by successive generations until settlement reached the Canadian Shield or the Appalachian Highlands.[22]

Little enough impinged from the outside on this habitant world. Seigneurial charges were low and often uncollected when seigneuries were sparsely settled, and in most seigneuries several generations would pass before the manor house was any more pretentious than the adjacent farmhouses. For years new settlements were served intermittently by missionary priests. *Curés* were eventually established, but tithes were lower than in France, and the *fabrique* (church vestry) never attained the importance of the *assemblée des habitants* with which it tended to merge in France. In Canada there was no royal *taille* or *gabelle* to apportion and collect, and few if any collective agricultural decisions to take; these were principal functions of the village plutocracy that comprised the assemblée des habitants in France. The Canadian bourgeoisie participated in the fur trade and in the commercial life of the towns and neglected a countryside where there was so little commercial momentum that after many decades of rural settlement there were still no agricultural villages. Within a few miles of Quebec or Montreal, the bourgeoisie owned perhaps 20 percent of the farmland; elsewhere, they owned virtually none of it.[23] French law, French officials, and most strata of French society had come to Canada, but the land that gave ordinary people a living and a stagnant agrarian economy that deflected the prosperous from the countryside allowed a Canadian peasantry a striking independence from the institutional and fiscal burdens of French peasant life. Long-lot farm, river, and forest produced a living, not much more. Occasional sales allowed occasional purchases. The core of this rural society was the nuclear family, and the core of its world was the long-lot farm with thirty or forty cleared acres, a small farm house, a few farm buildings, neighbours (who, in the older settlements, were likely to be relatives) in similar circumstances on either side and, not too far away, land that would absorb the extra young. Near the South African Cape, where land values were relatively high, where there was a regular market for some agricultural products, and where the capital costs (principally for land and slaves) of establishing an arable farm were several times those of establishing a stock farm in the interior, arable farming was controlled by a few wealthy farmers. Poorer arable farmers were in debt to these few; some white men worked as overseers and artisans on the estates of the prosperous. Yet only a few could be successful arable farmers, and as some of their sons moved off into the interior, where with little capital they could establish themselves as *trekboeren*, they created a society with almost no institutional control over the nuclear family.

This independence stemmed from the trekboer's remarkable economic self-sufficiency on his vast land holding.[24] Occasionally he drove stock the tens or hundreds of miles to the market at the Cape; occasionally he traded with pedlars to obtain guns, powder, coffee, or cloth; but the leeningsplaats was essentially a subsistent operation that supplied almost all the needs of the small cluster of ten to thirty people – the trekboer and his family, a few Khoekhoe workers and their families, and perhaps one or two slaves – who lived on it miles from anyone else. A feeble commercial economy and a dispersed population supported neither villages nor artisans, so that even the social interaction bred of some economic specialization was almost entirely eliminated. There was no local store, inn, or mill. As late as the 1770s, there were only two company officials (*landdrost*) beyond the Cape Flats. No local school, church, or social gatherings brought a region's trekboeren together regularly. Occasionally there might be a visitor, usually another stock farmer en route to or from the Cape. Occasionally the white men in a district might form an armed Commando to pursue a party of San. On

Sunday, perhaps daily, the trekboer would assemble his family and read from the family Bible, which, in all likelihood, was his only book; and every now and then relatives living hundreds of miles apart would assemble for a family marriage or anniversary.

In isolated, clay-walled houses – the roofs made of sod or reeds; the floors of hard-packed clay, bullocks' blood, and cow dung; and the inhabitants a mix of Europeans, pigs, poultry, and Khoekhoe – the trekboeren lived out their lives in conditions that appalled some European visitors but that met basic requirements of food and shelter. With game plentiful in the early years and later with hundreds of their own stock and with cereals and vegetables grown for domestic consumption, there was always enough to eat. Threadbare European clothing was interminably patched and darned; house interiors were cluttered with skins, guns, and powder horns on the walls, sheepskin bedding on the floors, and dried meat hanging from the ceiling. Life was crude, but among even the poorer trekboeren debts were usually less than 30 percent of gross assets while, judging by estate inventories, the richest trekboer was only four or five times as well off as the poorest.[25] The trekboer family lived secure in its basic needs as, in Holland, only the most prosperous peasants were able to do. European visitors commented on the monotonous sameness of trekboer life in the tiny, isolated settlements on the veld.

Settlers in Canada came from all over western France, and a few from the Midi probably did not speak French. The Dutch, German, and French-speaking immigrants to South Africa were from even more diverse regional backgrounds. Yet in both colonies diversity very quickly gave way to a common habitant or trekboer type. Most immigrants came as individuals, and as nuclear families reformed in new settings, relatively few spouses were from the same regional background. Not more than a quarter of Canadian marriages before 1663 were between people from the same French province; in the early years in South Africa, a small population and a shortage of women created integrative forces powerful enough to incorporate several former slaves into the predominantly white society.[26] In pioneer households distinctive regional characteristics blurred and merged; in any given population there were too few people from a common background to support its distinctive culture. Although a group of Huguenots had established themselves at Franschoek in the 1680s, French was not spoken in South Africa sixty years later. In Canada, the few *langue d'oc* and Breton speakers were even more quickly assimilated into the predominant French. Regional varieties in accent, dress, and housing met the same standardizing fate. Settlers had gone through the similar experience of establishing a farm, and they dealt, however infrequently, with the same administration; their offspring would intermarry, and many of them moved to new land, carrying with them a common culture.

A remarkable longevity characterized these simple socially and culturally undifferentiated rural societies, but eventually population pressure and improved markets increased the price of land. Rapid social change was the result. Agricultural land became scarce along the lower St. Lawrence early in the nineteenth century. The offspring of lowland farmers struggled to implant the family farm on the inhospitable terrain of the Canadian Shield, but more turned to the lumber camps, to a factory in New England or, eventually, to the slums of Montreal, Quebec, or Trois-Rivières. A landless proletariat emerged. Rural society perpetuated itself by exporting many of its young, but it became more stratified. Distinguished seigneurial manor houses emerged in the countryside, and a few prosperous habitants began to stand out against a growing base of rural poverty. In South Africa, Xhosa resistance along the Fish River before the end of the eighteenth century imposed a limit on the colony's eastward expansion that had not existed for the more than one hundred years since Jan van Riebeeck had planted a thorn hedge around the initial settlement at the Cape. For more than a generation, population pressure increased. Then, in the 1830s, South African settlement turned northward. The Great Trek, the vanguard of this northward migration of white farmers and their families, permitted the survival of the trekboer way of life into the twentieth century. At the Cape, on the other hand, where there was a market for wheat, wine, and meat and where arable land within a radius of reasonable travel cost from Cape Town was limited, rural society had long been dominated by a few wealthy families. This society had not been created by a different class of immigrants but by conditions that had made wealth possible for a few. In Canada before the early nineteenth century, this opportunity had been almost entirely urban.

In New England, commercial opportunities, spatially and temporally variable land costs, and the hierarchical and communitarian social vision of many early settlers created a more diverse rural society, yet one revealing the tendencies that were carried to such extremes in Canada and South Africa. Around the ports, population pressure and accessible agricultural markets raised land prices and encouraged social stratification, as near the Cape. Where markets were poor and land costs low, as in most of rural New England in the seventeenth century, the bulk of rural society comprised semisubsistent farm families whose farms, economic means and, eventually, social standing varied within a narrow range.[27] The nuclear family became the principal medium of spatial mobility and the essential unit of farm work.[28] Rural settlement was soon dispersed – even in the first generation nucleated settlement was uncharacteristic – fields were enclosed, and agricultural decision making became individual rather than collective.[29] Regional differences introduced from Britain were quickly blurred or lost.[30] Farm families lived in some isolation on freehold farms that, far larger than most English peasant landholdings, gave them their livelihood and a considerable independence. Artisans, shopkeepers, and a few professional people lived in most rural areas but, in comparison with almost any English parish, the occupational range had diminished and the average living standard had risen to the approximate level of the poorer English yeoman. The top and bottom of English rural society were pared away.[31] Honorifics became less important, and the sense of social grade diminished.[32] A society in which people knew their social place within a finely graded hierarchy had given way to a far more atomistic society built around the nuclear family in possession of the means to provide its subsistence.[33] If an extreme form of this condition endured for many generations in Canada and South Africa, it was short-lived in New England. Population pressure, improved and diversifying markets for rural products, and, the measure of both, rising land costs soon excluded some from land while favouring those in possession of it. In the oldest townships, this process was well underway before the end of the seventeenth century. Invariably, and often remarkably quickly, poor newcomers could not obtain land, family landholdings were divided, some of the township's young no longer had access to township land, and an older group of landed elite came into conflict with the young and frequently landless.[34] Moves to other parts of the townlands or to a newer township were inevitably the result. In a township in western Connecticut settled in the late 1730s, the first settlers' speculative opportunity to acquire cheap land was quickly curtailed; by the third generation, less than forty years after initial settlement, many farms were divided, rural poverty was growing, and a considerable percentage of the young faced landlessness or emigration. By the 1790s, New England as a whole was overpopulated. Its society was rapidly becoming more stratified economically, and the underemployed poor were a growing problem.[35] In many townships the condition of the region as a whole at the end of the eighteenth century had been reached much earlier as improved markets and rising land costs destroyed a relatively undifferentiated rural society as rapidly as the earlier cheapness of land within an essentially subsistent economy had created it.[36]

What appears to set New England most apart from early Canada and South Africa, however, is less the pace of change than the founding vision of an organic, hierarchical society based on Christian love. Love and brotherhood – the "Model of Christian charity" – would be the bonds of Winthrops' "Citty upon a Hill." England was a "sinfull lande," its central sin an acquisitive individualism that set the rich increasingly apart from the poor and undermined the bonds of social responsibility. New England was a setting in which the dream of a better society might become a reality, a place where "men would serve their fellow men ... as God would have them serve."[37] Its society would be ordered and hierarchical. For Jonathan Edwards, there was a "beauty of order in society, as when the different members of society, have all their appointed offices, place and station, according to their several capacities and talents, and everyone keeps his place, and continues in his proper business."[38] Wealth and power were held from God not man; "love, mercy, gentleness, temperance" were godly duties of those to whom much had been granted. It was this deeply conservative, Christian vision of an organic society that placed educated and prosperous Englishmen in the New England wilderness, that in some instances transplanted groups of several families from one English parish to one New England township, and that infused the early New England countryside with a deductive overtone that was entirely absent in rural Canada and South Africa.[39]

But in New as in old England, the idea was not to be the reality. Some communities in some early townships may have approached it for a time, perhaps even for a generation or two. It was embedded in the admonitions of countless sermons for over a century and, in an increasingly individualistic society, such sermons undoubtedly touched an enduring sense of social responsibility. Yet a shocked and saddened Winthrop had soon lamented "how little of a public spirit appeared in the country, but selflove too much."[40] The vision had been doomed on two counts. It was not the common conviction of all immigrants nor, unequivocally, even of those who espoused it most fervently. The saints were seventeenth-century English men attached to private property and land ownership, to the nuclear family, and to the principle of independence, attachments that would coexist uneasily with any communitarian vision. And, in various ways New England presented individual opportunity. It was to be found in the vigorous commerce that quickly developed in Boston and Salem, on the commercial farms near the ports, and in land speculating and horse trading in newly settled, eighteenth-century townships. In settings where individual initiative might quickly yield wealth and standing, society was sharply differentiated, but not within the Puritan vision of an ordered, loving society in which everyone knew their traditional place. In most rural areas, cheap land gave ordinary people access to family farms that furnished a livelihood and an opportunity for family-centred independence in a relatively unstratified society. The family work of establishing and tending a farm, the relative spatial mobility of individual and nuclear family, and inertia of the community at a time when there was a steady expansion of settlement – most basically, the opportunity for the nuclear family to get along on its own in the world – combined with the deep aspiration for family-centred independence, had simply overridden a collective vision to emphasize another sentiment that was far more deeply ingrained in seventeenth-century Englishmen.[41]

In New England, as in Canada and South Africa, family farms spread across the countryside. The availability of land reinforced the sentiment of the family, and before the end of the eighteenth century a now explicit liberal ideology reflected to a considerable extent the reality of the New England past if not, paradoxically, of its present. A well-blended stream of young New Englanders would move to the Old North West seeking the opportunity that was no longer available in New England.

GRANTING THE HARTZIAN point that Europeans tended to establish overseas drastically simplified versions of European society, I have attempted to show that often, and probably characteristically, the mechanism of simplification had less to do with the particular fragment of Europeans who came to a given colony than with the conditions any Europeans encountered when they got there. The confrontation with a new land seems to me to be fundamental to understanding these new societies, and the particular terms of access to land to have shaped their essential characteristics. In the early colonial societies discussed in this essay, the crucial European inheritance was a strong sense of family supported by a desire for the private control of land, assumptions that were common to most northwestern Europeans. When they were introduced to settings where land was cheap and agricultural markets were poor, the results were foregone: the very prosperous and the very poor would be stripped from the countryside, and a remarkably homogeneous society would emerge around the independent nuclear family. The circumstances of one family would be much like those of another and, except within the family, the opportunity for domination would be relatively slight. The essential characteristics of the predominant rural societies of early Canada, South Africa, and New England are explained by this simple equation. Similar farms and farmhouses, the homes of largely subsistent farmers and their families, were scattered in different patterns across the landscapes of these colonies, the reflection but also substantially the cause of the simple societies that inhabited them.

Such societies – particularly habitant and trekboer societies – were extreme examples of a tendency that was probably widespread as Europeans moved to middle-latitude environments overseas in the seventeenth, eighteenth, and even nineteenth centuries. Newly opened land was often relatively cheap, labour was correspondingly expensive, and markets were temporarily limited. Whenever these conditions arose, there would be the tendency for the rich and poor to disappear from the countryside leaving a relatively homogeneous, family-centred society; and then, as land values rose with population pressure and improved markets, for society again to become more stratified. Most rural areas must have gone through this cycle in some form, the differences between them depending essentially on the initial cheapness of land and the timing of rising land costs. Staple agricultural exports in the southern colonies created rapid and extreme social stratification in some areas, but there were also areas of farming on cheap land poorly connected to markets where far less differentiated societies had a considerable life. The rich farmland of southeastern Pennsylvania provided an initial opportunity for almost every man, if soon a growing concentration of wealth among the wealthy. In the nineteenth century, declining transfer costs and mass migrations ensured that cheap agricultural land would not long be available in any given area. Even so, for a time there was an opportunity for the emigrating poor on the land of early Ontario, Indiana, Nebraska, Saskatchewan, or New South Wales that was not available to them in the societies they had left. Of course, access to land should not be measured categorically. There were gradations of land costs in space and time and gradations of purchasing power. A land price that presented an opportunity to one settler was prohibitive to another. A land area that long since had been closed to the very poor by rising land costs (except as wage labourers) might still provide a base for an expanding middle class.

When access to land had closed in on the poor and society again became more stratified, it did so after an experience that Europeans had not had. This was the levelling initial encounter with a land that for a time – to different degrees in different settings – had given the nuclear family a remarkable independence from external institutional constraints. The task of settling on one's own, the confrontation farm by farm and family by family with the wilderness, the conviction that success had been achieved by the sweat of one's brow, and the family-centred autonomy that for many had become a reality intensified a deep-seated European craving for independence by giving it a tangible outlet. When the opportunity declined, the nostalgia remained to ramify in countless ways through literature, politics, and the popular imagination. The ideological result was not always liberal individualism. In Canada, the Conquest and impinging Anglo-Saxon settlement created a self-conscious French Canadian minority with a strong sense of the collectivity, as in South Africa did the presence of a nonwhite majority and the Boer War. Sturdy self-reliance and a generic image of the trekboer way of life combined in Afrikaaner nationalism; until recently, French Canadian nationalism included an equally strong agrarianism turned by devoted clerics into a vision of piety within the rural parish. Ideological currents flowed in fascinating distributaries but always carried the sediment of encounter with a new land.

Finally, and in the broadest view, migration to middle-latitude environments overseas presented a vast opportunity for hard-headed, practical, enterprising men – in land clearing, in trade, in primary resource industries, in commercial agriculture, in canal and railroad construction, in land speculation – an opportunity that Winthrop lamented in early Boston but that would be seized over and over again by larger or smaller segments of the population as the possibilities of new lands unfolded. For emigrating Europeans, new resources favoured action before meditation, entrepreneurship before aristocracy, emphasizing the virtues and vices of the rising middle class. One form of the European connection with a new middle-latitude environment has been described in this essay, a form that maximized participation but not profit. The vigorous commerce in early colonial towns created far more stratified societies as, for example, did the corporate assault at the end of the last century on the minerals and forests of the North American West. The fundamental constant in all of this is the overriding social importance at any given time in any given area of the particular nature of the European connection with a new land. Hartz would ignore this connection, which is to ignore a geographical perspective without which, it seems to me, the overseas expansion and simplification of Europe is incomprehensible.

Creating Place in
Early Canada

Two books on pre-Confederation Canada (one with
John Warkentin) and my long immersion in the first
volume of the *Historical Atlas of Canada* gave me ample
opportunity to consider the broad pattern of early
Canada. That pattern, I came to see, was a particular
composition of commercial capital, the imperial state
(including its military), and family farms; or, put more
geographically, of work camps, towns, and countrysides. Moreover, these basic elements of the composition of Canada were squeezed by rock and cold to the
north and by a political boundary to the south. The vast
abundance of the *pays d'Illinois* (the American Middle
West), which the French had reached but neither French
nor British power had held, passed to the United States.
British North America was left with a southern border
near or beyond the northern limit of North American
agricultural possibility.

From "Creating Place in Early Canada," *Journal of Canadian Studies* 49, 2 (2015): 7–24.

The arrangement of the basic geographical ingredients of early settler Canada in severely bounded space had a profound impact on the character of Canada, and I have frequently written about it. Of these writings, the article below, written for an invited lecture at an interdisciplinary conference on "Meeting Places" in Halifax in 2013, is the most recent, and perhaps the most comprehensive. I have omitted my discussion of John Ralston Saul's depiction of early Canada as a Métis society (because I consider this claim in the postscript), but otherwise reproduce my lecture as written.

A
S EUROPEANS SETTLED IN the northern lands that became Canada, they created innumerable places, some large, many more local and intimate. Different places overlapped, forming intricate, shifting, and now largely unrecoverable mosaics within which people situated their transplanted lives. The variety of places was great but tended to unfold within a small number of characteristic frames – within, to put it another way, a small number of generic places. This essay identifies these frames – the early towns, the work camps and trading posts associated with staple trades, the countrysides composed of small farms. Each section describes them (giving most attention to the countrysides, where most people lived) and suggests how they structured the lives lived within them. Treating the whole early country, it generalizes to the point of caricature but does so to highlight the few characteristic frames that underlay the intricate variety of local place making in early Canada.[1] These frames set boundaries, shaped outlooks, and largely defined the settings in which people understood, and here and there began to write about, their reconstituted lives. Moreover, the spatial arrangement of these frames in the bounded spaces of early Canada had profound consequences.

Towns

As Europeans began to move across the North Atlantic, they left behind a human geography dominated by towns and countrysides and in time reestablished both. Quebec, the first town in what became Canada, emerged in the 1680s,[2] Montreal a little later, Louisbourg after the Treaty of Utrecht (1713), and Halifax in 1749, in response to Louisbourg. In various combinations, these and other preindustrial Canadian towns were foci of administrative, military, and commercial power – the principal powers that underlay European towns and that reached into northern North America in the seventeenth, eighteenth, and early nineteenth centuries.[3] With them came many transatlantic ties, relevant personnel, and familiar institutions, values, and employments. So constructed, the towns in early Canada largely replicated the appearance, functions, and social organization of their transatlantic progenitors. Quebec and Montreal reproduced the architecture and the basic layout of the smallish towns of northwestern France, Louisbourg the French military architecture of its day, and Halifax the streetscapes of Georgian England. The powerful and wealthy in colonial society lived in these towns within transatlantic circuits of communication and trade and, like their counterparts in Europe, atop steep social hierarchies that ranged downward to the destitute. There were beggars in the towns; as well as a colony's most powerful officials, merchants, and military officers; and, variously calibrated between, labourers, stevedores, servants, prostitutes, soldiers and sailors of various ranks, tradesmen and artisans, clerks and shopkeepers, lesser merchants, and a few professional people (doctors, lawyers, or notaries), as in French and English towns of the day. In the late 1750s, Montcalm considered Quebec the equal of any French town after the first ten; some fifty years later in Halifax, Prince Edward, Duke of Kent, commanded a naval base and dined and danced in the town's handsome Georgian mansions. More than any other early European settlements in northern North America, the early towns were thick overseas reproductions of their equivalents in France or England.

Not exact reproductions, of course. Long urban pasts were not at hand. Whereas the population in small towns in France or England usually reflected local migration fields, the towns of early Canada assembled peoples from many regional backgrounds.[4] Their occupational structures seem to have been relatively fluid, and skilled artisans who made luxury goods (which tended to be imported) seem to have been relatively rare. A more telling difference was the relative salience of the state, a consequence of the ongoing threat of war. During the French regime in Canada, both governor and intendant acquired powers their offices did not have in France. Merchants in Quebec complained that public markets were far more regulated than in France. Soldiers patrolled the streets at night.[5] Long after the Seven Years War, British fortifications and garrisons in the towns were intended to counter threats from the south. A lesson British officials took from the loss of the Thirteen Colonies was that imperial control had been too lax, a mistake not to be repeated.[6]

These early towns, foci of systems of European power and loci of social reproduction, were one of the basic frames of immigrant life in early Canada. They were small, however, and levels of urbanization were low. Although in the 1750s troops and the accoutrements of war drove up the urban portion of the Canadian population to some 20 percent, after the war it fell to more normal levels. In 1800, only 7 percent of the Lower Canadian population was urban. As late as Confederation, Montreal, the dominion's largest city, had only 100,000 people. Barely 3.5 percent of the population of Ontario lived in Toronto; Prince Edward Island was 97 percent rural. The towns concentrated power, and they were hubs of administration, trade, and defence; yet they framed the lives of a small fraction of the population of early Canada.

Work Camps and Trading Posts

Nor were the towns nearly as old as the seasonal work camps, where commercial capital and labour combined to exploit a resource and ship it to Europe – the primary resource–based commerce that Harold Innis called staple trades.[7] The first of these camps, the shore installations of the inshore cod fishery, emerged early in the sixteenth century. They were located where the resource (cod), a site for processing it (usually a cobble beach), and the means of transporting it (by ocean-going ship from a suitable harbour) were all available. In these seasonal male work-places, men and boys recruited in the port towns of western Europe processed cod for shipment to European markets. Their social structure, like that on a ship, reflected the hierarchy of the workplace, and their culture reproduced fragments from the principal European sources of labour, while the work itself reflected the nature of the resource and the means of processing and transporting it. These basic patterns were re-peated in the Basque whaling operations along the north shore of the Gulf of St. Lawrence and again – however different the means of labour recruitment, resource exploitation, and transportation – three centuries later when lumber camps appeared in the pine forests of New Brunswick and along southern fringes of the Canadian Shield. The seasonal, male work camp, after the brief Norse incursions the oldest and most enduring type of European settlement in northern North America, is another characteristic frame of early Canadian society. If the resource held out, as it did for centuries in the fisheries, women and children would even-tually arrive, and the labour supply would become increasingly local.

The fur trade, another of Innis's staple trades, also withdrew men from the social complexities of established European societies while subjecting them to the discipline of commercial capital. Unlike the fisheries or even lumbering, however, it drew Europeans far into the continental interior where, because of the distances involved, European traders established year-round posts to which Indigenous hunters brought furs. Here and there, trading pidgins developed, many traders learned something of an Indigenous language, and the protocols of trade adopted many Indigenous ways. Fur posts often became hybrid places, especially when Indigenous women lived there, as they often did, as partners for lonely men and indispensable liaisons between worlds that in the continental interior of the fur trade tended to be increasingly confounded. A cultural middle ground probably emerged out of the tumultuous conditions west of Lake Michigan in the second half of the seventeenth century as refugees from the wars and epidemics that de-populated what is now southern Ontario, plus missionaries, coureurs de bois, authorized traders, and warring French troops, superimposed themselves on the peoples already there.[8] Much later, descendants of this mixture plus the merger of the Hudson's Bay and North West

Companies in 1821 (which closed many posts and discharged many men of mixed ancestry) created a critical mass that was neither Indigenous nor European and laid the basis for the emergence of a self-conscious Prairie Métis identity. The fur trade was complicit in such métissage. Moreover, it extended a British presence across the continent, and in so doing created the diplomatic leverage that underlay eventual boundary agreements with the United States. Its hunters and trappers, its principal labour force, were almost always Indigenous, however, and were far more numerous than the company employees in the fur posts. The fur trade transformed Indigenous ways, and in some basic ways, as Innis claimed, underlay the emergence of Canada; but, except here and there and then briefly, it was not a common frame of European settlement in Canada before or after Confederation.

Countrysides

As long as towns were small and staple trades modest employers, farming supported most of the early Canadian population, but it did so belatedly on land that was barely welcoming. Commercial capital sought primary resources, not agricultural land, and established itself accordingly. Agriculture, when it began, made do with sites chosen for other purposes. In Newfoundland, the abundance of the sea was matched by the penury of the land; even gardens planted in the hardiest European vegetables were barely feasible. Around the Bay of Fundy, which first attracted French fur traders, farming became possible only after the daunting labour of diking and draining tidal marshes. The uplands beyond the marshes were much less inviting. Along the lower St. Lawrence, the principal French entrance to the fur trade of the continental interior, the land was more attractive, although closely bounded northward by the Canadian Shield and southward by the Appalachian Highlands. Well inland, the growing season was longer and the land better and more abundant. The Jesuit Father Vivier, who served the French villages along the upper Mississippi (the Illinois Country) in the early 1750s, was astonished by the bounty he found there.[9] In 1783, however, when the Treaty of Paris established the border with the new United States of America, the Illinois Country became American territory. British North America was left with far more meagre agricultural prospects: patches of potential farmland close to the northern limits of North American agriculture bounded by an international border, cold, and rock.

While the countrysides that emerged in early Canada raised the hardier European crops and livestock, they did not reproduce European rural societies. The circumstances of rural life, most particularly the terms of access to land, had been radically transformed in North America.

The overwhelmingly rural France from which a few thousand people emigrated to Canada and Acadia was a country of 20 million people. The Ireland from which, later, many more immigrated to British North America, was a country of 8 million. Wherever in western Europe land could be farmed, either population densities were high or landlords excluded people. Rural life pressed against scarce land; the value of land was high and of labour was low. Those with land usually prospered. Those with little or none, and who sold only their labour, struggled at the edge of destitution. In some Irish counties in the early nineteenth century, where rural population densities exceeded five hundred people per square mile, a substantial farm was five acres. The value of a tenant right (that is, of the right to rent) to one acre of arable land was equivalent to the value of a year of manual labour. In the Western Highlands in the same years, landlords responded to the growing factory demand for wool by enclosing land for sheep and herded their tenants into three- or four-acre crofts along the coast where small gardens, various gatherings, and paltry wages from harvesting kelp yielded spare, scratched livelihoods. In the Scottish lowlands and throughout much of England, a hodgepodge of small farms had given way to improvers' landscapes of large, prosperous farms while opportunities for small farmers diminished, the number of rural landless increased, rural underemployment became chronic, and most rural people had no prospect of owning a farm.

Such pressures on land supported stratified, hierarchical rural societies and great extremes of wealth and poverty. Even within peasantries, the range was great. Those at the bottom, with no land, could easily slip into the ranks of the wandering poor. Those at the top – in England, prosperous yeoman farmers; in France the *gros fermiers* who were often the local *coq du village* – were able to afford hired hands and domestic servants and live very comfortably. A few were quite rich. Beyond this peasant world, although largely supported by it, was a mannered, elegant society dominated by landowners whose social standing among their peers usually also reflected the revenue they derived from land. The most landed and wealthy lived in castles or elegant manors. They surrounded their residences with manicured parks and their parks with miles of stone walls built by cheap, surplus, rural labour. These landscapes of privilege and power, most of them supported by the transfer of wealth from those who worked the land to those who owned it, dotted country-sides in all the source regions of immigration to early Canada.[10]

In these Old World countrysides, elite culture tended to reflect na-tional values and ways, and peasant cultures tended to vary over short distances. Accents changed, as did many items of material culture, as did stories and superstitions. Often people from only a day or two's walk away were strangers, not to be trusted. Local peasant cultures had long roots in times when overland transportation was slow, expensive, and dangerous, and when the state had little interest in the countryside except to tax and conscript. Much more than the state, the church sought to normalize rural behaviour, but not even Christianity had effaced the myriad local spirits and sprites that still inhabited these premodern countrysides. Gradually, overland transportation improved, the com-mon law replaced custom, and schooling imparted national standards. The localness of the countryside was increasingly under assault, but even in the early nineteenth century most British immigrants to Canada were as much from a particular locale – from Yorkshire or even from a particular vale; from the Hebrides or even from a particular isle – as they were English, Scots, or Irish.[11]

In leaving Europe for northern North America, and in attempting to farm there, immigrants left familiar, intricately known places and faced conditions that turned much of their experience upside down. They encountered winters the length and severity of which they had never known and boundless forests with animals like bears and wolves not seen in western Europe for centuries. They left densely settled land and high populations and found themselves at the edge of vast, sparsely inhabited tracts where, here and there, they encountered hunter-gatherers and their ways. Even fellow settlers, usually from different local backgrounds, were relative strangers. Moreover, the basic economic relationships that dominated European countrysides no longer held. Whereas land had been scarce and expensive and labour abundant and cheap, these relationships were now reversed. In short, the settlers of the patches of agricultural land available in early Canada were radically decontextualized; over the years, their lives and those of their descendants would be recontextualized in very un-European circumstances.

The low cost of land and the high cost of labour created opportunity for the poor, but between the opportunity and its realization were years of work to hew a farm out of the forest. Most of this pioneer work, waged relentlessly by all members of a family, is now invisible. There are no personal records of pioneering in Acadia or along the lower St. Lawrence during the French regime and few for other later settlements. It is known that lives went into clearing, grubbing, and building; that the margin between success and failure was thin; and that failure due to accidents, mental breakdown, or the overwhelming enormity of the task was common. Slowly, however, the forest yielded and farms appeared.

In Acadia, where political control fluctuated between France and England and colonial administrations were weak, settlers acquired land by squatting and rarely, if ever, paid annual seigneurial charges. Along the lower St. Lawrence, where the seigneurial system of land tenure was securely established, seigneurs conceded farm lots without initial charge in return for annual charges (usually waived for the first few years) amounting to some 5 to 10 percent of a farm's gross return.[12] In Upper Canada, the colonial government granted free farm lots then opened Crown land to private land companies and the land market. In the 1830s, an uncleared farm lot of eighty to a hundred acres in an area of new settlement in Upper Canada cost some thirty to forty pounds, which is what an agricultural labourer (who also received room and board) obtained for a year's work.[13] The same work that earned the right to rent one acre of arable land in Ireland earned a forested lot of eighty to a hundred acres in Upper Canada. Add to this the start-up costs of farming (about a hundred pounds) and it is apparent that after some four years of wage labour an immigrant who arrived in Upper Canada with little or no capital could reasonably expect to be working his own farm – the opportunity that underlay the momentum to immigrate to and settle in Upper Canada, as, within various terms of access to land, in all the pockets of developing agricultural settlement in the Maritimes. By the nineteenth century, there are some surviving letters home, including this one from Upper Canada: "Now I am goun to Work on My One frme of 50 Eakers wich I bot at 55L and have 5 years to pay it in.[14] I have bot Me a Cow and 5 pigs ... If I had staid at Corsley [Wiltshire, England] I never shuld had nothing. I like the Contry very Much – I am at librty to shout terky, Quill, Pigeons, Pheasants, Dear, and all kind of Geam wch I have on My Back Wood."[15]

Low entry costs for land, coupled with a type of agriculture that raised the common northern European crops and livestock and found limited markets, did not favour the emergence of a landed elite. There were no plantations. The family farm was the common unit of production, and most farms were semisubsistence operations that provided most of a family's food plus some surplus for sale. As late as Confederation, only a very unusual farm anywhere in Canada produced enough food for more than one or two other families.[16] In these circumstances, a mannered, land-based gentility had difficulty penetrating the countryside. Most of the seigneuries along the lower St. Lawrence, replicas in theory of the landed power of French feudalism, produced modest revenues for several generations until growing population pressures restored conditions that bore some relation to those in France. Even in the early nineteenth century, almost two hundred years after the concession of the first Canadian seigneuries, most of the seigneurial manors along the lower St. Lawrence were little more than very large farmhouses. Some Loyalist settlers in the St. John Valley, and the proprietors who held land in 20,000 acre lots on Prince Edward Island, dreamed of stratified, class-conscious, semifeudal societies, but dreaming of such societies was far easier than creating them. Farm lots on Prince Edward Island were leased (for 999 years) at a twentieth of the value of leasehold in Scotland. Prince Edward Island became a society of small farmers and tradespeople in which the most prosperous islanders were merchant-shipbuilders who seasonally employed thirty to forty people.

In the Eastern Townships of Lower Canada and in Upper Canada, a few gentlemen farmers tried, somewhat incongruously, to adopt the intensive methods advocated by European agricultural improvers; land companies prospered not by building rural estates but by selling farm lots.

Presenting advantage for the poor and little opportunity for the rich, the countrysides of early Canada tended to squash social hierarchies and produce far less stratified societies than their European counterparts. In extreme local instances, as when farm lots of equivalent size were taken up at much the same time by settlers of equivalent and limited means, the results a few years later were predictable and similar: on most lots a few acres cleared, a tiny house, minimal farm buildings, a few livestock, some rough fencing, and some crops among the stumps. Differentiation would increase as the years passed; all established countrysides contained both the very poor and the comfortably situated. Application, judgment or the lack of it, luck, start-up capital, an inheritance, a favourable marriage – any or all of them influenced the relative prosperity of farm families; and there were also merchants, shopkeepers, tradespeople, and millers, some of them very prosperous and holders of a good deal of rural debt. Yet the countrysides of early Canada produced nothing like the wealth that hung over their European counterparts. Rather, and basically, they produced a good proportion of farms that provided modest but adequate livelihoods for families. Judging by marriage age, number of surviving children, and mortality rates, farm households in early Canada tended to be better off, on average, than such households in France or Britain. The most comprehensive statistical study of inequality in an early Canadian countryside – by sociologists Gordon Darroch and Lee Soltow, and based on the Upper Canadian census of 1871 – shows that more than 60 percent of the province's farmers were landowners, that landowners with more than five hundred acres (less than 1 percent of all farmers) held 6.4 percent of all farmland, and that most farmers held about one hundred acres.[17] Even as late as 1871, when uncleared farm lots were no longer available in Upper Canada, Darroch and Soltow emphasize the breadth of access to modest farms and the countryside's relative social equality. The Upper Canadian towns, they write, "were islands of wealth accumulation and inequality in a wider sea of relative rural equality."[18] Upper Canada contained the best farmland in British North America. On other patches of agricultural settlement, where overall soils and climate were less favourable, there were relatively fewer prosperous farmers and more rural poor but also many small farmers and their families who were getting by.[19]

In some cases, emigrants from the same local area and culture crossed the Atlantic and settled together, but usually people from different local backgrounds met and mixed. The some ten thousand people who came to Canada during the French regime and left descendants were almost all French, the great majority of them from villages and towns in a large swath of western France north of the Garonne River.[20] Almost all of them spoke French of a sort, but they came out of different local ways that, in France, were geographically isolated from each other and that converged along the lower St. Lawrence. Similarly, the background of some 60 percent of the British immigrants to Upper Canada was Irish; they were a diverse lot, people who lived with their own local kind in Ireland and were thrown together (and with non-Irish) along concession line roads in Upper Canada. Transatlantic migrations transplanted individuals and families much more effectively than communities. They recontextualized immigrants and their descendants in different places with different people.

Specific, local Old World cultures could not survive such treatment. Different cultural memories, accents, and details of material cultures were abruptly thrown together. Some former ways fit the immigrants' new physical settings and were retained; others did not and were discarded. Faced with such pressures and changes, lives were being recalibrated. It was impossible to live at the edge of a North American forest amid a rearranged population as they had lived in a European countryside. Although the longer roots of habitant life along the lower St. Lawrence were in France, no French peasant existence was its close equivalent. Rather, a distinctive rural society emerged, shaped by its particular circumstances.[21] Similarly, none of the local peasant cultures of rural Ireland were replicated in Upper Canada, however much Irishness was in the air. Confronted with other ways, Irish ethnicity lost much of its vernacular content while becoming increasingly symbolic. The variety of regional backgrounds and Christian denominations represented in the small farms assembled along a typical concession line road in Upper Canada was worlds away from either the tight local world of the Irish peasantry or the hierarchical, deferential, and culturally fairly uniform society of an Anglican parish in rural England.

In these ways, countrysides of family farms, by far the most common frame of immigrant life in early Canada, rearranged the social hierarchy and the cultural geography of rural France and Britain – basic structural changes in the vertical and horizontal organization of rural life. Added to them were myriad less measurable differences associated, for example, with protracted winters, contacts with Indigenous peoples, the layout of settlements, the relative isolation of families, confrontations with forests and their creatures, the particular work of pioneering, and the psychological trauma of resettlement. In all these ways, lives were radically recontextualized, and rapid social and cultural change ensued.

Were these changes theorized, one might look to the existential philosophers, particularly to Martin Heidegger and his emphasis on the thereness of being. *Dasein* (being there) is the word Heidegger invented to convey his understanding that being and place are intertwined.[22] From this premise it follows that to change place, as immigrants did when crossing the Atlantic to farm in early Canada, is to change the nature of being. Although I agree with Heidegger, an abstract philosophical generalization, fundamental as it may be, that is silent about the nature or direction of change is not analytically useful. Karl Marx is more helpful. Whatever one makes of the full range of his thought, most will agree with him that systems of production powerfully influence social formations.[23] In chapter 33 of *Capital,* he writes briefly about land and labour costs and systems of production in settler colonial societies. He considers a Mr. Peel, who brought workers to Australia only to have them quit because, suddenly, they had access to their own farmland, and also Edward Gibbon Wakefield, the political economist who thought to cure Mr. Peel's problems by limiting the availability of land, thereby forcing settlers back to work while depressing the price of their labour. Wakefield, Marx thought, revealed an essential truth of capitalism: that it worked by curtailing labour's access to the fruits of its own independent production. In breaking capital's grip on labour, cheap colonial land had enabled settlers to vanish "from the labour market but not into the workhouse" – to become independent producers working for themselves.[24] Marx also noted that the settler experience in Australia and America had shown this opportunity to be temporary.[25]

The Problem of Land

The generational opportunity for farm families in early Canada depended on the availability of land. Usually, parents attempted to establish their offspring on land nearby, a feasible option when there were few settlers, low population densities, and available land. Sooner or later, however – the timing dependent on the rate of immigration and the quantity of locally available land – these conditions no longer applied. As it became harder to establish progeny, the generational politics of land intensified. The family farm could neither be divided into viable farms nor produce enough to enable one son to pay off debts to siblings for their equal shares.[26] In these circumstances, and where French civil and English common law prevailed, parents commonly passed the farm to one son, usually the eldest, and made some arrangements for their other children. Some landless progeny would find local work, but more would move away: in Lower Canada usually westward, towards the Montreal plain; in Upper Canada usually northward, towards Georgian Bay. An alternative strategy, intended to keep the family together, was to sell the family farm and move, parents and children together, to an area of pioneer settlement where land was cheaper and there was the prospect of acquiring several farm lots close at hand.

Along the lower St. Lawrence, pioneer farmland remained available, though in increasingly isolated locations, for almost two hundred years. Westward to Lake Huron, where land was more plentiful and immigrants more abundant, the pioneer opportunity to turn forest into farm lasted barely seventy-five years. In the Maritimes, where the smaller patches of arable land were often filled by a few initial settlers and the larger took only somewhat longer, agriculture was always limited by rock or sea. After the border settlement of 1783, not much arable land was left to British North America. Exposed to high rates of natural population increase and to massive immigration from the British Isles, it soon filled.

In a British North America dominated by rock and winter, agricultural settlements made up a thin archipelago stretched from a rockbound Atlantic coast to the eastern shore of Lake Huron. There was no continuous avenue for the westward expansion of pioneer farming and, as the St. Lawrence entrance to the continent became increasingly detached from the *pays d'en haut* of the French regime, the British North American West faded from popular view. Upper Canada ran into Lake Huron and stopped. Lower Canada ran into a settled Upper Canada. From anywhere in the Maritimes, the more westerly patches of British North American settlement were distant and taken. Those abandoning the meagre domestic economies of farm and forest along the Miramichi dreamed of an American West in Michigan or Wisconsin. In these years, North America's western momentum was American. From his perch in Massachusetts, Henry David Thoreau could urge his countrymen to walk west, away from the past, towards land that is "unexhausted and richer," towards freedom and the future, towards Oregon.[27] Progress itself, Thoreau maintained, moves from east to west. Such thought, situated in the vast landed opportunity that underlay the United States, was unimaginable in British North America. No one in Nova Scotia or New Brunswick dreamed of walking through generous land towards sunset and Vancouver Island. The difference is fundamental. The United States was fashioned out of welcoming land, Canada out of land that is bounded, parsimonious, and pinched.

As bounded patches of agricultural settlement filled, Canadians faced a common problem: where to establish the surplus young? Until the Canadian Pacific Railway reached Winnipeg in 1882, there was no accessible British North American West. A small percentage of the population was urban, and although the towns were beginning to industrialize, they provided little new employment, much of which was taken by recent immigrants.[28] In the Canadas at least, the North held out more potential. Its margins were at hand and their agricultural prospects were unexplored; when urban elites sought to open land for rural settlement, this is where their imaginations fixed. In Lower Canada, the impetus was clerical, their concern to protect faith and language by settling the young close at hand. In Upper Canada, businessmen eyeing the pace of American expansion sought to enlarge their Canadian markets. The most vigorous northern colonizer in Lower Canada, Curé Labelle, held that God had created the hilly southern fringe of the Canadian Shield and a vast arc of habitable farmland extending beyond to the Rockies for the settlement of the French Canadian people. In the mid-1850s in Upper Canada, the minister of agriculture concluded that the land between the Ottawa Valley and Georgian Bay – the Ottawa-Huron Tract – could support 8 million people. With such prospects in mind, colonization societies formed, and governments built colonization roads and offered free farm lots. Invariably, the results were meagre. The experienced took timber and left, the inexperienced struggled, and if they stayed, their progeny fled when they could. The urban elites were wrong. With only a few, small, local exceptions, the fringe of the Canadian Shield rejected agriculture. Its growing season was too short, its soils too thin and acidic, its black flies too numerous.

The only remaining option was to go south, and well before the middle of the nineteenth century all the British North American colonies were draining southward. Elites frequently disapproved of these migrations, and many who left intended to return, but few did. From Newfoundland and the Maritimes they went to the Boston states, from Lower Canada to the industrial towns of New England, from Upper Canada to a vast reach of land tending southwestward in the American Middle West. These were huge movements of people, comparable in scale if not in visibility to the migrations that had settled British North America. By 1900, as many Ontario-born probably lived in the United States as in Ontario.

Whereas westward migrations south of the border mixed different peoples within the United States, the southward migrations from British North America added people to American melting pots. They did not mix those in the different settled patches of British North America – places that exported many of their young and, without more agricultural land, provided little room for immigrants. Culturally, and in some local instances genetically, society tended to become more inbred. The different peoples who over two and a half centuries had taken up land and put down roots in northern North America – the French in Acadia and Canada, then the Loyalists, the Late Loyalists, the Irish, the Scots, the English, and a few others – had arranged themselves in different proportions in different places and worked out their North American lives in somewhat different ways. The southward migrations of many of the young tended to reinforce these differences. Something of the localism of earlier European countrysides reappeared. It would be possible, for example, for adjacent Newfoundland outports – one composed of Protestants from southwestern England, the other of Catholics from southern Ireland – to maintain separate accents and identities for generations. There was no space for immigrants; the young did not marry across religious boundaries and, when they left, they went to Boston. At a different scale, the southward migration of French Canadians, a product both of the early alienation of Upper Canadian land to others and of religious-ethnic prejudice, reinforced the cultural divide between a largely Protestant, English-speaking countryside in Upper Canada and a largely Catholic, French-speaking one in Lower Canada.

In summary, in rural Canada before Confederation, two differentiating sociocultural mechanisms, both of them tied to the particular circumstances of settlement, were at play. One differentiated settler societies from their European antecedents; the other stabilized, even augmented, the isolation of and differences between settler societies in different places. The former was a widely recurrent process that influenced social formation in most settler colonial societies. The latter was a social consequence of a distinctive Canadian relationship with a bounded and limited land, a relationship that was the opposite of the predominant American experience with land that was generous and yielding.

Canada at Confederation

Canada at Confederation was a scattered, irregular composition of these three frames of transplanted European life: towns, the camps and posts associated with staple trades, and countrysides. Except in the fur trade, the lives of immigrants and their descendants clung to a thin, southeastern edge of a vast, sparsely inhabited territory where Indigenous peoples were usually the only or the predominant population. The towns, the power containers of colonial societies and the principal colonial sites of European social reproduction, were centres of colonial government and defence and points of commercial, administrative, and social connection to the North Atlantic world. Apart from the towns along the St. Lawrence River, they were not well connected to each other; nor did the governments located in the principal towns yet have much capacity to normalize rural behaviour. A staple trade, the cod fishery, still dominated the Atlantic coast while now drawing most of its labour from residents, and another, the fur trade, had long since become a transcontinental enterprise. Requiring very few employees of European backgrounds, the fur trade incorporated Indigenous labour within the ambit of commercial capital (transforming and frequently undermining Indigenous livelihoods) and created the outline of a transcontinental British space that would eventually become Canada. The great majority of people in the settler colonies lived on small farms in patches of rock-bound countryside stretched along an international border between the eastern shore of Lake Huron and the Atlantic Ocean. Most of them knew little or nothing of the other patches. After the upheaval of migration and resettlement in circumstances very different from those previously known, they and their descendants lived refashioned lives in local communities. If they looked beyond, they were more likely to focus on a transatlantic place of origin or an adjacent edge of the United States than on other parts of British North America.

Such was the British North America about which the Fathers of Confederation sought to fashion a constitution. There had been no war of independence, and there was no John Locke. Overall, the reasons for Confederation, strongly backed by the Colonial Office, outweighed the reasons against. Political agreement owed more to a pragmatic response to what British North America was than to a vision of what it might be. In a British North America composed of sharp regional and ethnic differences – between Indigenous peoples and newcomers, French and

English, the isolated patches of English-speaking settlement with their somewhat different populations and ways – the protection of difference in the several levels of government within a confederation was a pressing issue. At their most original, the Confederation debates turned around it. The American constitution grew, as political scientist Samuel LaSelva has pointed out, out of a debate over the means of protecting republican liberty, the Canadian over the means of protecting identity,[29] a contrast embedded in the arrangements of people and land in the two countries and in their vastly different landed experiences.

The difference to which the Fathers of Confederation gave almost no attention, although it underlay the country for which they were writing a constitution, was that between Indigenous peoples and newcomers. *The British North America Act* assigned a federal responsibility for Indigenous peoples, no more. In this, the Fathers of Confederation were not out of touch with the popular mind. Early Canada was a unique arrangement of people and land, and it was in this whole arrangement, in which Indigenous peoples were a part among many, and the ways of life associated with it, that added up to the experiences, societies, and human geographies on which this essay has touched and for which the Fathers of Confederation were writing a constitution. No precedents quite fit the scattered mix of peoples and places with which they had to deal. The solution they came up with, to make the provinces the principal political representatives of difference, disguised the provinces' internal diversity and imposed a clear division of political and administrative authority on a thoroughly untidy reality. In the late 1860s and early 1870s, however, it was the acceptable geopolitical generalization that could be overlaid on the different ways of life, identities, and places in the British North America of their day.

The particular historical and geographical construction that worked itself out over several centuries in northern North America and that at Confederation became the Dominion of Canada was a composition in bounded physical spaces of the frames described in this essay. They reflected and generated different ways of being and, particularly in immigrant societies, different levels of retention of former ways. They worked variously to connect and to isolate and in countrysides encouraged the reformation of strong, local identities. This composition, like no other anywhere, would underlie a subsequent Canada. Ahead would lie the pressures and tendencies of a modernizing, globalizing world, but behind lay a stubborn past, the inductive creation of many years, that, willy-nilly, would complicate the evolving Canadian present.

PART 4

Reconfiguring British Columbia

The Making
of the Lower Mainland

After 1987, when the first volume of the *Historical Atlas of Canada* was finally completed, I was able to focus on British Columbia, where I was born and to which I had returned in the early 1970s. As a small boy in Vancouver, my only fleeting glimpse of Indigenous British Columbia had been the Musqueam woman who came to our house occasionally to trade baskets for used clothing my mother had saved. By the late 1980s, however, the issue of Indigenous title was in the air and the courts; it had become impossible to think about British Columbia without considering its Indigenous character. When the Geography Department at UBC produced a book on greater Vancouver (the Lower Mainland), I wrote on the period from 1820 to 1881, years when a deeply Indigenous space was transformed by an incoming settler society. The final pages of that piece, which

From "The Lower Mainland, 1820–81," in *Vancouver and Its Region,* ed. Graeme Wynn and Timothy Oke (Vancouver: UBC Press, 1992), 38–68.

describe the Lower Mainland in 1881, identify the basic
settler colonial ingredients: the intrusive power of
settler society, the pinched, continuing circumstances
of Indigenous peoples.

IN 1881 THE CENSUS enumerator in the Lower Mainland travelled
through a human geography that had not even begun to exist there
twenty-five years before. Figure 14 shows the new land surveys. Of
course, much of this recently introduced geography had existed elsewhere. Neither town nor countryside nor resource camps nor innumerable details within them were invented in the Lower Mainland. All these
components of the outside world were somewhat rearranged there, but
most of the elements of the composition had been introduced.

The Lower Mainland was suddenly part of a much larger world, part
of the ways in which it organized and controlled space. The traders at
Fort Langley had not sought or been able to exert such control, and when
Indigenous peoples dominated the Lower Mainland they organized it
in ways that, in most respects, were virtually the opposite of those that
held sway in 1881.

The complex of power that had suddenly assumed control in the
Lower Mainland ultimately depended on brute geopolitical force. It was
what Thomas Hobbes would have called sovereign power, vested in a
monarch and expressed, in this case, through a Colonial Office backed
by the Royal Navy and, briefly, the Royal Engineers. Edward Bulwer
Lytton, the colonial secretary, told Colonel Moody that while civil societies should manage themselves, their internal stability required "the
unflinching aid of military discipline" in the background. Moreover,
"wherever England extends her sceptre, there, as against the Foreign
enemy, she pledges the defence of her sword." This was the language
of imperialism and of sovereign power, and, as the Cowichan heard it

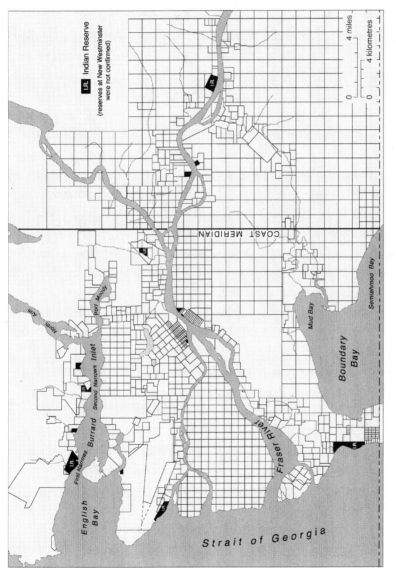

FIGURE 14
Land surveys, the Lower Mainland, 1876

from Governor Douglas, the language of conquest. Battles were unnecessary; shows of force and a few summary executions did much to establish the new realities. In a newly acquired territory where other forms of control were unavailable, the quick, brutal, episodic application of sovereign power established its authority, and fear bred compliance.

Once the realities of sovereign power were established, other less brutal and more disciplinary forms of power could begin to be put in place. These included codes of law, judges, police, and jails, and also public schools (and residential schools for Indigenous children), industrial work discipline, institutionalized religious practices, and a land system – almost all of which white immigrants took for granted. In a newly settled place where, as far as immigrants knew or cared, there was no prior system of landed property, the land system itself became the most powerful single agent of disciplinary power. It defined where people could and could not go as well as their rights to land use, and it backed these rights, as need be, with sovereign power. The two Cowichan who killed a shepherd they thought was on their land experienced the power with which the newcomers defended their own conception of property. The point so made, the land system itself became powerfully regulative. Survey lines and fences were pervasive forms of disciplinary power backed by a property owner, backed by the law, and requiring little official supervision. Moreover, Indigenous peoples could not acquire land of their own and many of them lived on reserves, an imposed spatial discipline which, given the mobility of former Indigenous ways, had a profound capacity to modify Indigenous life.

The de facto establishment of sovereignty and a regime of property with their inherent opportunities and controls provided protection for development. Farmers could acquire land knowing that title was secure and the colony safe for settlement. Townspeople could buy lots and live within the familiar guarantees of civil society. An immigrant society, especially its elite, could begin to put its world back together. But not, of course, entirely, if only because the setting had changed, and because societies and their settings are not separate categories. Immigrants on pioneer farmsteads or in lumber camps lived in unfamiliar relationships with the land; all immigrants lived without a local past and amid a strange mix of peoples. Such mixing brought ideas of ethnicity and race to the fore, weakened somewhat the idea of class, and tended to turn what in other more homogeneous settings were the unremarked details of everyday life into explicit and increasingly symbolic elements of difference. Of these, whiteness became the most generalized and powerful symbol, and, as it did, racism was built into the landscape of settlement. The Lower Mainland was certainly not a replica of any other place, yet its emerging human geography did convey a complex of power that did come, broadly, out of the English-speaking North Atlantic world of the mid-late nineteenth century.

Indigenous power over the Lower Mainland and, to a considerable extent, earlier Indigenous lifeworlds had collapsed. Many Indigenous settlement and spatial routines were radically different from those that had existed a short generation before. Most Indigenous people were ostensibly Roman Catholics, and at the church-run residential school at Mission, not far upriver from Langley, Indigenous children were being taught in English and meticulously disciplined so that "savagery" would yield to civilization. How much the Indigenous cognitive world has changed is another question. Most Indigenous people still spoke little or no English. Spirits still haunted Burrard Inlet near Deep Cove; Indigenous people would not go there. For some of them, Christianity offered a new trail to a familiar land of shades and dancing ghosts. The most that can now be said, perhaps, is that changes in the Lower Mainland were such that Indigenous cognition would not long survive unaltered.

In 1881 the future of the Lower Mainland was at hand. The land had been restructured and, as it had, way had been made for a railway, ever-more-modern sawmills and canneries, a largely British and eastern Canadian middle class, a city, and a metropolis. Indigenous peoples, pushed to the margins, would turn increasingly to the heart of their problem, the land issue, and, in so doing, run squarely into the geographical reality of a place remade by others.

The Struggle with Distance

The settler colonial appropriation of British Columbia
entailed a protracted struggle with distance, first to
bring a remote corner of North America within range
of the world economy and then to open up the insides
of a huge, angular territory to settlers and capital. In this
excerpt, I discuss the means by which the external and
internal constraints of distance were reduced in settler
colonial British Columbia and, in conclusion, reflect on
the relationship between the assault on distance and
the distribution of social power as settler society implanted itself in what had been Indigenous space.

From *The Resettlement of British Columbia* (Vancouver: UBC Press, 1997), 161–62, 182–93.

THE WORLD ECONOMY began to emerge in the sixteenth century, slowly expanded into the corners of the world that were least accessible to Europe, and, more than two hundred years after the first Spanish galleons crossed the Pacific from Acapulco to trade Mexican silver for Chinese spices and silks, reached the Northwest Coast of North America. After the Spanish and British encounters in the 1770s, and the beginning of the trade in sea otter pelts in the 1780s, the process of incorporating this coast and the cordilleran massif beyond it into the world economy accelerated slowly, then with a rush after 1850. The costs and delays of transportation and communication decreased, items other than sea otter pelts became "resources," and more corners of land became accessible. In the process, distances shrank; the territory that became British Columbia was repositioned and restructured.

From their earliest encounters, Europeans had begun to remake this territory in their own terms: mapping it, renaming it, claiming possession of it, bringing it within reach of the European imagination. They created a cartographic and conceptual outline of what, for them, was a new land, placing its coast and principal rivers on their maps, identifying the land as wilderness and its peoples as "savages." These abstractions were agents of European colonialism, as many general analyses of what has come to be called "colonial discourse" have convincingly shown.[1] Complementing them were changes in transportation and communication that, in effect, actualized the immigrant presence on the ground. As the high costs and inconveniences of distance were reduced, more elements of the outside world could enter this distant place, reaching more corners of previously inaccessible land. With enormous cost and effort, distances were diminished and thresholds of exclusion reduced. The conquest of distance, partial as it was, was at once a central motor of colonization, enabling an immigrant society to impose its ways; and of modernization, facilitating the spatial economies, disciplinary tactics, and many of the assumptions of advanced industrial societies.

In the years from early contact to about 1850, external connections were dominated by preindustrial technologies: sailing ships at sea, canoes and pack horses inland. Over the next forty years, modern distance-diminishing technologies – particularly steamers, telegraphs, and railways – ushered in a period of sharp time-space compression. Whereas return letters between Victoria and London could easily take a year and a half before 1850, in 1890 they took about a month, and telegraph messages a few days. As much as in any area of recent European expansion, the principal towns of British Columbia had become integrated components of the larger, modernizing world. It was another matter, however, to extend this degree of connectivity across the length and breadth of British Columbia. Rather, a few corridors of modern transportation and communication were constructed, and from them a host of more local strategies, many improvised on the spot, reached into some of the spaces between. All these developments opened up new economic opportunities and imposed new powers on peoples and land. None, as Harold Innis understood years ago,[2] was politically or culturally innocent. A territory and its peoples were being reconfigured within a set of assumptions and practices that immigrants brought to British Columbia and that conformed to their sense of its future.

[...]

Here and there, these developments drew on Indigenous precedent, but for the most part they did not. Immigrants considered Indigenous ways irrelevant, treated British Columbia as a *tabula rasa,* and constructed their own systems of transportation and communication essentially from scratch. These systems were among their principal achievements, the framework on which the province's changing human geography was hung. As such, they were enormously powerful, for they shaped many of the spaces in which British Columbians lived and, in so doing, many of their social relations.

The relationship between empire and the media of transportation and communication has been widely explored, in this country first, and perhaps most suggestively, by Harold Innis in his studies of the Canadian Pacific Railway (CPR), the fur trade, and the bias of communications. Railways, steamers, and telegraphs were admirable tools of imperialism, incorporating into empires the territories won by the overwhelming superiority of European firearms.[3] As much as troops on the ground, a nineteenth-century empire depended on the capacity of interlocking networks of rail, steamship, wire, and mail to overcome distance. As space collapsed, territory awaited the powerful, and the rhetoric of expansion became more and more self-evident. Strong states, it was held, would inevitably expand and should absorb weaker, less civilized societies.[4] The question was not of the right to expand, which was taken for granted, but of which strong state would expand the most – the impetus, for example, for the rush of European states to carve up Africa. Geopolitical thinking flourished in this climate. A telegraph line connecting Washington, DC, and Moscow was a vision of American commercial and cultural empire. The Trans-Siberian Railway was an alarming instrument of Russian power in the Pacific; the British geographer Halford Mackinder thought that railways had tilted the balance of world power landward and would shift global power towards the state (Russia) that occupied the great Eurasian heartland of the world.[5] British Columbia was not detached from such geopolitical thinking. The CPR, for example, consolidated a transcontinental state and enabled central Canada to reach quickly outward, as it did by both railway and telegraph when putting down the second Métis resistance (the second Riel Resistance) on the Prairies. The CPR was also a link between Britain and Asia; together with the empress ships that sailed out of Vancouver and that, by prior agreement, the admiralty could commandeer at any time and convert to troop carriers, it provided an alternative route to India should the Suez Canal be blocked.[6] The Grand Trunk Pacific, built with millions of British pounds, was the final, imperial northwest passage in the railway age.

Within British Columbia, imperial visions merged with the realities of colonialism. As distance diminished, newcomers were able to possess the "wilderness" more comprehensively. Edward Said has suggested that the construction of the Suez Canal "destroyed the Orient's distance, its cloistered intimacy away from the West" and that, unsheltered, the West could now possess it. "After de Lesseps no one could speak of the Orient as belonging to another world ... There was only 'our' world."[7] So too in British Columbia as distances were undermined. Claiming political control of a territory was an act of imperialism, coming to know it was often another, but using it was far more intrusive than either. Improvements in transportation and communication enabled the world economy to use British Columbia's space not through Indigenous intermediaries, as during the fur trade, but by distributing Western technologies, labour, and settlers across the land. They allowed the state greatly to expand its reach, providing the channels by which it collected information, distributed regulation, and imposed order. Although it would not be quickly possible to extend the state uniformly over British Columbia's territory – a characteristic, according to sociologist Anthony Giddens, of modern societies – the thrust, facilitated by the decline of distance, was in this direction. From an Indigenous perspective, white territorial claims, place names on maps, and exploration and survey parties were being followed by a far more tangible form of colonialism: white workers, settlers, and their machines using Indigenous land for their own purposes. As long as Indigenous peoples had been able to hunt, fish, and gather in their former territories, the small reserves the reserve commissioners laid out for them had little meaning; however, the implications of reserves, and the exclusions they entailed, became ever more apparent as non-Indigenous people occupied and used the surrounding land. A logging operation in a mountain valley previously used for seasonal hunting marked a huge transformation of land use and power. For those experiencing it, colonialism was enacted locally, on the ground.

Viewed in this light, the systems of transportation and communication that spread into British Columbia were the capillaries of colonial appropriation. They allowed non-Indigenous people into the land, not as explorers, visitors, or passers-through, but as users and settlers. Coupled with a regime of property rights validated by the state, they effected a vast transfer of local power from Indigenous peoples to immigrants. They did so not as the result of any one event but incrementally, as a flume was built here, a corduroy road laid out there, a donkey engine brought into the bush. This pervasive geographical expansion, superimposed on a depopulated land and backed by the immigrants' cultural confidence, technological superiority, and force of arms, was itself a diffused form of power that prized open more and more nooks and crannies of an alien land and civilized them in terms a modern immigrant population could understand. French social philosopher Michel Foucault has insisted upon the relationship between social power and the configuration of space, but whereas Foucault's examples turn around prisons, asylums, and reformatories, in British Columbia the prime example is the land itself, reconfigured into new patterns of appropriation and social control.[8] Colonialism and colonization were about the control of land; land use itself defined new rights, exclusions, and patterns of dominance; and strategies for the effective control of land operationalized colonial rhetorics and discourses. In British Columbia, immigrants were preoccupied with the challenges and opportunities of a remote land into which global imbalances of power and the British Empire had incongruously brought them; as they reduced the problems of distance and gained access to the land, immigrants relegated the former population ever more to the sidelines. A Foucaultian analysis of the decentred strategies of disciplinary power is shifted in such settings, becoming more preoccupied with land and the disciplinary power associated with reaching and possessing it.

Closer to the British Columbian mark, in some ways, is the work of two other French philosophers, Gilles Deleuze and Félix Guattari, on what they call the "desiring machine" of capitalism,[9] or what the geographer David Harvey calls, with some of the same meanings, capitalism's "spatial fix."[10] Harvey argues that capitalism required new space both for profits and to quell social unrest within established capitalist societies. As capital travels – in British Columbia, along routes largely constructed for itself – it "is perpetually deconstructing ... social power by reshaping its geographical bases."[11] Deleuze and Guattari treat capitalism as a surface of desire that transcends individuals and, machine-like, stamps its own rules across the land. For them, capitalism had to deterritorialize societies that were otherwise constructed, in the process decoding their social rules, and then reterritorialize land and recode the social rules to fit its own requirements. Only then could it function. The desiring machine consumed otherness and regurgitated its products in spaces remade around its own assumptions about markets, money, property, and objectively known nature.[12] Such analyses are obviously relevant to the changes explored here, with the qualification, in my view, that capitalism was only one source of a reterritorialization that was as much grounded in cultural assumptions that were pervasive in an immigrant society as in the spatial logic of capital.

There is yet another side of the colonial question: the extent to which new systems of transportation and communication were themselves agents of Indigenous cultural change. This is a matter awaiting exploration, but it is worth bearing in mind Jean and John Comaroff's conclusion, with respect to Protestant missions in South Africa, that colonized peoples often "reject the message of the colonizers, and yet are powerfully and profoundly affected by its media." The very meeting of different ways, they suggest, had the capacity to redefine "the taken-for-granted surfaces" of everyday worlds. In the missionaries' implicit assumptions, rather than their explicit evangelical narratives, lay the "hegemonic forms" that shaped "colonial subjects."[13] If a steamboat or a railway were less conventionally articulate than a missionary, they perhaps took as much for granted: clock time, linear distance, rational empiricism, a revised geographical relationship with space and with other peoples, an instant relativity that situated the local in the world. A railway that ran past an Indigenous village was more than an intrusive symbol of white power; it redefined the "surfaces" of life in that place, making local people more self-conscious, situating them within a global, rationalized civilization, taking away their local integrity. A talking wire, the telegraph, initially perceived as another form of white spirit power, eventually led to a wholly other way of thinking about the world.[14] Such connections remain to be examined, but it can hardly be doubted either that new media of transportation and communication powerfully imbalanced white-Indigenous interactions or that they were themselves powerful colonizers of Indigenous consciousness.

From the newcomers' perspective, most of this was invisible. The land was wilderness awaiting development. The few legacies of an Indigenous past were irrelevant to an immigrant future; British Columbia was a beginning. In terms of the media of transportation and communication, this meant not only that systems were constructed de novo but also that they were constructed without interference from the past. Liberated from the past, they faced an open, untrammelled relationship with the future, a relationship affected by the terrain through which they would pass, but not by prior human geographies. Immigrant British Columbians knew this. The location of their future was still very much up in the air, an uncertainty that was the source of the strident boosterism with which they promoted this or that settlement. Transportation schemes frequently underpinned such boosterism, also for obvious reasons. Transportation would provide the links with other places; in good part, settlements would grow in proportion to the strength of such links; and a railway or other form of modern transportation was often the difference between an efficient connection and none at all. The transportation system, in short, was seen to have enormous power, not to complement or supplement, but to create; and there was abundant evidence at hand that it did.

Victoria, the first town, grew out of the HBC's main Pacific depot and moved from the lower Columbia River to southern Vancouver Island in 1843, less in anticipation of the border settlement three years later than, as Richard Mackie has recently shown, to secure an accessible harbour for the company's growing Pacific trade.[15] New Westminster emerged during the gold rush as a classic gateway town, a river-mouth, steamboat port on the main route to the diggings. Vancouver, which superseded New Westminster, was a creation of the railway, and its spectacular growth to metropolitan dominance reflected its location at the junction of the main corridors of transportation affecting the province: railway routes east, coastwise steamer traffic, and deep-sea shipping.[16] At no other point in a network dominated by a few channels was there anything like equivalent access to goods and information. By the time Prince Rupert became the Pacific port for the Grand Trunk Pacific, the pattern of urban dominance was already set; Prince Rupert could not begin to compete with the many linkage advantages, both within the city and beyond, that already had accrued to Vancouver. And small railway-dominated towns emerged at divisional points, to a railway approximately what roadhouses were to a wagon road.

Another category of towns, all of them small in early British Columbia, emerged at points where local resources and access to distant markets were available. Nanaimo, the first, was a colliery town on the coast, accessible to shipping. Across Georgia Strait and later, Britannia was a company town beside a concentrating mill, at the junction of two transportation systems: a tram bringing copper ore to the mill from mountainside mines and ships loading concentrates. At Hedley in the Similkameen Valley, and at many other small hard-rock mining towns, the pattern was essentially the same. The closer the town to the resource base on which it depended, the more ephemeral it was likely to be.

Phoenix, atop a copper mine in Boundary Country, became an open pit; Anyox, another copper town on the coast north of Prince Rupert, closed down with its mine. Sandon, a silver-lead town in the Kootenays, faded away as its small mines closed; Kaslo, on the other hand, a gateway to the Sandon mines via a narrow-gauge railway from Kootenay Lake, survived. Small developments that provided short-term employment remained as camps: perhaps an adit, rock dump, a few mine buildings, and bunkhouse accommodation for men high on a mountain. A logging railway might produce a sawmill town, like Chemainus, but logging alone produced camps, though the distinction between camp and small town was often blurred. The camps of the salmon fishery were seasonally occupied canneries, located close to the resource and accessible to steamers; at the mouth of the Fraser, enough canneries bunched together to create the small town of Steveston. In the few places with dispersed farming populations, as in the lower Fraser Valley, the Okanagan, and the Peace River, small towns emerged as rural service centres. Some towns combined several of these functions. All these different towns and camps were at advantageous locations in a new matrix of transportation and communication, which was a necessary condition for their existence.

Regional economies and land uses were also being reworked as distances declined and the reach of the international market expanded. Here, as elsewhere, the market's influence was to commodify land and specialize land use. Trees began to be calculated in board feet, salmon in the number of twenty-four-can packs. Clearcuts were products both of techniques of logging and hauling and of the market's unrestricted access to forests. Various forest tenures gave clear title; Indigenous peoples were on reserves; and, apart from their discounted, largely inaudible voices, there was no interference from past or current populations with other agendas. The equation seemed greatly simplified: wilderness and market bound, as it were, by logging railways and donkey engines. Provincial land policies that allocated land for specialized purposes, such as forestry, mining, agriculture, provided institutional support for an international market economy that depended on the division of land and the functional integration of economic space as much as on the division of labour. In older societies, regional specializations tended to be imposed slowly in the face of a good deal of resistance from prior, more regionally self-sufficient economies. In British Columbia, however, such specializations were the abrupt accompaniment of the virtually simultaneous arrival of settlers, low-cost transportation, and the market. Ranching, logging, or mining quickly dominated particular regions; at various scales, heartland-hinterland relationships were quickly introduced. Economic specialization tended to create ecological simplifications, such as agriculture or, later, tree plantations. In these restructurings was a whole new geographical order of things – Deleuze and Guattari's reterritorialization. Compared to what had gone before, a thick layer of difference was imposed across the land.[17]

In short, introduced systems of transportation and communication incorporated British Columbia within the modernizing world and created patterns of settlement and land use that bore many characteristic stamps of modernity. But modernity is itself a collection of shifting relationships, and relocation adjusted the complex of modern ways that reached British Columbia from the east. These adjustments were bound up with the particular flows of goods, people, and information into and within the province.

Most immigrant British Columbians could remain closely in touch with the places they had left. Letters and all manner of printed materials followed them, keeping them in close contact with distant families, prevailing opinion in home societies, and world news. Letters were particularly awaited, and protracted correspondences, lifelines between distant worlds, were common. Newspapers and magazines were sent from home, and books not locally available were ordered. Mail order catalogues displayed current fashions and consumer goods, some of which were usually available in even the smallest dry goods stores. Few immigrants came to British Columbia to escape the modern world, and those few hardly could, for a modern communicative environment was at hand with a vast capacity to distribute information. At the same time, immigrant and home societies communicated with each other out of different contexts, which over the years diminished their capacity for mutual understanding. Daisy Phillips, prim, brave, and as unprepared as the British army officer-turned-orchardist she had recently married, lived surrounded by forest on a terrace clearing in the Windermere Valley in southeastern British Columbia and corresponded with a mother and sister in a four-storey Georgian town house on High Street in Windsor, England. She knew their world but could not reproduce it, and they could only imagine hers. A Chinese coal miner living in the spare male accommodation of Nanaimo's Chinatown received a scribe-written letter from his wife in a peasant village near Canton: husband and wife living in vastly different settings thousands of miles apart. A pioneer woman learned about the latest domestic science at a local meeting of the Women's Institute and returned to a log cabin with a water barrel in a corner. A colonial secretary, writing from Downing Street, communicated a theoretical experience of empire to officials in British Columbia, who somehow had to accommodate such theory to their sense of local realities. Texts, in short, travel more readily than contexts, and to the extent that both are required for communication, British Columbians were on their own. Most fundamentally, perhaps, British Columbia reproduced neither space nor time as they were commonly understood in Europe.

Colonization appeared to have simplified space. This was partly because immigrants considered that they had left the past behind, an assumption encouraged by their deeply implicit assumptions about the location of civilization, "savagery," and plummeting Indigenous numbers. To take the past out of space was to eliminate most of its human texture, an unimaginable subtraction even in a rapidly urbanizing, industrializing Britain, the heart of the modern world, but an obvious fact of immigrant life, apparently, in British Columbia. Moreover, immigrant activities tended to be spatially segregated by the uneven distribution of resources, and the specializing tendencies of the international market. One region was dominated by the equipment, work routines, logistics, and, after a time, the subculture of logging; another was similarly dominated by mining; another by ranching. Regions changed as resources were depleted and technologies and markets evolved; they variously overlapped, but large stretches of land tended to be dominated by a few particular strategies of resource extraction. The economy of British Columbia as a whole depended on a few resource industries, each with its characteristic, much repeated human geography. Vancouver's metropolitan dominance was another form of spatial specialization, in this case around flows of goods and information. Simplified space was also partly the creation of people who wanted to avoid complexity and relocated it when they could: by legislating reserves for Indigenous peoples or by the constant pressure of racism that largely created Chinatowns and Japtowns.[18] As Edward Said has pointed out, people who are themselves dislocated and threatened by the unknown and the previously distant tend to fall back on their own basic texts; in the case of British Columbia, immigrants drew on beliefs about the superiority of European civilization and the inferior otherness of the rest of the world.[19] Essentially, a relocated, simplified version of loosely "British" culture sought to contain the unfamiliar complexities of its new situation.

This textual agenda and associated spatial strategies, coupled with the denial of a local past, and the territorial specializations inherent in international market economies and supportive government policies, encouraged new, simplified constructions of space. Men worked in camps, enclaves of capital and labour largely abstracted from social contexts (other than ethnicity, itself an abstraction) and relocated in wilderness. Because there were often no other media, the lines of industrial transportation became those of social interaction. Men in mountainside bunkhouses rode the ore tramways to nights out in the bars below. Men leaving the coastal logging camps or canneries caught the steamer to Vancouver; there was nowhere else to go. The drab toil of a work camp, the bright lights of a city; the tough maleness of a work camp, the softer, civilized femaleness of home: simple spatial dichotomies within simple constructions of space. Much of the interior dry belt was quickly known as cattle country and recognized as such in provincial land policy, but the very speed of such homogeneous regional identifications is a measure of the lack of perceived alternatives. Even in Vancouver, rows of California bungalows emerged on the west side of the city, their occupants white, English-speaking, middle-class people who lived, as much as possible, within networks linking others of their kind in Vancouver and to home societies in eastern Canada or Britain. Modernizing British Columbia denied many of the novel elements of complexity within it.

And the province appears to have jumbled time: displacing it, destroying its linearity, mixing elements from the past like raisins in a pudding. There was little continuous British Columbian time, rather, essentially, a present and its future. The European past was relevant but distant; it contained the history of most people who came to British Columbia but not of the place where they lived. Yet artefacts from this geographically displaced past crept in. Settlers built log cabins, dwellings not seen in western Europe south of Scandinavia since the medieval forests had been cleared. Packhorse trails and railways intersected. Wherever transportation costs were high, local labour and preindustrial technologies were viable alternatives to imported manufactures, as when Hawaiians pit-sawed lumber at Fort Langley and the fort blacksmith made tools that, in Britain at the time, were factory-produced. In such ways, immigrants lived with introduced anachronisms. One, perhaps, was the ethnographers' quest for traditional Indigenous culture. I suspect that this was neither disinterested curiosity nor colonial appropriation but a quest for the original uncivilized Europe. In this light, British Columbia appeared to contain the beginning and the current end of Europe, together with a few intervening artefacts.

Finally, the elimination of distance has been a primary tactic of power in modernizing British Columbia. Distance at first fended off the outside world, while the progressive conquest of distance allowed ever more of that outside world in. The conquest permitted government to extend its influence through most of the province, giving what initially was an abstract geopolitical space, British Columbia, concrete political meaning. It enabled capital to reach out to ever more land, exploit the land's resources, and then connect them to the world economy. It enabled immigrants to settle, knowing that they would be in touch with home and with many familiar ways. From an Indigenous perspective, it ushered in a barrage of land appropriation and cultural change that could be resisted in various ways but hardly stopped. The assault on distance was too pervasive, too central to the agendas of colonialism and modernity. A road might be blockaded here or there, but to hold off the changed relationship with space that was being forged in the modern world, and the new land uses and human geographies that accompanied it, was another matter altogether.

Indigenous Space

The detachment of the Indigenous peoples of British Columbia from most of their land was not a simple process, and I wrote a book, *Making Native Space: Colonialism, Resistance, and Reserves in British Columbia* (2002), to describe how it came about. By the time reserve allocations ended in the 1930s, they comprised about a third of 1 percent of the area of the province. Intricately worked out Indigenous land uses no longer fit these assigned spaces. Near the end of my book, I considered the relationship between the assault on Indigenous custom in British Columbia and earlier assaults on customary land uses in the British Isles and also the enormous challenge for Indigenous peoples to make anything like secure livelihoods in the new configurations of space – on and beyond their reserves – in which their lives had become situated.

From *Making Native Space: Colonialism, Resistance, and Reserves in British Columbia* (Vancouver: UBC Press, 2002), 265–75.

THE ALLOCATION OF RESERVES in British Columbia defined two primal spaces, one for Indigenous peoples and the other for virtually everyone else. By the 1930s, the space set aside for Indigenous peoples consisted of more than 1,500 small reserves scattered across the province, a reserve geography with no close North American equivalent. Basically, it was the product of the pervasive settler assumptions, backed by the colonial state, that most of the land they encountered in British Columbia was waste, waiting to be put to productive use: or, where Indigenous peoples obviously were using the land, that their uses were inefficient and therefore should be replaced. Such assumptions, coupled with self-interest and a huge imbalance of power, were sufficient to dispossess Indigenous peoples of most of their land. They were located in many small reserves rather than a few large ones (as many had advocated) for a variety of reasons: the provincial government argued that small reserves would force Indigenous peoples into the workplace, there to learn the habits of industry, thrift, and materialism, thus becoming civilized; and also (less stated) to provide cheap seasonal labour for burgeoning industries – arguments that joined self-interest and altruism. In the early years there was concern that concentrations of Indigenous peoples could pose a military threat to settlers. Moreover, government officials soon found that Indigenous peoples were intensely attached to their habitual places and that there was not the military and bureaucratic power at hand to move them or to make the moves stick. Given, then, that reserves would be located within traditional territories, there was some attempt, more at some times than at others, to allocate the places that were most precious to Indigenous peoples, such as their villages, grave sites, cultivated fields, and fishing sites – none of which required much space. Indigenous peoples identified such places to the reserve commissioners. They never convinced the provincial government to allocate reserves for commercial logging or, for that matter, to allocate much agricultural land that settlers might be able to use. Nor was the Dominion, the legal custodian of Indigenous rights but also a partner in Confederation, ever quite prepared to take the province to court, with the result that the reserve map of British Columbia reflected the agenda of the provincial government backed by the prevailing values of a settler society.

This reserve geography functioned as intended. It opened almost all provincial land to capital and settlers (insofar as access and topography allowed) and, for all practical purposes, extinguished the rights of usage, custom, and Indigenous law on which, not long previously, the human geography of the northern Cordillera had depended. Another geography was quickly emerging, one dependent on another regime of property. This one derived primarily from Britain and from the long struggle, which was essentially over by the mid-nineteenth century, to detach ownership of land from use rights to it and, thereby, make it more accessible and responsive to the market. By the time British Columbia was being resettled, most immigrants took a regime of private property rights, backed by the state, for granted. The policy that Indian reserve commissioners could not interfere with the rights of private property, legally obtained, was neither deviated from nor debated. These rights were assumed to be at the heart of a civilized society in which owners should be entitled to do what they wished with their lands: fence them, sell them, or evict trespassers. If these rights were transgressed, the law and the state were at hand to punish the transgressors. Such, very generally, was the regime of property–law–state that had repossessed the former Indigenous lands of British Columbia and constituted the matrix in which the province's many small Indian reserves were situated.

The reorientation of land away from custom and towards the market was not unique, of course, to British Columbia. It had happened many times before, not only in earlier settler societies but also in the British Isles, whence many of the settlers in early modern British Columbia had come. There, the centuries-long struggles over enclosure had been waged between a great many ordinary folk who sought to protect customary-use rights to land (on which livelihoods often depended) and landlords who wanted to dispense with the clutter and relative unprofitability of customary usage and use their lands as they saw fit. In the western Highlands at the end of the eighteenth century, to take one example, landlords sought to clear the land of tenants and, with them, the stone-and-turf villages (*clachans*), surrounded by open arable fields, surrounded by common grazings, surrounded by upland pastures (*shielings*), from all of which in myriad ways the ordinary Gaelic-speaking people of the western Highlands had wrested their livelihoods.[1] As wool and meat prices rose during the Napoleonic Wars, landlords found it more profitable to run sheep, and tenants without formal contracts (the great majority) could be evicted "at will." They were. Their former lands came to be managed by a few sheep farmers: their intricate local land uses were replaced by sheep pasture. The displaced were relocated in small plots (crofts) along the coast, where they supplemented the meagre returns of inadequate farms and paid the exorbitant rents for them with poorly paid work, collecting and burning kelp (to make alkali) in a glutted labour market created by the landlords – conditions reflected in landlord mansions and crofter destitution. Out of them, eventually, came much of the Scottish migration to eastern Canada.

In Windsor forest, to take another example, were not only the King's deer, but thousands of people who used the forest in varied ways and whose livelihoods were threatened by attempts to assert property rights at the expense of custom. The Black Act of 1723, brilliantly analyzed by E.P. Thompson in *Whigs and Hunters,* turned deer hunting and many other venerable uses of the forest into capital offences, thereby raising the stakes of the struggle between those who blackened their faces and hunted deer and the wardens who tried to stop them. Crime was being defined by the propertied and was increasingly conceptualized, Thompson argues, as offences against things rather than as injuries to people. "This enabled the law to assume," he claims, "the postures of impartiality: it was neutral as between every degree of man, and defended only the inviolability of the ownership of things."[2] However defended by those who depended on it, the practical, vernacular economy of the forest was slowly being eaten away as the law increasingly favoured notions of absolute property ownership, backed them up if need be with hangings, and left less and less space for what Thompson calls "the messy complexities of coincident use-right."[3] As in the western Highlands, thousands of ordinary people were detached from the land – that is, from familiar livelihoods – as the sway of exclusive property rights expanded.[4]

These developments in the western Highlands and Windsor forest were approximately reproduced in British Columbia, as elsewhere in North America,[5] as a regime of exclusive property rights overrode a fisher-hunter-gatherer version of what historian Jeanette Neeson calls "the economy of multiple occupations."[6] Crofts, like reserves, were small spaces for the dispossessed. Even the rhetoric of dispossession – about lazy, filthy, improvident people who did not know how to use land properly – often sounded remarkably similar in locations thousands of miles apart.[7] But if colonial settings provided fresh opportunities for the expansion of exclusive property rights and the market economy, the context of these developments had changed and, with it, both the nature of the argument and the balance of forces involved.

The arguments over land in Britain were, essentially, class arguments within societies that recognized themselves as such: their outcomes revealed only too vividly the reality of class relations. The argument, such as it was, between settler society and Indigenous peoples over land in British Columbia was not a class argument but rather one between different societies and cultures that, out of altogether different historical experiences, had only recently encountered each other. British settlers had met a much more other "other" than any stratum of British society, one that easily could be racialized (and usually was) and that, because assumed to be savage, was thought to have nothing to say to civilized people. And so the argument against custom, multiple occupations, and the constraints of lifeworlds on the rights of property and the free play of the market became, in a colonial setting like British Columbia, not an argument between classes about the distribution of wealth, nor even an argument between different economies, but rather a far more elemental, polarized, and characteristically racialized juxtaposition of civilization and savagery.

This, I think, partly explains why there was such unanimity among settlers about the exclusive rights of private property when many of their near ancestors had fought tooth and nail to protect the rights of custom and usage. Now such use rights were seen to be associated with completely different and apparently savage peoples. The argument had been placed in another register and, so situated, there was no choice in the matter. Moreover, before they migrated, most emigrants were already well detached from regimes of customary rights, and migration had only deepened the rupture. There was no regime of custom to fall back on, rather, in a sense, its antithesis, the symbol of the prosperous, socially aspiring farmer or, more generally, of the hard-working, up-wardly mobile individual. This symbol, new land, the absence of cus-tom, perhaps even the memory of the loss of livelihoods because of the absence of clear title to land – these were ingredients in the settler commitment to exclusive property rights, an entirely understand-able construction of self-interest in late nineteenth- and early twentieth-century British Columbia. In such circumstances, the use rights of a different and, in most settler eyes, a lesser people were essentially in-visible, and a regime of private property rights in an open market economy flowed into the province. Like the crofters or the folk in Windsor forest, Indigenous peoples resisted it as they could but with even less power, as colonized and marginalized peoples, to fend it off or to mitigate its effects.

Accompanying this regime of property and, in a sense, providing social cohesion in the absence of local custom was a complex apparatus of surveillance – the regime that French philosopher Michel Foucault called disciplinary power and associated with "biopower," the control of bodies. Foucault claimed that disciplinary power operated through an enveloping array of technologies, assumptions, and channels that eventuated in the docile and normalized body. He thought that such power was pervasive in modern societies and used the spatial metaphor of Jeremy Bentham's Panopticon (a prison in which inmates were ob-served but could not see their observers) to suggest the type of surveil-lance and control that it imposed.[8] His analysis of the modalities of such power turned on explorations of discursive strategies of normal-ization, and of the institutions, such as prisons, reformatories, asylums, and courts, in which they were expressed. He did not explicitly consider colonial settings, but he was a theorist of the spatial relations of power, and insisted that disciplinary power was preoccupied with, as he said, "the analytical arrangement of space."[9] He went further, holding that disciplinary power had solved a number of problems that had eluded the old economy of power (which he called sovereign power and con-sidered to rest on spectacle, terror, and the taking of life). Essentially, he thought that disciplinary power had found the means to reduce multiplicity (difference, variety) to manageable and useful order – ultimately to the normal – and that this new "machinery" of control was deeply spatial. He held that "discipline fixes; it arrests or regulates movements; it clears up confusion; it dissipates compact groupings of individuals wandering about the country in unpredictable ways; it establishes calculated distributions."[10] Some years before Foucault, Frantz Fanon made similar points about colonialism in North Africa,[11] an indication, perhaps, of the relevance of Foucault's thought to the analysis of a colonialism preoccupied with both discipline and space. Had Foucault worked in colonial settings, I venture that he would have offered a less institutional version of the carceral metaphor and made less of the disciplined individual while making more of strategies associated with the deployment of land and the management and normalization of groups.

As it was, Foucault's most famous example after the Panopticon was the reform school at Mettray, where the young inmates were constantly watched and subjected to rigorously managed routines. Their overseers, Foucault said, were "technicians of discipline," and he went so far as to describe the school as "the first training college in pure discipline."[12] In such institutions he saw early models of a form of power that would eventually slip beyond the walls of any particular institution to become lodged in the human sciences, law, bureaucracies, and even beyond them, in "the innumerable mechanisms of discipline" of, virtually, the whole society – all bearing, as Foucault saw it, on the eradication of deviance and the creation of the normalized individual.[13]

In this light, a Foucaultian analysis of colonial practices in British Columbia might well start with the residential schools, where, somewhat as at Mettray, Indigenous children were subjected to rigorous space-time disciplines, watched, weaned as much as possible from their Indigenousness, and remade, at least in principle, as English-speaking members of a civilized, modern society.[14] Or it might begin with the missions, places that the missionaries usually sought to set apart from the rough edges of settler society so that their sequestered converts could be tutored in God's truth and watched to see that the message had stuck.[15] If souls defied watching, bodies were more visible, and almost all the missionaries were moral watchdogs on the lookout for sin, particularly for those of the flesh. When they could not be present, many of them appointed Indigenous watchmen in their stead, and sometimes watchmen of the watchmen, a system of espionage and double espionage directed at the management of bodies (biopower) that Foucault would have explored with relish. He would also have noted that these settings functioned not so much to create normalized, disciplined individuals as to remake deviant cultures. Savages were being civilized and brought to God. Those were the primary objectives, of which the normalized individual was, in a sense, a byproduct.

Although Foucault did not develop the analysis, he was well aware that land itself could be a crucial factor in the disciplinary equation. He considered the possibility that Paris could be organized as a carceral city, reshaped in a geopolitics of disciplinary power.[16] He was fascinated by accounts of a vagabond, Béasse, a person of no fixed address, no timetable, no master, no identifiable work; and by the judicial process that sought to normalize such indiscipline – such deviance – by tying it down to a particular place, a particular job, and a recognized station in life.[17] Had he worked in British Columbia, he might well have concluded that Béasse was Taku Jack, the Tlingit Chief who refused to be placed because he moved everywhere across his land and who lived but did not work. Disciplining Taku Jack and Béasse became a matter of fixing both of them on the ground, but whereas Béasse, the vagabond, was a marginal character at the edge of a French society composed overwhelmingly of people who did have fixed addresses, Taku Jack was a Chief, and the spatial restrictions that an Indian reserve commissioner sought to impose upon him had been resisted, in one way or another, by all Indigenous peoples in the province. Moreover, Béasse lived within the complex, enveloping hierarchy of a French society with a vast, intricate capacity to provide sharp, finely nuanced social definition and to monitor deviance. Taku Jack lived where there were, at most, a handful of people in any hundred square miles and where the institutions of settler society and its governments were only beginning to express themselves. There were not, in such circumstances, many disciplinary technologies at hand. Discipline, I think, had come to rely on a few salient practices, of which, in particular circumstances, missions and residential schools were undoubtedly important examples. Underneath them, as it were, was the more pervasive discipline imparted by the differential allocation of land in the province, backed up, of course, by laws, courts, and jails. For mobile hunting, fishing, and gathering peoples accustomed to using many different places in many different ways, the discipline imparted by a land system that defined where they could and could not go would have enormous effect. It may have been the primal disciplinary strategy in many colonial societies as, I think, it was in British Columbia.

The land system and the discipline associated therewith required and superseded maps. Indian reserves were mapped, named, usually numbered, and surveyed and, so treated, entered a grid of calculation. It became an easy matter to look up a reserve, check its location on a map, and fit it into a classification of land uses. The reserve acquired a fixed place in the Cartesian space of the survey system and in the minds of officials and settlers.[18] On the maps of the Indian reserve commissioners who laid them out, reserves were displayed rather like insects on pins, exhibits mounted on blank sheets (Figure 15). Such mapping situated the reserve within an official ambit of sovereignty, surveillance, and management while detaching it from its surroundings as well as the complex land uses and spatial patterns of former Indigenous lifeways. In some ways, this was an illusion – Indigenous lives were never entirely confined to these little patches – but in other ways it was real enough. The rather arbitrary boundaries identified on the reserve maps had become legal realities. Rights differed on either side of them, as Indigenous peoples, Indian agents, and settlers all became well aware. From an official perspective, the map focused the disciplinary gaze, albeit from afar.

Closer at hand was an Indian agent, of whom by 1920 there were sixteen in the province. These agents were responsible for the protection of Indigenous rights, such as they were, for instructing Indigenous peoples in civilized ways (e.g., in agriculture), and for their general well-being. Some agents were appreciated by their charges, others were detested, and many were considered irrelevant – it was often said that they never did anything. The province was large and the agents few and not always competent or sympathetic: many Indigenous peoples hardly ever saw one. Other eyes, embedded in the land system, usually were more insistently at hand, and from the perspective of Indigenous peoples their disciplinary power was more tangible and disruptive. These eyes

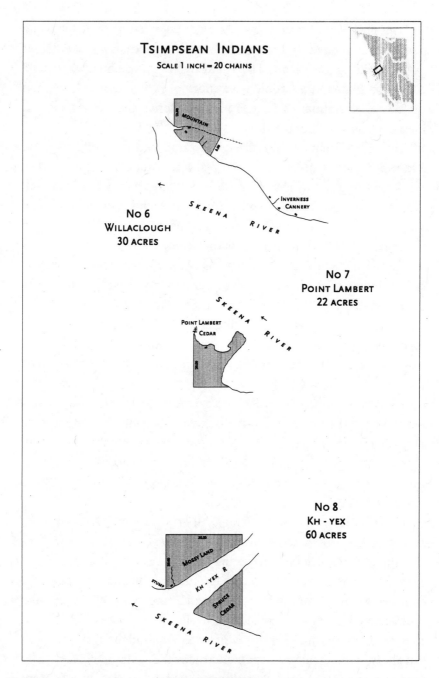

FIGURE 15
Reserves as exhibitions

belonged to all those people who owned property nearby, or who held land under licence or lease. Some of them were absentee owners, and some turned a blind eye, but in general they watched, thereby securing their rights to their properties. Such watching, backed by the law, turned Indigenous peoples into trespassers. It defined where they could and could not go, and as they had once moved everywhere within tribal territories, and as livelihoods and lifeways had been tied to these movements, the management of movement associated with property rights was the most essential discipline imposed on them. Its effects were most pervasive where most Crown land had been alienated and the settler population was considerable,[19] but even in areas where non-Indigenous people held little or no land and reserve boundaries, therefore, had little initial meaning, immigrants would acquire trapping, hunting, timber, or mineral rights sooner or later, and the constraints imposed by the non-Indigenous control of land would come into play. The metaphor of the Panopticon does not describe such watching: this was a decentred gaze that emanated from many eyes in many landed properties, fixed on Indigenous subjects, and tended to normalize their movement within a few acceptable channels.

The McKenna-McBride commissioners, to take one body of evidence, received complaints about such discipline almost wherever they went. Outsiders controlled off-reserve land and resources, which Indigenous peoples could no longer use. Chief Peters at Seton Lake: "Now at this particular time we have a hard time to make our living – the whites tied up the salmon and the whites tied up the game, and the whites they have tied up everything outside the Reserves marked on this map."[20] Chief Retasket at Lillooet: "Our friends the whites they have been taking our lands away from us, and there is nothing left to us, and everything that we use – they stop us from using it."[21] Chief David at Bridge River: "Some of the Indians are pretty poor now; we can only hunt a small piece of land up here, the other places are all tied up."[22] Such was the general problem, the details of which were sometimes spelled out. Chief Adolph at Fountain: "The Indians built a road right up to the spot where we want the land. A white man came along and he preempted the land right inside that road, and he took part of that wagon road. He told the Indians that we were not to go through there again. He said 'It is all my own' ... One of the Indian men went over to chop a tree down, and this white man told him to leave that tree alone, because he said 'that is my wood, and I am going to sell it in Lillooet.'"[23] At Ashcroft, the same. Chief Samson: "[The white men] have put gates across our roads, so that we cannot use them. It does not matter what we do, the white men are around and try to put us in gaol. If we want to go and kill deer and birds we are stopped. Even firewood, they wont allow us to take what we want."[24] Also at Douglas Lake: "The white man has fenced all the land around us and we can do nothing with them."[25] At the Koskimo hearings (north end of Vancouver Island), there was this request: "Can't we cut the dead trees that would be useless to the white man – We use those for drying the fish?" and this answer: "You can't go on other peoples land without the owner giving you permission to do so."[26] So with fishing. Chief Legence at Alert Bay: "I mean that years ago when I was a young man, they were able to use the traps all along to get the salmon and we sold them from these traps; but now we are not allowed to use the traps and sell them from the traps. The sockeye salmon we have been stopped from selling the fish at any time of the year."[27] And with hunting. Charles Jules at Coldwater: "Look at me, I am poor, and all the white people they watch me pretty sharp – If I go out to get game they watch me, and haul me right up and put me in gaol for it."[28] A few voices, recorded in the transcripts of a royal commission, from Indigenous peoples on the receiving end of a spatial discipline that regulated, watched, and owned, and that tended to create, even in the vastness of British Columbia, what Frantz Fanon once described as a world without spaciousness.[29]

In such comments are glimpses of the reconfigured geography of Indigenous life. It was anchored on the reserves, but they were small. Some of them contained some agricultural land but usually not enough for commercial farming sustained over the long term, never enough to support a band. Few reserves contained any merchantable timber, while throughout the long dispute over the reversionary interest the little timber on those that did could not be sold. Many reserves had been set aside as fishing stations where, with permits, Indigenous people could catch food for their own consumption (the Indigenous food fishery). Beyond the reserves were all the resources formerly incorporated in the seasonal round of Indigenous life but increasingly controlled by others and presented as an array of new employments. Fragments of older seasonal rounds remained for a time – in some places far longer than in others – but were increasingly curtailed by competition and regulation. This was the compartmentalized world in which Indigenous peoples had been fitted: the largely subsistent economies of the reserves, inadequate year in and year out to support them; dwindling connections with former regional economies of resource procurement; and wage labour in the larger immigrant economy that turned on its own logic, was controlled by others, and in relation to which (depending on changing technologies, markets, and prices) Indigenous peoples might or might not be relevant.

For them, life became a matter of working out the spatial strategies that would allow them to survive in such circumstances. Old regimes of custom had been weakened or broken, and something else had to be put in their place. In Europe, the common alternatives for ordinary people to the assault on custom were emigration overseas or migration to the industrializing cities. The former was not an option for the Indigenous peoples of British Columbia, and the latter has become one only in recent decades. In the late nineteenth and through much of the twentieth century – for many, until the present day – their challenge, rather, was to find some mix of on- and off-reserve occupations that would allow them to keep body and soul together while maintaining a connection with the particular land of their ancestors. They tried to do this in innumerable ways. Combinations that worked for a time in one place tended not to work in different times or other places. Sometimes nothing worked, sometimes incomes were fairly good, but the context was always changing in ways Indigenous peoples had little capacity to predict or control. Living outside the mainstream of settler society as they did, racially judged by it, and allocated a tiny fraction of provincial lands, their livelihoods tended to be found in precariously maintained negotiations among shifting and uncertain options in a new configuration of places.

PART 5

Theorizing Settler Colonialism

Making an
Immigrant Society

British Columbia in the late nineteenth and early
twentieth centuries, like Acadia and Canada two centuries before, was predominantly an immigrant, settler
society. As such, all three raise the same basic questions
about social and cultural change in places where migration had abruptly changed the context of individual
lives. And so, as I turned to the study of British Columbia,
I addressed issues that I had considered before, but
this time with a far larger and more diverse body of
immigrants, a far more dispersed and varied pattern of
settlement, and far more data. I could do no more than
probe this complexity, and here reproduce an article
that attempts to do so.

From *The Resettlement of British Columbia* (Vancouver: UBC Press, 1997), 250–75.

*B*ORN IN WARE, ENGLAND, *Topaz Edgeworth grew up in a wealthy industrial family, surrounded by servants, connections in high places, Methodist piety, and Victorian respectability. She remembered when the Duke of Wellington died – the Edgeworth family went into mourning – and admired Gladstone's principles and integrity all her adult life. She went to Mrs. Porter's School for Young Ladies at Brighton, to receive an "English reflection of a classical education." After her mother and stepmother died, and eventually, at a ripe age, her father as well, Topaz, unmarried and fifty, moved with her elder sister, Annie, and niece Rachel to Vancouver, where three of her nephews already lived. The three women and a somewhat corrupt Chinese cook named Yow (he went to jail for stealing from a subsequent employer) moved into a large house in the West End, the elite residential area in the city, when they arrived in the late 1890s. They soon settled in, aware that there seemed to be "more mixing-up of people here than in Ware" – Yow, Americans with unusual table manners, and others – but secure in their position near the top of the social hierarchy. The three women's "at home days" – tea and talk – were always well attended. Topaz joined the Minerva Club, a select group of ten literary ladies who met in West End homes to discuss Browning or an Elizabethan poet. She adored the royal family and wrote regularly to the Queen. The replies from the Queen's Lady in Waiting were published in a local paper. When the war came, Topaz organized the knitting of scarves for the troops. Late in her life, and to her boundless delight, she had a private audience with the Queen. At her death, one hundred years old, she was still very much the voluble Topaz from Ware who had come to Vancouver fifty years before.*[1]

Nan Bourgeon (née Capewell) grew up in a Methodist working-class family in Derby, England. Taught by her grandmother, she became a seamstress and was eventually employed by a titled family to make school outfits for the children. She moved into a life that alternated between a country estate on the edge of what remained of Sherwood Forest and a town house in London, lived within the ordered hierarchy of the servants' quarters, and was taught never to laugh or show the slightest emotion when Milord or Milady or any of their family or friends were about. Such, for a number of years, was her world. In 1911, Nan Capewell visited the Emigration Office in London, came back with literature on various colonies, and wrote to a sister in Vancouver. When she decided to leave, Milady was gracious: she presented Nan with a prayer book and offered to give her references.

In Vancouver, Nan worked as a dressmaker and as a waitress; then, caught by the depression of 1913, she got a job in the Grand Trunk Pacific Café opening in Prince Rupert. She went north by steamer and worked in the café for three months, then quit to escape a manager's unwelcome advances. She took the second Grand Trunk Pacific train out of Prince Rupert, winding up some 400 kilometres to the east in Aldermere in the Bulkley Valley, with five dollars to her name. There, Nan found work for the local entrepreneur as the cleaning woman in his small hotel. From time to time, Joe Bourgeon, a local farmer and livery man, asked her to ride in his buggy. Although he was French Canadian and Roman Catholic, she became known as Joe Bourgeon's girl, and eventually, though not with much enthusiasm, she married him. Joe wanted a farmwife, and Nan, poor and thirty-four years old, sought a measure of security.

It was not an easy marriage. Their cultural backgrounds were exceedingly different, and they clashed over many details of house and garden. Once, the priest, suspicious of Nan's Protestantism, threatened to take her children away. She left her husband shortly after their first child arrived, going to her sister in Seattle. But there was no work there, and when Joe sent her money for the trip back, she returned. Nan and Joe got by, coping with and needing each other but hardly close. Joe was a good, practical farmer, and after a time his farm was one of the more successful in the valley, a family operation that shipped fluid milk by train to Prince Rupert. Joe became president of the Farmers' Institute; Nan was an occasional midwife and an organizer of community social activities. Eventually, the Bourgeons were among the valley's most respected citizens.[2]

At seventeen years of age, Leong May-ying, a beautiful young woman living in a rural village near Canton, was told that she would become the second wife, the concubine, of Chan Sam, a peasant from another village in Guangdong Province, who was then living in Gum San (Gold Mountain or North America). He had paid a high bride price, and the matter was settled. May-ying could go or commit suicide. She went, entered Canada in 1924 (the year after the Chinese Exclusion Act) on a falsified passport, was met by Chan Sam in Vancouver, and found herself working as a waitress in the Peking Tea House to pay off the money he had borrowed for her bride price, passage, and passport. The tea house took her wages; Chan Sam took her tips. Four years later, they and their two daughters returned to China to live for a year in her husband's village with his first wife. When May-ying was again well pregnant, she and Chan Sam left the two daughters with the first wife, their official mother, and returned to Canada so the expected son would have a Canadian passport.

At the beginning of the Depression, May-ying was the more employable. She worked in tea houses in Vancouver and Nanaimo while relations with the frequently idle Chan Sam deteriorated. Eventually, she prevailed on him to pay another visit to his first wife in China; her earnings paid for his passage, and, instalment by instalment, for the house, the largest in the village, that he would build there. She worked in the tea houses, gambled after hours, and, increasingly, drank and turned to prostitution. Her daughter Hing (the "son" was female) grew up in rooming houses and hotel rooms at the edge of her mother's world and within her mother's determination to be a traditional parent of an obedient child. May-ying regularly beat her daughter, who then, sobbing, would kneel and repeat, "I will be obedient. I admit I was naughty. I will be a good girl." When Sam returned, he and May-ying soon separated. Her drinking, gambling, and prostitution increased. Hing went to the government school and to a Chinese school after hours. Covered with eczema, she was the best student in either class. May-ying's separation from Sam was followed by a long, intermittent relationship with a professional gambler, as quick witted as May-ying herself, with bouts of drinking, and incessant gambling, increasingly on credit. As a young woman, Hing was allowed no social contact with boys; eventually, she left, and her mother, try as she would, did not choose her husband. With the gambler out of the picture, May-ying came to live for a time with Hing's young family, but the arrangement did not work: too much drinking and lying, too many dark memories, and too much generational tension between mother and daughter. May-ying returned to cheap rooms in cheap hotels. Her grandchildren, when they saw her, remarked on how Chinese she was. Eventually, she was killed in a car accident, a frail Chinese woman in broken health who spoke no English and had never wished to.[3]

After the mid-1880s, the majority of British Columbians were immigrants, most coming directly or indirectly from the British Isles, but others from continental Europe, and a considerable number from across the Pacific. The Indigenous population, a small fraction of what it had been before outsiders and their diseases arrived, was declining rapidly. In 1891, Indigenous peoples accounted for a little more than a quarter of the provincial total; in 1921, they were 4 percent. In short order, a largely immigrant society had been put in place and largely immigrant human geographies created. British Columbia, a territory invented by British diplomacy, had acquired a new social and geographical reality. This new society was, itself, a late product of and an active participant in the processes of colonialism, yet such was the extent of its domination that most immigrant British Columbians were oblivious to the impact of their society on the peoples they had largely displaced.

What sort of society was this? Most British Columbians would have said that it was a modern society, part of the British Empire, part of the Dominion of Canada, part of the reach of European civilization and progress. They would have struggled to be more analytical, and their analytical problem remains. This was not a modern society that had evolved in situ, as in Europe. Nor was it a colonial society, where a small European elite and its troops and retainers presided over a large Indigenous population, the situation considered in almost all the recent literature on the strategies and tactics of colonialism and resistance.[4] Nor, even, was it much like the immigrant societies that had emerged in eastern, preindustrial North America, where agriculture was the predominant activity and forests yielded to the dispersed labour of axe and plow. Models of social change derived from such circumstances do not fit British Columbia very well, and the province as a whole remains rather uncharted social space.

To understand this society in some comprehensive way is to come to terms, I think, with its largely immigrant character. It was hugely influenced, of course, by industrial capitalism and the tactics of social control of the modern nation-state. But cutting across these dimensions of modern life were the basic facts of immigration: most British Columbians or their recent ancestors had left one setting, usually their home, for another; and in this new place they encountered a different land inhabited by a different mix of peoples. A society was being composed out of extreme displacements and disaggregations: a severely disrupted Indigenous population and a largely immigrant population detached from the circumstances of former lives, juxtaposed to unfamiliar peoples and ways, and perched amid some of the most dramatic terrain in the world. People no longer lived in anything like the full societies they had come from but commonly in small fractions of those societies assembled where resources and transportation combined to offer some economic opportunity. A certain astonishment was in the air, a quality that some of the province's best writers have caught.[5]

It is not easy to translate astonishment into analysis, especially when the main models of social change in modernizing societies have been framed in somewhat different circumstances. I doubt that British Columbians understand their society very well, a malaise of modernity perhaps, but probably accentuated here by recent immigration and the radically reworked land associated with it. Put somewhat abstractly, immigrants and capital had abruptly deterritorialized the prior inhabitants of British Columbia and had reterritorialized themselves.[6] The creation of an immigrant society in a reconfigured geographical space was a culminating colonial process, and here I offer some thoughts about the formation and shape of such a society.

I start with the simple proposition, increasingly taken for granted by social theorists, that societies and the places they occupy are part and parcel of each other.[7] The one is not the stage on which the other evolves. Nor are societies made by their settings, as environmental determinists once thought, or settings the simple effects of human activity. The two are interrelated, each affecting the other in complex, ongoing interaction. It follows that to take people out of one setting and relocate them in another, radically different, is to change their social relations. It follows that different types of settlement in British Columbia express different types of social relations. The same society cannot be in different settings.

Three other propositions follow. First, immigrants reestablish elements, but never the sum, of former ways. If for no other reason than that already given, a society and its geographical context in all their complexity are untransferable. Immigrants live within lean replications of the world they have left behind. Second, they also live within a host of new experiences related to the novel setting (for them) to which they have come, the places they have constructed therein, and the unfamiliar people who are suddenly at hand. Third, both these deletions and these encounters are sources of social change.

These simple propositions may begin to provide a framework for analysis. One might say that the dialectic between the intertwined processes by which, on the one hand, a tradition is simplified and, on the other, it is introduced to new dimensions of complexity largely shapes the character of an immigrant society. One might then inquire by what particular means a tradition is simplified and what form such simplification might characteristically take.[8] One might inquire whether there is a pattern to the ways in which a relocated fragment of a former society deals with the other fragments it encounters and how different fragments begin to borrow from each other. Something of the shape of an immigrant society might begin to be discerned by such an analysis. This, at least, is a line of attack, one that I am inclined to follow.

Deletions

A long tradition that includes the early nineteenth-century English political economist Edward Gibbon Wakefield and the late nineteenth-century American frontier historian Frederick Jackson Turner has held that when Europeans moved overseas into the depopulated middle latitudes, they encountered new environments that stimulated social change.[9] For both Wakefield and Turner, cheap land was the decisive ingredient of these new environments. Wakefield thought that it destroyed social bonds and created a rabble, Turner that it loosened the bonds of tyranny and provided context for American democracy. The one sought to seal the frontier and raise the price of land, the other lamented the frontier's passing, but both agreed about the social importance of a sudden change in land values. A rapid decrease in the value of land, relative to labour, had upset European property relations and the grid of custom and inheritance surrounding them. The result, they thought, was that segments of European social hierarchies could not reestablish themselves, a failure they either applauded or deprecated. For both Wakefield and Turner, a new environment put selective pressures on European ways, tending to accept some and reject others. The motor of social change was a new environment, particularly its new terms of access to land.

A very different approach to thinking about immigrant societies was suggested more than thirty years ago by the American political scientist Louis Hartz.[10] Hartz argued that only fragments, rather than the sum of European societies, migrated overseas and that in these new settings the ethos of the fragment, suddenly detached from the constraints of a larger social formation, became the ethos of a whole society. The United States, Hartz held, was a liberal bourgeois fragment of Europe, New France a feudal fragment. Compared to their progenitors, Hartz thought immigrant societies had been drastically simplified, a process of social change he associated with the selective migration of elements of European society. Hartz, a political scientist interested in political ideas, was struck by how much of the European political debate was virtually absent in the United States and believed he had identified the cause.

The point of agreement in these otherwise very different analyses is the common assumption that immigrant societies had pared back the complex social worlds from which they had sprung. I argued some years ago that this was an important insight but that Hartz had got the mechanism of simplification wrong.[11] Ideas, I suggested, have been remarkably mobile, not only "big" ideas about political life of the sort

Hartz was after, but a host of more ordinary, everyday ideas and as-sumptions about social organization, work, and the details of daily life. Such ideas travelled in the thoughts and memories of travellers, part of their invisible baggage wherever they went. Any substantial group of people represented, at least in principle, an enormous capacity to transfer ways of life from one place to another because of the store of knowledge that accompanied them. On the other hand, not all, by any means, of this intellectual and cultural baggage was relevant to new settings. Ideas and cultures had been decontextualized. It availed little to remember how to build a particular roof if the materials were not at hand, or if others, previously unavailable, were now cheaper and better. It availed little to plan for a gentry life if the economy would not produce the revenue to sustain it. The paring back of former ways in immigrant settings had much less to do, I held, with the particular groups that came than with the conditions in which they found themselves.

I remain of the view that a Hartzian analysis does not begin to explain the social structure of immigrant societies and still broadly agree with Wakefield and Turner that the interaction of people and environment in the New World has been a powerful source of social change. But I have increasingly realized that the Hartzian analysis is relevant in ways Hartz did not intend. It does not explain social structure, but it does bear on the transfer of regional cultures. In effect, two selective processes tended to affect different segments of the Old World heritage. A new environment shaped, first and foremost, a society's terms of access to land – its relationship with property. These changed relationships bore particularly on the vertical structure of Old World society. They tended to mean that some components of intricate Old World social hierarchies were favoured and that others were not. In settings, for example, where land was relatively cheap and markets poor, a relatively generous space was opened for the ordinary family, and relatively little space for the upper echelons of Old World society. Where markets were accessible and resources attractive, capital and labour rushed in. On the other hand, the selective migrations of people from Old World societies tended to affect the horizontal structure of Old World culture, repre-senting different cultures quite unevenly and mixing cultures up. Over-all, such migration left behind a great deal of the regional cultural complexity of the Old World. It was never possible to reproduce a regional culture, much less anything like the intricate horizontal range of Old World cultures; one reason for this cultural attrition was a migratory process in which a few people were drawn out of a much larger society and relocated across an ocean. Simply put, selective emigration emphasized some Old World regional cultures more than others. This was the other basic way in which the sum of Old World societies was drastically pared back in their extensions overseas. Some ideas were lost because they did not fit and others because they did not come.

In sum, these two processes of social and cultural change tended to work at right angles to each other; together, their capacity to eliminate large parts of immigrants' Old World backgrounds was enormous. Some clusters of ideas did not reestablish themselves because the context was wrong. Others were not established because they never came or because they came in so few individual memories that there was an insufficient critical mass for their social reproduction. Unfamiliar environments tended to rework social structures and pare back many former regional cultural ways; selective migrations tended to transfer only fragments of the intricate cultural mosaic that was spread across the Old World.

Immigrant British Columbia was a recently depopulated land that the time-space compressions of the mid-late nineteenth century had suddenly brought within reach of world markets. Its minerals, forests, and fish were attractive, particularly to western American capital, which was close at hand and experienced in these resource industries. As British Columbian resources came within range, capital poured in, often building the systems of transportation and communication it required and opening industrial work camps at favoured resource locations. Over the years, capital reached into ever-more-remote interstices of a vast, rugged land to develop resources and, inadvertently, to create new human geographies. With it, sometimes preceding it, came labour and particular techniques of resource exploitation, most of western American origin. In this, rather than in pioneer agriculture, was the principal momentum of settlement and economic growth in an emerging, immigrant British Columbia. A work camp in the "wilderness" and a line of industrial transportation to the outside world, rather than a pioneer farm tucked in a clearing, was the more basic geography of the place.

This huge, ongoing effort of development created abundant space for, and emphasized the social importance of, capital and labour. There were investments to make; practical jobs to be done by hard-headed, practical people; and, especially in the earlier years, an enormous amount of back-breaking physical labour. The basic arteries, economies, and settlements of a new human geography were being constructed. This vast practical effort drew selectively on prior social structures, emphasizing some elements and discouraging others. A British miner, reflecting on the gold rush society he had observed in the Cariboo in the 1860s, saw it this way.[12] Educated people, he said, should stay away. Their place was in "polished appreciative communities." Capital could take its chances. The real opportunity was for labour (he wrote about placer mining, which was not capital intensive). Old World societies were "overburdened with men of muscle"; there, "muscle bears so small an interest that the labourer cannot hope to attain a higher grade than that at which he started." But new societies had reversed these conditions. In them "life is simplified ... man is brought more directly in relation with mother earth ... and the only middlemen are traders and artisans [who] have no aristocracy of birth, wealth or position." He was offering, crudely, an analysis of the relationship between social organization and the factors of production in new societies and arguing approximately the same case as Wakefield and Turner.

The miner's analysis fits some parts of British Columbia better than others, but, overall, there was a tendency for the workplaces of the province to emphasize the values of the bourgeoisie and the working class. The cleavage between capital and labour became a dominant axis of the social structure of the immigrant society, leaving a lasting mark on the province's polarized political culture. In work camps, where labour overwhelmingly predominated, the values and aspirations were those of the working class; in early elections, labour candidates expected to do well in such settings. In the small towns dominated by primary resource industries, capital and labour were both well represented. Shopkeepers, somewhat in the middle, sided with one or the other.

Often the struggle between them was intense, as when mine owners' associations and militant unions battled in isolated mining towns. At stake was the apportionment of a great deal of new wealth. In the cities, where the occupational structure was much more varied, class alignments were less sharp. Yet the cities, Vancouver in particular, were essentially points of exceptional connectivity in the commercial-industrial economy. They organized the local primary resource economy, maintained external trading connections, and were enthusiastic boosters of their own progress and development. Their most successful citizens were entrepreneurs, speculators, or business managers; some had made fortunes in the real estate game. Such cities were not a world apart; they were another physical creation of capital and labour. They were spatially divided along class lines and reflected, in only somewhat attenuated form, the class divisions that ran through much of the province.

If there was a haven from the dominance of capital and labour, it was in farming. Mountainous as it is, British Columbia admitted farming to many of its valleys, though farming neither had the economic momentum of the primary resource industries nor became a defining regional presence, as it had on the Prairies and in much of eastern Canada. Still, agrarian visions were strong, and farming was vigorously pursued, both where it was possible and where it was not. By and large, farmers struggled with problems common to much of North American agriculture of the day: farms that were too small for the economies of scale of increasingly mechanized production; a cost-price squeeze associated with declining agricultural prices and rising equipment costs; and inaccessible, distant markets. In these circumstances, most agriculture was not very profitable, and the characteristic farm had a high subsistent component. It was usually subsidized by the low cost of family labour – on Chinese market gardens, usually by male family or village labour. Except in ranching, capital was hardly interested in agricultural investments, and the few attempts to create landed estates and lives of gentlemanly ease foundered on economic realities. Compared to the primary resource industries, farming tended to produce weakly stratified societies in which the tensions between capital and labour were largely absent, and the values of the farm family and, to a degree, those of the local rural community tended to come to the fore. Essentially, farming provided a niche, somewhat apart from the modern commercial economy, for families.

In this, farming contrasted strikingly with the primary resource industries, which tended to extend the growing separation of place of work from place of residence in modernizing economies to the point of excluding families altogether.[13] Work in the resource industries was for men, with the exception of salmon canneries, which employed Indigenous and Japanese women. The work was often temporary, in settings with few amenities for families or, because of the shifting location of work, little incentive to create them. In such circumstances, much of the labour in the resource industries was performed by single men, a mobile labour force moving among the camps, bunkhouses, and cheap hotels associated with a particular resource industry. The Chinese labourer, unmarried or with wife and family in a peasant village near Canton, was part of a larger pattern. Wives and families appeared in the larger camps, but many workers in the resource industries never married or, if they did, lived apart from their wives for much of the year. Working lives over, elderly bachelor men lived out their lives in cheap rooming houses at the dilapidated edge of downtown.

The brawny maleness of most work in the resource industries and the scarcity of outside work for white women probably tended to reinforce the gendered separation of workplace and residence associated with industrializing societies. For many men, the domestic values of home became a particular locus of civility, a retreat from a competitive, isolated, and often exceedingly dangerous workplace. Women, in this view, were identified with domestic virtues, an identification that contributed to their isolation from outside work.[14] On pioneer farms, the gendered separation of workplace and residence tended to break down, as it did for immigrant nonwhite women, for whom there was a variety of poorly paid outside employments.

The resource industries also excluded a huge variety of skills associated with former work, skills that could not be transferred to new industrial workplaces because the factors of production were differently arranged and technologies were unfamiliar. The resource industries in British Columbia tended to rely on skills and technologies that had evolved in analogous settings in the far western United States and had diffused rapidly northward. The axis of immigration crossed that of technological diffusion. This, coupled with the facts that the range of different employments was often greatly diminished and that many immigrants found themselves engaged in what, for them, were novel occupations, meant that a large part of the former ways associated with daily male work was suddenly irrelevant. New skills had to be learned, and in most of the resource industries they could be, to some acceptable level, fairly quickly. A strong back, confidence, and adaptability, rather than a prolonged apprenticeship, were required.[15] As men were reskilled, they tended to be identified with their occupations; they became miners, or loggers, or fishermen, occupational identifications that ignored the particular backgrounds from which they had come.

Each resource industry illustrates this. Technologies of placer mining came north from mining camps in California, as did the first miners. Later, more miners came from the east into what, for them, were extraordinary circumstances. There was very little work other than placer mining, very little society other than placer miners. The skills of placer mining, unfamiliar to many, could be learned fairly quickly: they had far more to do with hard work, practical ingenuity, and some experience than with science, engineering, or craftsmanship. To be a placer miner in a remote camp suddenly assembled in what miners took to be wilderness was to acquire a few new ways and leave an enormous amount behind. So it was in hard-rock mining and logging. Much of the technology of hard-rock mining in the mountains of southeastern British Columbia had evolved in American hard-rock camps, just as much of the technology of coastal logging came from American redwood and Douglas-fir forests. Experienced miners and loggers moved north with these technologies, but more immigrants who eventually became loggers or miners had no previous experience with this work. The huge coastal forest, a double-bitted axe, a ten or twelve-foot crosscut saw, wedges and screw jacks (the basic tools of logging in British Columbia until the Second World War), a bunkhouse, a few other loggers: this was a powerful new environment of work. It fashioned loggers and rendered prior occupations irrelevant. As an individual became a logger, or a miner, prior skills slipped away. Even agricultural skills changed, often drastically. Experienced farmers (most who tried to farm in British Columbia were not) found that the relative cost of land and labour had changed and that familiar crops were unsuited to new environments. In the Interior, horticulture required irrigation, and ranching depended on a Hispanic cattle culture of Mexican origin, both new to immigrants from more humid regions. Almost wherever practised, farming was an ongoing experiment with unfamiliar conditions. Such, perhaps, was the condition of agriculture in any modernizing society, but to the usual uncertainties were added those associated with pioneering in unfamiliar environments. In sum, a particular distribution of resources and relationships among the factors of production and with markets had created types of work in British Columbia that were new to many immigrants. To earn a living, they usually had little choice but to adopt these ways; by so doing, they discarded much of the work experience associated with their place of origin.

Outside (predominantly male) work was more affected by these changes than inside (predominantly female) work. The former was exposed to the competitive market economy and conformed to its efficiencies; the latter, somewhat shielded from the market, could reflect other values. For this reason, domestic female work tended to be far more conservative than outside male work. The nature and arrangement of furniture, the pictures on the wall, the stories told to children, the garments knit or sewed, the meals prepared, perhaps the language spoken: all this could reflect a home elsewhere, and often did. On a farm, there were often two landscapes: the fields tended by the man and conforming to the common regional practices of commercial agriculture; and the kitchen garden, tended by the woman and reflecting the preferred vegetables, flowers, and herbs from home. In the logging or mining camps that were big and permanent enough to admit families, a worker's cabin might have a tiny garden, with bits of lace from home in the windows: pinpoints of another place and culture in landscapes dominated by the terms and conditions of industrial work. A man would return from forest or mine not only to a family but also to a few touches from another place once lived in. Often the touches were weak because the women were limited by what they could afford, what was available in the stores, the peer-group-dominated interests of their children, and the opinions of neighbours. Farming was culturally more conservative than the primary resource industries due to the primacy of the nuclear family and the considerable place it accorded for domestic work.

Within this, values associated with gentility and refined living had a tough time. Such values found a certain amount of space, but generally around the margins of a society with another momentum. They had neither a local economy nor a local past to fall back on. And yet the late nineteenth-century to early twentieth-century emigrations from the British Isles to British Columbia included a good number of educated, upper-class people. There was a fair share of Oxbridge educations and venerable family names. Some of these people brought money, but most came with little more than public school educations, well-developed imaginations, and an educated upper-class English civility. Such ways had little practical relevance in the primary resource industries and made little headway there. There was more opportunity for the genteel English in agriculture, a socially acceptable pursuit for this class, but their farms tended to be long on picturesque landscapes and short on practical experience. The few pioneers who became successful farmers and left an established commercial position to their progeny were rarely of this group. Overall, the educated English were perceived to be haughty and useless. Indeed, their record of practical achievement is not good; at one extreme, men listed in *Burke's Peerage* lived in shacks in the Cariboo; at the other, young English blue bloods played polo on a terrace overlooking the Thompson River while Chinese workers built an elaborate irrigation system and planted an ill-conceived orchard.[16] The lives of such people had been radically decontextualized; old meanings and ways had lost their social fit. The shock was less in Vancouver, Victoria, and some rural areas – the Cowichan and Coldstream Valleys, a few enclaves in the Kootenays – where settlers with mannered English ways converged, but, overall, British Columbia provided little economic base or social context for imported gentility. It considerably accelerated a process of social change that was taking place in Britain.

Such were some of the pressures that new terms of land access and new work environments placed on the ways of life that immigrants had previously known. Overall, these pressures tended to emphasize the social relationships associated with industrial capital and to weaken other forms of sociability. On pioneer farms, however, they emphasized the nuclear family and tended to fend off capital. They favoured a few new, dominating technologies and discouraged others; inside work, shielded from these technologies, was culturally more conservative than outside work. These pressures were never very conducive to the social reproduction of gentility.

This was not the only axis of simplification. Immigrants came from many different cultural backgrounds in widely different parts of the world. No individual culture could be replicated in British Columbia. Invariably, they were pared back, some much more drastically than others, but always to a fraction of what they had been. As this happened, ways that had survived the process of migration were recontextualized; their meanings changed. For many immigrants, their own ethnicity was being invented.

Before the Second World War, the great majority of immigrants were of British background, most coming directly from the British Isles and most of the rest from eastern Canada. The considerable majority of those coming directly from Britain were English, unlike the predominantly Scottish and Irish migrations to early Ontario and the Maritimes. The eastern Canadians were usually two or more generations removed from the British Isles, as were the Americans of British background who entered the province. In 1931, these people – British born or of British background – were 73 percent of the non-Indigenous population of British Columbia, quite enough to ensure that English would be the province's predominant as well as official language. These "British" people were, however, a culturally diverse collection. The British Isles were still a cultural mosaic, if one increasingly dominated by the English language and a standardizing national culture. Eastern Canadians brought different ways, bred of their North American years, from immigrants directly from Britain. The Scottishness of Cape Breton was not the refashioned Irishness (Catholic or Protestant) of much of southern Ontario or the sixth-generation Loyalist culture of the St. John Valley of New Brunswick. Such, and more, was the regionally variegated Britishness that entered British Columbia.

Regional differences within the concept of British could hardly be sustained in British Columbia. People were mixed up; there was not a critical mass – whatever, precisely, it might be – of people from a particular regional background, and there was little will to maintain such differences. People of different backgrounds married; the census identified their progeny as British, but the connection with Yorkshire or the St. John Valley was gone. Differences in accent and dialect thinned out, not overnight and not entirely, but the drift was towards a regional English accent that combined eastern Canadian, English, and north-western American influences. A generalized British diet tended to survive; so, too, for the most part, a generalized enthusiasm for Britain and the Empire. Expatriate Scots got together on Robbie Burns night to sing his songs, drink, and feel Scottish. Expatriate Irish did much the same on St. Patrick's Day. Anglicans built Gothic revival churches and, where they could, planted and tended English flowers in the church-yards, replicating patches of Ruskinesque England. This diverse group, which collectively comprised both the cultural majority and social elite within a British colony endowed with British institutions, gave British Columbian society a British tone. It was not, however, a particular cul-tural replication, rather an amalgam of different regional ways that omitted a great deal from any one of them.

In 1931, 27 percent of the non-Indigenous population of British Columbia was not of British origin. Some 19 percent were from con-tinental Europe, principally from Germany, Sweden, Norway, Italy, and Russia. Just over 7 percent were from East Asia: China (4 percent) and Japan (3 percent). There was a sprinkling of others. These people found themselves as cultural minorities in a society dominated by the English-speaking and the reworked "British" culture described above. Many had no intention of staying; they were in British Columbia to earn some money and return home. Whether or not they came to stay, a great many did, and their British Columbian lives unfolded in a place where mi-gration had turned them into an identifiable cultural and, in some cases, a racial minority. There were many coping strategies. Some tried to integrate as quickly as possible; as a group, the Germans were perhaps foremost in this approach. Most sought out people of their own kind, partly for the familiarity of language and culture, partly for security against the perceived and often real hostility of the larger society. Even in the resource industries, workers of particular regional backgrounds stuck together when and where they could. Italians lived in residential "Little Italys" in the Kootenay mining towns. Swedes took over a corner of a bunkhouse. Societies and associations perpetuated various links with home. In some cases, children were sent to special classes after the public schools closed to learn to read and write their parents' language. Such efforts to maintain links with home were always an uphill struggle; the assimilative pressures were enormous. The first generation of British Columbian–born could usually speak their parents' language yet hardly read or write it; the second generation usually knew only a few words. The overall decline of many details of cultures rooted elsewhere may have been roughly in proportion to the decline in languages. Domestic ways always tended to be more resistant than those associated with the cash economy, but old ways were under assault everywhere. In time, they often survived only in special ceremonial occasions, such as weddings or national days, and perhaps in a few basic values, such as deference to parents. British Columbian Japanese could be embarrassed when presented to high-ranking Japanese officials visiting the province; they had forgotten the correct form of polite address because they no longer lived in a society in which such forms had social meaning.

There was always a small minority of immigrants who came to British Columbia to preserve an Old World social vision. Such were some of the upper-middle-class English, who no longer had the means to sustain their social pretensions in England and considered a farm or ranch in a British settler colony a socially acceptable safety valve. Such, indirectly, were the missionary agendas for Christian utopias – European inspirations without European space – among Indigenous peoples, whom they believed lived in darkness and sin but who could be led to light and salvation in isolated settlements shielded from the nefarious influences of other whites.[17] The utopian impulse was expressed most directly in various communal settlements that sought, in some tucked-away corner in the mountains, a little space and isolation from the values and demands of an encroaching world. Of these, the most conspicuous were the Doukhobor settlements in the Kootenays. The Doukhobors, an ascetic, Christian-anarchist sect from the Caucasus, sought to live communally apart from the state, apart from the corrupt values of the larger society. As Hartz would have put it, they sought to make the ethos of a fragment – their peasant Doukhobor communities – their whole social circumference, an ambition they partly achieved in British Columbia for more than a generation. The Doukhobors are an idiosyncratic example of the common immigrant tendency, made almost inevitable in circumstances where comprehensive social reproduction was impossible, to focus on some parts of the former social whole and let the rest slip away. For the Doukhobors, as for others with an explicit utopian vision, the rest was a welcome riddance.

In all of this, former ways of life were being reproduced in increasingly abstract and symbolic form. To live in a village in County Armagh, Ireland, or in Guangdong Province, China, was to live in a regional culture that affected most details of daily life yet was virtually invisible. Cultural assumptions were shared. The lifeworld was pervasive, enveloping, and apparent only when strangers came along or local people travelled and were reminded of their difference. In situ, the stranger seemed odd, but travel turned people into strangers who, as they moved away from the familiar, began to feel odd themselves. To settle down in another place, among different people and different ways, was constantly to be reminded of one's own difference. What was implicit had been made explicit. People discovered their own ethnicity. When, at the same time, there was a great deal of cultural loss, as invariably there was, this explicit identification focused on a declining number of markers. Increasingly, for those inside an expatriate culture, these markers became symbols of where one had come from and who one was. Such was the significance of the "ethnic" wedding. Ethnicity was no longer invisible and implicit in a way of life. It had become spare, symbolic, and altogether explicit, and, so abstracted, it could be exceedingly powerful. It could be said that migrations tended to destroy cultures and invent ethnicities.

This change took place in different ways with different groups and individuals. The more centrally people were placed in the British migrations, the more of their own ways they were able to retain, and the less explicitly they were likely to be held. These people were least likely to discover their own ethnicity; they thought others were "ethnics." For cultural minorities, the process of explicit ethnic identification was very much to the fore. Some people fled it to assimilate as quickly as possible.

Others did not have this option or did not seek it. Ethnic definitions were strong, especially when reinforced by race. They defined many people to themselves and to each other and comprised another basic axis of social differentiation in an immigrant society.

Recombinations

If one followed migration paths from their origin in the Old World to their destination overseas and compared the ways of life in the two locations, one would often be struck by how little of the former lifeworld had been transferred to the latter. I have suggested what seem the basic reasons for these common, and frequently drastic, deletions. But migration paths originating in very different, geographically distant cultures converged in places like British Columbia. People who had lived apart – and had been aware of each other only in the most general terms, if at all – met abruptly on unfamiliar terrain. The land and the means of earning a living thereon, as well as the people around, were often exceedingly strange. Immigrant life was located at the intersection of what, for the people involved, were two radically novel circumstances: an attenuating connection with a distant home, and an expanding connection with the ingredients of a new setting. Immigrant society reflected both these sets of relationships.

People migrated to British Columbia, as elsewhere, for a great many reasons, most economic in one way or another. The few who came for cultural reasons did so to protect, or modify, some aspect of the culture they left behind. Almost no one was drawn to a new mix of cultures. Because it seemed the route to prosperity, some immigrants tried to assimilate quickly into what they perceived to be the dominant culture, but many were more wary. The common reaction was to fend off otherness as much as one reasonably could. People sought to get ahead and retain something of their own cultural identities. I have mentioned some of the strategies of cultural conservation and their common result: an increasingly reified ethnicity based on a declining number of increasingly symbolic markers. But the success of immigrants' attempts to draw boundaries around their own ways of life and keep strangeness somewhat at bay varied with the size and power of the immigrant group. A small, non-English-speaking immigrant minority, with little access to government and not much capital, had little power – beyond an intense local struggle waged at the scale of the family and of community organizations – to defend its own cultural boundaries. Immigrants of British background, a solid majority with the levers of economic and political power at their disposal, were in an altogether different position to defend themselves and their way of life. They set out to define a territory in their terms and make it theirs, in the process creating boundaries that they used to fend off or control others.

British immigrants to British Columbia assumed what Edward Said, in *Orientalism,* has called an "imaginative geography" of the world. In this geography, there was Europe, the centre of civilization, and there was the rest of the world, less civilized, less ordered, somewhat mysterious, essentially "barbarous" or "savage." This divide was a cultural construction, not so much a geography of the world as of the European mind. Therein lay its power. It enabled Europeans to define and locate themselves in relation to the world in, for them, an altogether satisfactory way. They, more than any others, were the bearers of civilization and progress; the rest of the world was identified by stereotypes that served to emphasize the superiority of Europeans and hide the achievements and variety of non-Europeans. This imaginative geography underlay orientalism as a field of study, ran as a pervasive strand through European art and literature, and provided moral validation for European imperialism. It accompanied European technology and military might out into the world, discourse and physical power validating each other.[18] British immigrants to British Columbia, like Europeans elsewhere in various nineteenth-century empires, took the discourse entirely for granted; they knew they were among the civilized. But they were not in Europe, not even on the Atlantic Ocean, rather in a distant corner of the world with Asia beyond the horizon and a "savage" population at hand. To the extent that their new location was on the wrong side of an imaginative geographical divide, it was a geography to be corrected. In September 1858, late in the first summer of the gold rush, Governor Douglas addressed a large congregation of miners at the foot of the Fraser Canyon, only weeks after miners and Indigenous people had been fighting a few miles to the north. He welcomed them, assured them of the protection and value of British law, and then, addressing the British miners, said that he was "commanded to say to all Her Majesty's Native born subjects that this is their country."[19] Considering where he was, and when, this was an extraordinary statement. It was not just that a new colony was being added to the Empire; rather, settlers were welcomed to a colony that was to become "their country" approximately as England or Scotland had been. British Columbia was to be added, in effect, to the geography of a greater Britain, part of a greater Europe, the locus of civilization.

Such a project could only involve keeping others out, or, if this could not be done, containing them in as little space as possible. Boundaries became exceedingly important: the boundary of a colony (later of Canada) could be used to exclude immigrants, and, internally, boundaries could be used to separate those who were welcome because they were civilized, and those who had to be put up with because they were not. In drawing these latter boundaries, it could easily seem a moral duty, from the perspective of the civilized, to be as parsimonious as possible with the uncivilized.

The drawing of boundaries was enormously facilitated by the idea of race, which gained in currency and, apparently, scientific foundation during the nineteenth century. The Enlightenment idea of the fundamental unity of all people still found expression in the British government's abolition of slavery in 1833 and in the Treaty of Waitangi with the Māori in New Zealand in 1840, but gave way, from the mid-nineteenth century on, to increasingly racial classifications of people. It was a relatively small step, especially in the light of Darwinian theories of selection and of the survival of the fittest, to identify advanced and backward races – different stages, apparently, of evolution.[20] This "binary typology" of race, as Said has called it, readily complemented the far older European discourse about the location of civilization and savagery; it gave the discourse scientific validity, casting the difference between Europeans and non-Europeans into an immutable, biologically determined fact. Most late nineteenth-century imperial discourses were racialized in this way, and a lively idea of race became part of the baggage of European emigrants. In British Columbia, such ideas, somewhat abstracted from Europe, encountered their object in a place where social and cultural change was the common lot and an immigrant society, of somewhat uncertain future, was being constructed. These encounters and uncertainties, superimposed on a broad background of racist opinion, generated a particularly virulent racism. The moral and physical failings of the "yellow race," considered the most threatening in British Columbia, were elaborated in detail, the dangers of contamination widely described. In a society given to increasingly symbolic social representation, race became the preeminent symbol. It defined simply and effectively, with no need to go into details, who was acceptable and who was not.

So armed, a white and British majority population set out to police its boundaries. From its vantage point, the simplest solution was to keep other races out. The province's demands for exclusionary immigration policies, often more extreme than the federal government was prepared to go, steadily raised racial barriers. A head tax on Chinese immigrants set at $10 in 1884 became $50 the next year and $500 in 1904. Still, the Chinese arrived, and in greater numbers than ever in the years just before the First World War, when their labour was required to complete two new transcontinental railways. When the railways were built, the Chinese Exclusion Act (1923), supported by the overwhelming majority of voting British Columbians, stopped Chinese immigration. Restrictions on the Japanese were only slightly less severe. An agreement with Japan in 1908 allowed 400 Japanese men and their wives into Canada each year; in 1928, the number was reduced to 150. East Indians, almost all Jat Sikhs, faced another version of the same racial politics. More than 5,000 arrived between 1904 and 1908, anti-"Hindoo" sentiment intensified, and in 1908 the Canadian government, unable to ban immigration from another British colony, required that each East Indian immigrant have $200 on arrival. East Indian immigration virtually stopped. Combined, these measures had essentially sealed off British Columbia to nonwhites by 1930.

Those who had entered before these barriers were erected, or had managed to cross them, faced other exclusions. People of Asian heritage could not vote. In most cases, they could not purchase Crown land or logging licences. In 1923, the number of fishing licences for "orientals" was reduced sharply. Because they did not vote, they did not have access to the professions. They were excluded from most unions. Many found a little space in unorganized corners of the economy: as house boys, cooks, or gardeners; as launders or restauranteurs; as market gardeners. Others found wage work where reliable, inexpensive labour was required for work that whites would rarely perform. Some became fishermen or boat builders. A few became successful shopkeepers, importers, or labour brokers. All these activities faced the constant pressure of a white majority that assumed such people did not belong. At times, prejudice turned into racial riots. More common were the ubiquitous boundaries that could not be crossed. "Orientals" could not ride streetcars in New Westminster at one time; even the private land market often would not sell to them. The prejudice of the majority, coupled with the minority's protective response and tendency to gather together, created Chinatowns and Japtowns: racialized ghettos on cheap land at the least inviting edge of frontier towns. Kay Anderson, in her study of Vancouver's Chinatown, has shown how ideas of race and place were mutually reinforced within this geographic construction.[21] White racial discourse required Chinatown, a place apart for Chinese; and the social pathologies associated with a largely male population jammed into such a place only reinforced pejorative, racialized stereotypes. In British Columbia, the idea of race drew sharp boundaries.

In the eyes of most British Columbians, the other main racial minority was Indigenous, but after the epidemics, Indigenous peoples were perceived to be much less threatening. By 1900, perhaps much earlier, the white majority knew that it was well in control. There was no large Indigenous population lurking elsewhere, as with the Asians. There was, rather, a remnant non-European people – "backward," "uncivilized," and "savage" – who, in the racialized discourse of the late nineteenth century, might be assimilated to a point but could not become white, neither racially nor culturally. Even the missionaries, who considered all people equally precious in God's eyes and assumed that devout Christians would meet in heaven, hardly anticipated such equality on earth. For most British Columbians, Indigenous peoples stood in the way of progress and development. The reserve was the solution, another place apart required by a white discourse of otherness. There, the Indigenous other would be tucked away, given as little land as possible, marginalized in its own territory. For most of the majority, this was entirely appropriate, not only because of the realpolitik of power, but because they were civilized and Indigenous peoples were not. The civilized knew how to use land effectively. Another racialized space, reserves, appeared as tiny patches across the map of British Columbia.

Such boundary drawing was intended to deny the un-European complexities of a new place. The white British majority could cope with new technologies and terms of work: in them was change but also opportunity as the majority understood it. They could cope, with more or less grace, with other Europeans; despite lapses here and there, they too were among the civilized and would be assimilated into an English-speaking society. They could cope, often with much regret, with the loss of ways from home. What they could not cope with – in this, they were prisoners of their own beliefs – was a drastic assertion of un-Europeanness, and they did what they could to keep the un-European out of a place that was thousands of miles from Europe.

Boundaries, of course, were never watertight; there was always seepage. There continued to be white-Indigenous marriages, though not nearly as many as in the fur trade years. There were whites who learned Indigenous languages fluently and devoted years to the study of Indigenous cultures. One of them, James Teit of Spences Bridge, became a central, trusted adviser when, before the First World War, Chiefs of many Indigenous groups began to forge a collective voice on the issue of land title.[22] There were missionaries who became absorbed in the lives of their Indigenous congregations, creating complex, cross-cultural relationships with ramifications both ways. One of them, a young Englishman who arrived in Lytton in 1927 fresh from Canterbury, asked, years later, that his ashes be spread over the grave of the Nlaka'pamux woman who had taught him the language and something of Nlaka'pamux culture.[23] There were others, like Emily Carr, creative nonconformist souls who ventured some appreciative distance into Indigenous worlds; and many other people, more ordinary and unremembered, whose lives overlapped with Indigenous society in various ways.

The Asian-European boundary was probably sharper, partly because there were few Asian women in British Columbia, partly because Asians were not a "curiosity" and were considered threatening. Before the Second World War, there were almost no white-Japanese or white-Chinese marriages in British Columbia. But even to have a Chinese cook in the house, a Chinese peddler delivering vegetables, or Chinese workers in a bunkhouse next door was to identify individuals in the mass and begin, however slightly, to weaken a stereotype and its boundary-making propensities.

Some seepage, certainly, but essentially the boundaries held. In the eyes of most of its white inhabitants, British Columbia had become what its name implied: an integrated part of the British Empire within, as things had turned out, the Dominion of Canada. Its future was assumed to be white, English-speaking, and primarily British. By the early twentieth century, most British Columbians rarely saw an Indigenous person. Asians and whites lived in closer proximity, and their paths crossed more frequently, but interaction was almost always constrained by differences in language, culture, and social power, as well as by prejudice. Continental Europeans, especially the Protestants, were being drawn into the predominant culture. Their progeny and those of British immigrants increasingly intermarried. There were many interpersonal cultural exchanges, but as no one continental European nationality amounted to over 2 percent of the population before the Second World War, none had much capacity to influence a derivative British culture. It could easily be said that British Columbia risked becoming a narrow, expatriate British society, shorn of much of its British background, increasingly attached to symbols or abstractions of itself (particularly its whiteness), and determined to fend off novel connections and complexities that offered, potentially, some of the more creative opportunities in its new setting.

And yet, for all the rigidities that many sought to impose, immigrant society in British Columbia was an evolving New World creation. I have discussed some general tendencies that shaped the province's composition. The salience of capital and labour – most starkly represented in the industrial work camps, but far more widely expressed – was undoubtedly crucial, as were their associated work environments, new to most immigrants. From this, agriculture stood apart, space primarily for nuclear families in weakly stratified societies. Mannered gentility found little space anywhere. None of the regional cultures from which immigrants had come could be reproduced in toto, though majorities transferred more than minorities. The primarily British migrations to British Columbia produced an English-speaking population that increasingly melded different regional shades of Britishness, in the process discarding many regional ways and creating a regional culture (in detail, several regional subcultures) with no precise antecedents. Minorities struggled to hold on to cultural fragments, in the process creating an increasingly symbolic ethnicity while, particularly among immigrants from continental Europe, ways of life merged more and more into an expanding majority culture adjusted only a little by their presence. The tendency to turn ways of life into symbols was pervasive, and when the racialized European colonial discourse of the late nineteenth century was superimposed on the uncertainties of an emerging immigrant society, race became an overriding symbol. Whiteness became the first and most essential marker of social respectability. From the idea of race followed a number of boundary operations intent on affixing space for insiders and outsiders and ensuring that the former had most of it. While never entirely successful, they produced and sustained a powerful set of exclusions.

Out of these tendencies, with their myriad tensions and cross-currents, emerged an immigrant society. Robert Young, one of the best current analysts of colonial discourse, has remarked that a "culture never repeats itself perfectly away from home." Of this there is no doubt. However, when Young goes on to say that "any exported culture will in some way run amok, go phut or threaten to turn into mumbo-jumbo as it dissolves in the heterogeneity of the elsewhere,"[24] one such as I, who lives in the mumbo-jumbo and the heterogeneity of the elsewhere, is suddenly uneasy. Such phrases are vivid but empty; they provide no analytical assistance and virtually deny the possibility of understanding. What, Young implies, can be made of mumbo-jumbo? Yet it is possible to identify some of the principal structuring tendencies in the disaggregated and dislocated societies that emerged overseas. I have tried to do this here, suggesting something of the overall shape of British Columbia's immigrant society and locating some of the lives that comprised it.

AND SO I AM led back to the three lives with which I began. Topaz Edgeworth, who lived her British Columbian years amid respectable society within the domestic economy in the elite West End, was as insulated from social change as an immigrant life could be in British Columbia. She was largely oblivious to what was different in her new setting. She saw a lot of Yow, but as a cook with a remote culture. She admired the north shore mountains and the seagulls in the park, but knew next to nothing of this un-English nature. One night at the family cottage, Topaz decided to sleep on the porch, only to flee inside when the small noises of the night – island deer cropping the grass, a boom of logs squeaking rhythmically in the swell – took her back, terrified, to Mrs. Porter's School in Brighton and the Greek god Pan, whose fluting turned those who heard it mad. In this, as in so much else, her thought led back to England, an orientation that could just be maintained, in her comfortable circumstances, for the second half of a life.

Nan Bourgeon's life, on the other hand, had begun English but had become something else. An English social hierarchy was not in the Bulkley Valley; deprived of its social context, Milady's reference had lost its meaning. Nan lived there within a barely stratified local society tied to semicommercial family farming. On the other hand, she was exposed to cultural differences, particularly in the person of her French Canadian husband, that she could not have encountered in England. Her family itself became a primary locus of cultural interaction and change. Her children grew up in a sociocultural context and within a weakly developed social hierarchy that Nan, as a young girl, could not have begun to imagine.

Leong May-ying was caught, partly by her own conservative assumptions drawn from peasant China, in a social world where such assumptions no longer quite fit. She struggled with this disjunction throughout her Canadian life, a talented soul tossed into extraordinary circumstances. The subsequent generations had changed. Hing, whose teachers thought she should be a doctor, had had no such opportunity; she trained to be a psychiatric nurse then left the profession when she married. One of Hing's daughters became an economist and senior economic adviser in Ottawa, married a white man, and wrote a remarkable book about her grandmother. The processes of social change in an immigrant society work themselves out through the generations.

If one adds up such lives, and keeps adding, one returns, I think, to the patterns I have attempted to describe. An immigrant society has to be studied with immigration, and its effects, in mind. One should also remember that immigrants did not occupy a wilderness. In the background, nearer or farther, are those who were displaced by the resettlement of British Columbia and for whom colonialism is not so much about events in the past as an ongoing engagement with an invasive society that imposed itself across their territories then extolled its own energy while denying the destruction it wrought. For the May-yings, Nans, and Aunt Topazes of this world, Indigenous peoples were virtually invisible. Now, many of us should be able to see our own circumstances more clearly. If we better understood the tensions inherent in an immigrant society and realized that immigrant opportunities in this remarkable place have always rested, and continue to rest, on the displacement of Indigenous peoples, we would, I think, live here more thoughtfully and much more gently.

How Did Colonialism Dispossess?

After various writings on British Columbia, and particularly after my book (*Making Native Space*) on the reserve system, I felt that I had begun to understand the array of powers that enabled a settler colonial society to override other, prior, ways of life. At the same time, I was increasingly uneasy with colonial discourse theory, mainly because I thought that, in acquiring a great deal of academic momentum, it tended to ignore other forms of colonial power and, in so doing, was unable to assess its own relative significance. Rather than starting with the cultural analysis of texts, I thought one should start on the ground, at the sites of colonial dispossession, and there inquire how dispossession came about. In that way it should be possible to discern the different powers at play and assess their interconnections and relative salience. Thoughts such as these lie behind the article reproduced here.

From "How Did Colonialism Dispossess? Comments from an Edge of Empire," *Annals of the Association of American Geographers* 94, 1 (2004): 165–82.

INFLUENCED BY MICHEL FOUCAULT'S analysis of the relationships of power and knowledge,[1] by Edward Said's examination of orientalism,[2] by textual theory harnessed to colonial discourse analysis, and by many studies of the values and ideologies enmeshed in particular colonial encounters, most postcolonial scholars now identify culture and associated procedures of knowledge generation as the dominant power relations associated with colonialism. Whereas Frantz Fanon[3] emphasized violence – the power of the gun – and Marx, to the extent that he wrote on colonialism, the aggressive reach of capital, postcolonial research and writing situates the momentum of colonialism in the culture of imperialists and colonists. A central goal, therefore, of colonial discourse theory is to identify the assumptions and representations inherent in colonial culture – in the binary of civilization–savagery, in the erasures of Indigenous knowledge of time and space, in assumptions about race and gender, in the concept of the land as empty (*terra nullius*), and so on – and then, insofar as possible, to expose their contemporary manifestations. This work has focused much scholarly energy and has yielded important theoretical and practical results, but it is less clear that it has revealed the principal momentum and power relations inherent in colonialism.

Originating in literary and cultural studies, colonial discourse theory – indeed, postcolonial scholarship generally – privileges the investigation of imperial texts, enunciations, and systems of signification. In so doing, it exposes implicit modes of seeing and of understanding that are held to infuse and validate colonialism while imparting much of its momentum. If Said offered broadly inclusive descriptions of colonial culture, and if others, more recently, have emphasized the variety of colonial voices and the importance of a local, contextual appreciation of different colonial cultures,[4] in either case, culture is treated as a primary locus of colonial power. Moreover, as elements of colonial culture are assumed to have outlived formal colonial regimes, their identification becomes an active political project – the decolonization of representation.[5] In itself, this is commendable enough, but if studies of colonial culture are not contextualized among other forms of colonial power, then it is well nigh impossible to assess the particular work and the relative salience of colonial culture itself. A study of travel writing, for example, may yield an appreciation of the inflected seeing of travellers and of the complicity of such seeing with colonial projects while not beginning to address the relative importance of travellers' seeing and writing in the whole colonial enterprise. Given its focus, it cannot. At best, it can yield a nuanced understanding of traveller perceptions and values and suggestive ideas about their relationships with colonialism. Colonialism's complexity may be affirmed, so too, perhaps, the discursive construction of reality – comments tied more closely to theory than to a situated knowledge of colonial practices and power relations.

In the hands of some of its most able practitioners, postcolonial scholarship is a potent means of exploring the reworking ("provincializing") of European thought at and for the margins of empire.[6] However, most postcolonial scholarship is written out of British or American universities and emanates from the heart of a recently superseded empire or of a recently ascendant one that hesitates to acknowledge its own imperial background. American postcolonial scholarship is not preoccupied with America.[7] In the background of such scholarship are European theorists, particularly Foucault, Derrida, and Gramsci; in the foreground, European colonial thought and culture. In these circumstances, as many have pointed out, it tends to be Eurocentric – or as the Australian anthropologist Patrick Wolfe puts it, occidocentric.[8] So positioned, it is well placed to comment on the imperial mind in its large diversity, and even – especially in the hands of scholars like Homi Bhabha and Dipesh Chakrabarty who grew up in former colonies – on the ways in which European thought has been inflected and hybridized by its colonial encounters, but not on the diverse, on-the-ground workings of colonialism in colonized spaces around the world. A central claim of the distinguished Indian subaltern historian Ranajit Guha is that if British historical writing on the subcontinent reveals something of Britain and the Raj, it reveals nothing of India.[9] Somewhat similar criticisms have been made of much of the postcolonial literature: that it (or parts of it) anticipates a radically restructured European historiography, that it allows for nothing outside the (European) discourse of colonialism, that it is yet another exercise in metatheory and in European universalism.[10] As the literary theorist Benita Parry puts it, the postcolonial emphasis on language and texts tends to offer "the World according to the Word"[11] – and the word tends to be European. But unless it can be shown that colonialism is entirely constituted by European colonial culture (a proposition for which it is hard to imagine any convincing evidence unless the concept of culture is understood so broadly that it loses any analytical value), then studies of colonial discourse, written from the centre, must be a very partial window on the workings of colonialism.

The discipline of geography has responded to postcolonial thought in a variety of ways.[12] Among others, studies of colonialism itself have come into vogue, most of them written in Britain, a few from the edges of empire. I am struck by how much the character of these studies has been influenced by the locations of their authors. Consider, for example, two recent books by historical geographers: Felix Driver's *Geography Militant: Cultures of Exploration and Empire*[13] and Frank Tough's *"As Their Natural Resources Fail": Native Peoples and the Economic History of Northern Manitoba, 1870–1930*.[14] From opposite perspectives, they treat a fairly similar period of British colonialism. Driver analyzes the culture of exploration, particularly the sites and nature of its production and consumption – as at the Royal Geographical Society. His is a study of the ways in which the British imperial mind, both popular and academic, processed explorers' information. Tough's work is embedded in the materiality of a declining fur trade in the northern Manitoba bush. It deals with forts and trade routes; with economies and survival strategies as a two-hundred-year-old system of commercial capital vacated the region; and with Indigenous livelihoods found in a precarious balance between what remained of a hunting, fishing, and gathering economy and intermittent employment in uncertain industrial resource economies. Each is an authentic study, yet they have little to say to each other, and this is basically, I think, because one is written from London, the heart of an empire, and the other from the Canadian Shield, one of its many colonial margins. At least, as Derek Gregory has put it, "what seemed plausible in the lecture hall of the Royal Geographical Society in London ... might well become a half truth on the ground."[15] The distinction, perhaps, is between studies of imperialism and of colonialism: imperialism ideologically driven from the centre and susceptible to conceptual analysis, colonialism a set of activities on the periphery that are revealed as practice.[16] Only a few geographers have tried to bring both the imperial mind and the particularities of local colonial circumstances into focus.[17]

But if the aim is to understand colonialism rather than the workings of the imperial mind, then it would seem essential to investigate the sites where colonialism was actually practised. Its effects were displayed there. The strategies and tactics on which it relied were actualized there. There, in the detail of colonial dispossessions and repossessions, the relative weight of different agents of colonial power may begin to be assessed. If colonialism is the object of investigation, then Tough's sparse Canadian Shield is promising terrain. It was not detached from London, of course, and may have been profoundly influenced by elements of imperial thought and culture, but the extent of this influence cannot be ascertained in London. Rather, I think, one needs to study the colonial site itself, assess the displacements that took place there, and seek to account for them. To do so is to position studies of colonialism in the actuality and materiality of colonial experience. As that experience comes into focus, its principal causes are to be assessed, among which may well be something like the culture of imperialism. To proceed the other way around is to impose a form of intellectual imperialism on the study of colonialism, a tendency to which the postcolonial literature inclines.

The experienced materiality of colonialism is grounded, as many have noted, in dispossessions and repossessions of land. Even Edward Said (for all his emphasis on literary texts) described the essence of colonialism this way: "Underlying social space are territories, land, geographical domains, the actual geographical underpinnings of the imperial, and also the cultural contest. To think about distant places, to colonize them, to populate or depopulate them: all of this occurs on, about, or because of land. The actual geographical possession of land is what empire in the final analysis is all about."[18] Frantz Fanon held that colonialism created a world "divided into compartments," a "narrow world strewn with prohibitions," a "world without spaciousness." He maintained that a close examination of "this system of compartments" would "reveal the lines of force it implies." Moreover, "this approach to the colonial world, its ordering and its geographical layout will allow us to mark out the lines on which a decolonized society will be reorganized."[19] Along the edge of empire that was early modern British Columbia, colonialism's "geographical layout" was primarily expressed in a reserve (reservation) system that allocated a small portion of the land to Indigenous people and opened the rest for development. Indigenous peoples were in the way, their land was coveted, and settlers took it. The line between the reserves and the rest – between the land set aside for the people who had lived there from time immemorial and land made available in various tenures to immigrants – became the primary line on the map of British Columbia. Eventually, there were approximately 1,500 small reserves, slightly more than a third of 1 percent of the land of the province. Indigenous peoples had been placed in compartments by an aggressive settler society that, like others of its kind, was far more interested in Indigenous land than in the surplus value of Indigenous labour.[20] Figure 16 illustrates the scale of dispossession. At these sites of colonial dispossession, it seems particularly fruitful to ask by what means it came about. The common emphasis in the colonial discourse literature is reversed. By starting not with texts, language, and strategies of representation, but with the dispossession of colonized peoples of their land – with, as it were, Figure 16 – the relative weight of different colonial powers is not prejudged, and the question becomes simply: How was colonial power deployed to achieve this geographical effect? Rather than writing from the imperial centre, rather than investigating colonial subtexts within a particular category of texts, the analysis turns on the primary effect of a particular settler colonialism and on the gamut of colonial powers that facilitated it. So situated, the distinctive roles of different components of the colonial arsenal should begin to come into focus (including maps like Figure 16). The cultural discourse of colonialism should begin to be contextualized, and some basis should be established for the evaluation of salience. Moreover, different theoretical points of attachment should come into focus, and it should be possible to sketch the work that particular bodies of theory accomplish.

This essay is a rather schematic attempt to undertake such an analysis and, on that basis, to offer some preliminary conclusions. In a recent book on the reserve system in British Columbia, I provide more texture for those who wish it.[21] Yet the very starkness of an article that surveys

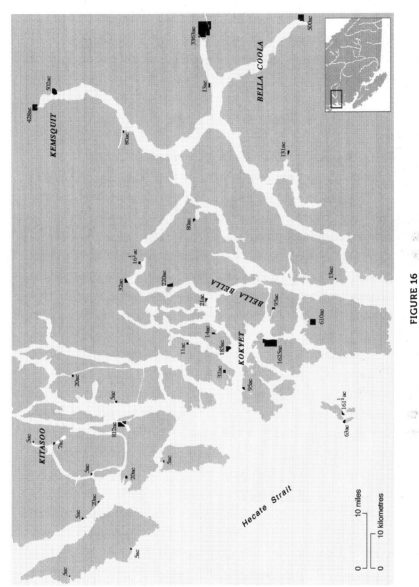

FIGURE 16

Reserves in a portion of the Bella Coola Indian Agency, coastal British Columbia, 1916

an array of colonial powers may serve to emphasize my argument and encourage the discussion of the relationships among different forms of colonial power – and of different ways of theorizing them – out of which, I think, a more balanced geographical contribution to the study of colonialism is likely to emerge. I deal with British Columbia while assuming that my arguments bear, to some fair extent, on other theatres of settler colonialism.

The Power to Dispossess

The problem of reserves in British Columbia arose with the establishment of colonies and settlers some seventy years after people of European background began to frequent its coastal waters. After commercial capital reached the coast in the 1780s and 1790s, and the interior in the first decade of the nineteenth century, trade became the basis of the relationship between Indigenous and non-Indigenous peoples. The relationship was frequently mediated by violence, sexual liaisons of various sorts, and cross-cultural borrowing, but land was not at issue. Except for the few acres within their palisaded forts and, in some cases, a little land beyond for a farm or two, traders did not need it. For their purposes, it was sufficient to insert a handful of outsiders in ships or forts into Indigenous space.

But a territory had become known to the outside world, and its outline had been mapped. In French sociologist Bruno Latour's terms, such "inscriptions" were transported to distant "centers of calculation."[22] Sketchy information about a distant corner of North America was processed, thousands of miles from its source, within complex calculuses of diplomatic ambition, ideology, cultural stereotypes, and raw geopolitical power.[23] Spain relinquished any claim to sovereignty along the north Pacific Coast in 1795. Britain and the United States contended much longer, an intricate diplomacy at times verging on war that was settled only in 1846, when the border between British North America and the United States was extended along the forty-ninth parallel to the Pacific. This agreement, the Oregon Treaty, was a legal understanding between distant governments "respecting the sovereignty and government of the territory on the northwest coast of America." It did not mention Indigenous peoples. In the eyes of the governments involved, the issue of sovereignty was settled. Three years later, in response to the American settlement of Oregon and the news of gold in California, the British government established the proprietary colony of Vancouver Island. Then, in 1858, following a rush of underemployed miners from California to the Fraser River, it established the Crown colony of British Columbia. As Daniel Clayton puts it, "native space was reproduced as an absolute space of British sovereignty,"[24] although initially, in the aftermath of the Treaty of Waitangi and judicial rulings in New Zealand, officials in the Colonial Office were uncertain about the extent to which British sovereignty in these colonies was burdened by Indigenous title.[25]

With the creation of these two colonies, land was framed in a new problematic. Colonies entailed settlers, and settlers required land, which could be got only by dispossessing Indigenous peoples. A relationship based on trade was replaced by one based on land. As their land was taken away, Indigenous peoples had to be put somewhere. A solution with many precedents in other settler colonies was to put them on reserves. Dispossession began in the 1850s and continued through the rest of the century. Physical violence, the imperial state, colonial culture, and self-interest all underlay it.

Violence. The establishment of colonies on Vancouver Island and the mainland changed the nature of violence there. It had long accompanied the fur trades. Coastal trading ships bristled with arms, greed was rampant on both sides, cross-cultural misunderstandings were frequent, and killing was the common result.[26] In the Interior, an axiom of the land-based fur trade was that perceived assaults on the personnel or property of the traders would be met with quick, spectacular displays of violence – sovereign power in the Foucaultian sense, though without a validating regime of rights.[27] Nor was the gold rush peaceable. Miners arrived with the latest weaponry (including six-shooters and spiral-bored rifles) and tactics of Indian fighting worked out in the American southwest. At the first sign of trouble, they organized themselves into companies, elected officers, and advanced in paramilitary formation. But with the creation of settler colonies, a new level of organization and calculation – the British military – was built into the equation of violence.[28] British warships operated along the coast; a detachment of Royal Engineers was sent out to survey land and maintain order. Such power was more often displayed than used – a few quick and very public hangings of suspected murderers after summary trials on the quarterdeck of one of Her Majesty's warships, or a few villages shelled and destroyed – spectacles intended to instill fear. Officials considered such power "a grand persuasive." Some held that it saved lives by preventing settler-Indigenous wars. Frequently, they judged it sufficient to anchor a warship just off an Indigenous village and ostentatiously prepare the guns.

In the Interior, the space beyond the reach of a ship's guns, the military equation was more balanced. In the 1870s, as settlers were moving in and preempting land, many Indigenous leaders talked of war. Settlers feared, perhaps with justification, that an Indigenous uprising could wipe all of them out in a single night. But, as the Chiefs knew, a short-term victory was one thing; keeping at bay settlers and the armies that, sooner or later, would back them up was quite another. The results of wars across the border in which Indigenous warriors (some from British Columbia) had fought federal US troops, was evidence in hand. Those who counselled war did so out of desperation. One Chief put it this way: "A war with the white man will end in our destruction, but death in war is not so bad as death by starvation."[29] Overall, the balance of physical power lay overwhelmingly with the state.

The imperial state. From the vantage point of London, Vancouver Island and British Columbia were two remote and relatively inconsequential colonies. Imperial attention focused, rather, on India and Ireland. After the advent of free trade in 1846, the role of settler colonies in the imperial scheme of things had become increasingly murky. Earl Grey, secretary of state for the colonies when the colony of Vancouver Island was created, held that colonies returned important image value for a great power and also that the honour of the Crown required it to protect British settlers overseas (who had chosen to settle within the British Empire) and also to protect Indigenous peoples from settlers, who, left to their own devices, would probably exterminate them.[30] Yet the coffers of the Lords of the Treasury opened reluctantly for honour, and British settler colonies around the world were expected to support themselves. Moreover, the duty of the Crown to protect Indigenous peoples from settlers conflicted with the Colonial Office's growing willingness to accord responsible government. As liberal humanitarian sentiments about the essential oneness of human kind and the opportunity to create a world of civilized, Christian people faded, responsible government came to dominate protection in Colonial Office thought.[31] In settler colonies, where access to land was the predominant issue, only a hollow form of responsible government would exclude land policy from colonial jurisdiction. In effect, by the late 1840s and 1850s, the Colonial Office had no clear, consistent Indigenous policy. As a result, when the colony of Vancouver Island was created, it was readily inclined to turn over the management of Indigenous peoples to the Hudson's Bay Company (which, it thought, had handled them much better than the Americans) and to rely on the judgment of the fur trader–cum–governor (George Douglas), who managed both colonies until his retirement in 1864. Thereafter, land policies were formulated by local settler politicians. The Colonial Office hardly interfered, and in 1871, when British Columbia became a Canadian province, land policy, now constitutionally a provincial responsibility within the Canadian confederation, remained in the hands of these same politicians. The state created a framework for the ordered development of a settler society but did not, itself, provide the momentum for the development of that society or for the dispossessions and repossessions of land that accompanied it. When power passed to local politicians, they reflected the values and interests of their constituents.

Culture. The assumptions about the colonized other analyzed in the colonial discourse literature were pervasive in early modern British Columbia. Hardly a white person questioned the distinction between civilization and "savagery" or the association of the former with Europeans and the latter with Indigenous peoples. Nor did they question the proposition that civilized people knew how to use land properly and that "savages" did not. From these assumptions it followed that until Europeans arrived, most of the land was waste, or, where Indigenous people were obviously using it, that their uses were inadequate. Nor was there room for alternative understandings of civilized modernity. Rather, thought about Indigenous peoples focused on a simple binary: civilization and savagery with little of consequence between. From this it followed that if Indigenous peoples did not become civilized, and if, in a changing world, it was no longer possible for them to be savage, then they would die out, a common prediction in British Columbia well into the twentieth century. These social constructions were assumed, not debated.

They pervaded thought about Indigenous peoples in the Colonial Office; in political, administrative, legal, and missionary circles in British Columbia; and in the settler mind. An Indian reserve commissioner, charged with laying out reserves, said this to an Indigenous audience on Vancouver Island in 1876:

> Many years ago you were in darkness killing each other and mak-
> ing slaves was your trade. The Land was of no value to you. The trees
> were of no value to you. The Coal was of no value to you. The white
> man came he improved the land you can follow his example – he
> cuts the trees and pays you to help him. He takes the coal out of
> the ground and he pays you to help him – you are improving fast.
> The Government protects you, you are rich – You live in peace
> and have everything you want.[32]

At the time, few if any white settlers would have disagreed. There were arguments about how quickly Indigenous peoples could be assimilated and, therefore, about how much land should be allocated to them. Some settlers, biological racists to the core, considered Indigenous peoples utterly lazy, degenerate, and unredeemable; but a few found much to appreciate or pity in Indigenous lives, were well disposed towards Indigenous people nearby, and now and then supported their pleas for more reserve land. But even kindness – tinged by an educated, romantic appreciation of nature and, therefore, of lives assumed to live close to nature – was situated within the assumptions of the civilization-savage binary. So was salvage anthropology, which in the influential presence of Franz Boas reached the coast late in the nineteenth century, there intent upon recovering the uncontaminated "primitive" condition. Boas had little interest in the Indigenous societies around him (which, he thought, were becoming civilized) except insofar as they supplied informants about earlier precontact times.

These values had not been invented in British Columbia. As a considerable literature has shown,[33] some of them were as old as the European connection with the New World and had surfaced in the first European theorizing about their rights there by the Spanish theologian Francisco de Vitoria in the 1530s, or by the Dutch legal theorist Hugo Grotius a century later. They were powerfully and influentially elaborated by John Locke in his labour theory of property.[34] Locke held that God's gift of land to Adam and his posterity acquired value only as labour was expended on them, and that labour justified individual property rights. Those who did not labour on the land wandered over what Locke called unassisted nature, land that yielded little and lay in common. This, he thought, was the condition of America before European settlers arrived. The land was "a wild common of Nature," the original condition of the world before labour was expended on land and benefits accrued therefrom. Hence his famous dictum: "In the beginning, all the world was America." In all the early settler colonies, ordinary (frequently illiterate) settlers – people who had never heard of Vitoria, Grotius, or Locke – held unsophisticated versions of these views.

By the mid-nineteenth century, these old and pervasive ideas were powerfully reinforced by an increasingly strident racism and the achievements of industrial production. These years were the high-water marks of "scientific" racism. The ideas of phrenologists, craniometricians, and polygenesists were in the air, and after Darwin's *The Origin of Species* (published in 1859), it could be argued that, even if humans shared a common origin, there had been ample time for evolution to take different courses and produce different peoples. The very achievements of industrial society were the measure, it seemed, of an evolutionary advantage. The lurid tales of the massacres of English women and children at Morant Bay in Jamaica or at Lucknow and Cawnpore during the Indian Mutiny confirmed in many minds the absurdity of treating Indigenous peoples as the equal of whites. Such judgments reached British Columbia. Even more important, I think, as the historian Michael Adas has pointed out, was the growing technological gulf between Europe and the rest of the world and the tangible measure it provided of the disjunction between civilization and savagery.[35] European weaponry and military discipline had made conquest relatively easy.[36] Contrasts between Europeans and others seemed obvious: machine power versus animal or human power, progress versus stagnation, science versus superstition. The whole material paraphernalia of European modernity was a tangible yardstick of superiority, and the idea of progress, conceived in these material terms, was in the air as never before. Moreover, as the historian Mark Francis has shown, if civilization and progress came to be equated with technology and material wealth, then a measurable standard had been invented that Indigenous peoples could not attain.[37] They could be mannered, but they could not match European technologies or material wealth. Nor did they have the Europeans' growing ability to dominate nature, another measure of progress. People who marked the land lightly and lived within the rhythms of nature were obviously unprogressive and backward. If civilization were measured in these terms, then Indigenous societies must be savage. For British Columbians of European background, the conclusion was obvious, and the rhetoric surrounding civilization, savagery, and unused land awaiting development was pervasive and uncontested.

Self-interest. Missionaries excepted, immigrants had not come to British Columbia to civilize Indigenous peoples. They had been attracted by the prospect of unused land. Indeed, by any standard with which they were familiar, such was land in British Columbia. In 1881, the first date for which there is a general census, fifty thousand people were scattered across an area larger than Britain and France combined.[38] After the epidemics (smallpox, measles, influenza) and before substantial immigration, the population of this recently defined political space was lower than it had been for perhaps a thousand years. Indigenous numbers had declined in the previous century, perhaps by as much as 90 percent, and some parts of British Columbia were almost completely depopulated. Moreover, the time-space compressions of the mid-nineteenth century had repositioned this distant corner of North America in the world system. In 1830, the travel time from London to the Northwest Coast, whether by way of Hudson Bay or the Horn, was six to seven months. By 1890, it was three weeks. Telegraph messages took three days. Usable land had been recently opened up to the outside world, facilitating the opportunity to which the momentum to develop and settle was the response.

In these circumstances, the commercial economy of the fur trade soon yielded to industrial economies focused on mining, forestry, and fishing. The first industrial mining (for coal) began on Vancouver Island in the early 1850s, the first sizable industrial sawmill opened a few years later, and fish canning began on the Fraser River in 1870. From these beginnings, industrial economies reached into the interstices of British Columbia, establishing work camps close to the resource and processing centres (canneries, sawmills, concentrating mills) at points of intersection of external and local transportation systems. As the years went by, these transportation systems expanded, bringing ever more land (resources) within reach of industrial capital. Each of these developments was a local instance of David Harvey's general point that the pace of time-space compressions after 1850 accelerated capital's "massive, long-term investment in the conquest of space"[39] and its commodifications of nature. The very soil, Marx said in another context, was becoming "part and parcel of capital."[40]

As Marx and, subsequently, others have noted, the spatial energy of capitalism works to deterritorialize people (that is, to detach them from prior bonds between people and place) and to reterritorialize them in relation to the requirements of capital (that is, to land conceived as resources and freed from the constraints of custom and to labour detached from land). For Marx the "wholesale expropriation of the agricultural population from the soil ... created for the town industries the necessary supply of a 'free' and outlawed proletariat."[41] For Gilles Deleuze and Félix Guattari[42] – drawing on insights from psychoanalysis – capitalism may be thought of as a desiring machine, as a sort of territorial writing machine that functions to inscribe "the flows of desire upon the surface or body of the earth."[43] In Henri Lefebvre's terms, it produces space in the image of its own relations of production.[44] For David Harvey it entails the "restless formation and reformation of geographical landscapes" and postpones the effects of its inherent contradictions by the conquest of space – capitalism's "spatial fix."[45] In detail, positions differ; in general, it can hardly be doubted that in British Columbia industrial capitalism introduced new relationships between people and with land and that at the interface of the Indigenous and the non-Indigenous, these relationships created total misunderstandings and powerful new axes of power that quickly detached Indigenous peoples from former lands. When a Tlingit Chief was asked by a reserve commissioner about the work he did, he replied, "I don't know how to work at anything. My father, grandfather, and uncle just taught me how to live, and I have always done what they told me – we learned this from our fathers and grandfathers and our uncles how to do the things among ourselves and we teach our children in the same way."[46] Two different worlds were facing each other, and one of them was fashioning very deliberate plans for the reallocation of land and the reordering of social relations.

In 1875 the premier of British Columbia argued that the way to civilize Indigenous peoples was to bring them into the industrial workplace, there to learn the habits of thrift, time discipline, and materialism. Schools were secondary. The workplace was held to be the crucible of cultural change and, as such, the locus of what the premier depicted as a politics of altruism intended to bring Indigenous peoples up to the point where they could enter society as full, participating citizens. To draw them into the workplace, they had to be separated from land. Hence, in the premier's scheme of things, the small reserve, a space that could not yield a livelihood and would eject Indigenous labour towards the industrial workplace and, hence, towards civilization. Marx would have had no illusions about what was going on: Indigenous lives, he would have said, were being detached from their own means of production (from the land and the use value of their own labour on it) and were being transformed into free (unencumbered) wage labourers dependent on the social relations of capital. The social means of production and of subsistence were being converted into capital. Capital was benefitting doubly, acquiring access to land freed by small reserves and to cheap labour detached from land.

The reorientation of land and labour away from older customary uses had happened many times before, not only in earlier settler societies but also in the British Isles and, somewhat later, in continental Europe. There, the centuries-long struggles over enclosure had been waged between many ordinary folk who sought to protect customary-use rights to land and landlords who wanted to replace custom with private property rights and market economies. In the western Highlands, tenants without formal contracts (the great majority) could be evicted "at will." Their former lands came to be managed by a few sheep farmers; their intricate local land uses were replaced by sheep pasture.[47] In Windsor Forest, a practical vernacular economy that had used the forest in innumerable local ways was slowly eaten away as the law increasingly favoured notions of absolute property ownership, backed them up with hangings, and left less and less space for what E.P. Thompson calls "the messy complexities of coincident use-right."[48] Such developments were approximately reproduced in British Columbia, as a regime of exclusive property rights overrode a fisher-hunter-gatherer version of, in historian Jeanette Neeson's phrase, an "economy of multiple occupations."[49] Even the rhetoric of dispossession – about lazy, filthy, improvident people who did not know how to use land properly – often sounded remarkably similar in locations thousands of miles apart.[50] There was this difference: the argument against custom, multiple occupations, and the constraints of lifeworlds on the rights of property and the free play of the market became, in British Columbia, not an argument between different economies and classes (as it had been in Britain) but the more polarized, and characteristically racialized, juxtaposition of civilization and savagery that I have alluded to above.

Moreover, in British Columbia, capital was far more attracted to the opportunities of Indigenous land than to the surplus value of Indigenous labour. In the early years, when labour was scarce, it sought Indigenous workers, but in the longer run, with its labour needs supplied otherwise (by Chinese workers contracted through labour brokers, by itinerant white loggers or miners), it was far more interested in unfettered access to resources. A bonanza of new resources awaited capital, and if Indigenous peoples, who had always lived amid these resources, could not be shipped away, they could be – indeed, had to be – detached from them. Their labour was useful for a time, but land in the form of fish, forests, and minerals was the prize, one not to be cluttered with Indigenous use rights. From the perspective of capital, therefore, Indigenous peoples had to be dispossessed of their land. Otherwise, nature could hardly be developed. An industrial primary resource economy could hardly function.

In settler colonies, as Marx knew, the availability of agricultural land could turn wage labourers back into independent producers who worked for themselves instead of for capital (they vanished, Marx said, "from the labour market but not into the workhouse").[51] As such, they were unavailable to capital and resisted its incursions, the source, Marx thought, of the prosperity and vitality of colonial societies. In British Columbia, where agricultural land was severely limited, many settlers were closely implicated with capital, although the objectives of the two were different and frequently antagonistic. Without the ready alternative of pioneer farming, many of them were wage labourers dependent on employment in the industrial labour market, yet often contending with capital in bitter strikes. Some of them sought to become capitalists. In M.A. Grainger's *Woodsmen of the West,* a short, vivid novel set in early modern British Columbia, the central character, Carter, wrestles with this opportunity. Carter had grown up on a rock farm in Nova Scotia, worked at various jobs across the continent, and fetched up in British Columbia at a time when, for a nominal fee, the government leased standing timber to small operators. He acquired a lease in a remote fjord and there, with a few men under towering glaciers at the edge of the world economy, attacked the forest. His chances were slight, but the land was his opportunity, his labour his means, and he threw himself at the forest with the intensity of Captain Ahab in pursuit of the white whale. There were many Carters.

But other immigrants did become something like Marx's independent producers. They had found a little land on the basis of which they hoped to get by, avoid the work relations of industrial capitalism, and leave their progeny more than they had known themselves. Their stories are poignant. A Czech peasant family, forced from home for want of land, found its way to one of the coal towns of southeastern British Columbia and then, having accumulated a little cash from mining, homesteaded in the province's arid interior. The homestead would consume a family's work while yielding a living of sorts from intermittent sales from a dry wheat farm and a large measure of domestic self-sufficiency – a farm just sustaining a family, providing a toehold in a new society, and a site of adaptation to it. Or, a young woman from a brick, working-class street in Derby, England, coming to British Columbia during the depression years before the First World War, finding work up the coast in a railway hotel in Prince Rupert, quitting with five dollars to her name after a manager's amorous advances, travelling east as far as five dollars would take her on the second train out of Prince Rupert, working in a small frontier hotel, and eventually marrying a French Canadian farmer. There, in a northern British Columbian valley, in a context unlike any she could have imagined as a girl, she would raise a family and become a stalwart of a diverse local society in which no one was particularly well off. Such stories are at the heart of settler colonialism.[52]

The lives reflected in these stories, like the productions of capital, were sustained by land. Older regimes of custom had been broken, in most cases by enclosures or other displacements in the homeland several generations before emigration. Many settlers became property owners, holders of land in fee simple, beneficiaries of a landed opportunity that, previously, had been unobtainable. But use values had not given way entirely to exchange values, nor was labour entirely detached from land. Indeed, for all the work associated with it, the pioneer farm offered a temporary haven from capital. The family would be relatively autonomous (it would exploit itself). There would be no outside boss. Cultural assumptions about land as a source of security and family-centred independence, assumptions rooted in centuries of lives lived elsewhere, seemed to have found a place of fulfillment. Often this was an illusion – the valleys of British Columbia are strewn with failed pioneer farms – but even illusions drew immigrants and occupied them with the land.

In short, and in a great variety of ways, British Columbia offered modest opportunities to ordinary people of limited means, opportunities that depended, directly or indirectly, on access to land. The wage labourer in the resource camp, as much as the pioneer farmer, depended on such access, as, indirectly, did the shopkeeper who relied on their custom. In this respect, the interests of capital and settlers converged. For both, land was the opportunity at hand, an opportunity that gave settler colonialism its energy. Measured in relation to this opportunity, Indigenous peoples were superfluous. Worse, they were in the way and, by one means or another, had to be removed. Patrick Wolfe is entirely correct in saying that "settler societies were (are) premised on the elimination of native societies," which, by occupying land of their ancestors, had got in the way.[53] If, here and there, their labour was useful for a time, capital and settlers usually acquired labour by other means and, in so doing, facilitated the uninhibited construction of Indigenous peoples as redundant and expendable. In 1840, in Oxford, Herman Merivale, then a professor of political economy and later a permanent undersecretary at the Colonial Office, had concluded as much. He thought that the interests of settlers and Indigenous peoples were fundamentally opposed and that, if left to their own devices, settlers would launch wars of extermination. He knew what had been going on in some colonies – "wretched details of ferocity and treachery" – and considered that what he called the amalgamation (essentially, assimilation through acculturation and miscegenation) of Indigenous peoples into settler society to be the only possible solution.[54] Merivale's motives were partly altruistic, yet assimilation as colonial practice was another means of eliminating "native" as a social category, as well as any land rights attached to it – as, everywhere, settler colonialism would tend to do.

These different elements of what might be termed the foundational complex of settler colonial power were mutually reinforcing. When, in 1859, a first large sawmill was contemplated on the west coast of Vancouver Island, its manager purchased the land from the Crown and then, arriving at the intended mill site, dispersed its Indigenous inhabitants at the point of a cannon.[55] He then worried somewhat about the proprieties of his actions and talked with the Chief, trying to convince him that, through contact with whites, his people would be civilized and improved. The Chief would have none of it but could stop neither the loggers nor the mill. The manager and his men had debated the issue of rights, concluding (in an approximation of Locke) that the Chief and his people did not occupy the land in any civilized sense; that it lay in waste for want of labour; and that if labour were not brought to such land, then the worldwide progress of colonialism, which was "changing the whole surface of the earth," would come to a halt. Moreover, and whatever the rights or wrongs, they assumed, with unabashed self-interest, that colonists would keep what they had got: "This, without discussion, we on the west coast of Vancouver Island were all prepared to do."[56] Capital was establishing itself at the edge of a forest within reach of the world economy and, in so doing, was employing state-sanctioned property rights, physical power, and cultural discourse in the service of interest.

A discourse that treated colonial land as waste awaiting development and its inhabitants as backward and lazy was exceedingly service-
able. It allowed the improvement of a people's habits *and* land uses to
become a cultural imperative, part of the civilizing mission, and a
manifestation of progress. It validated the dispossessions and repossessions intrinsic to settler colonialism – as it had the consolidation of
market economies in western Europe – while adding a veneer of altruism. But, apart from missionaries who came to win souls for God and
civilize Indigenous peoples in the process, it did not provide the momentum for settler colonialism, which came, rather, from the interests
of capital and settlers in what both perceived to be the profits/livelihoods
associated with new, land-based opportunities. Although, as the example of the sawmill on Vancouver Island suggests, these different
colonial powers were interrelated in many ways, they tended to comprise
different parts of the system of power that introduced colonialism to
British Columbia. Of this system, the following points can be made.
Physical violence and the framework of the colonial state appear as
necessary preconditions for successful settler colonialism. The impetus
for such colonialism appears to be associated primarily with the interest
of capital and settlers in land. To the extent required, the legitimation
of the dispossessions and repossessions of land associated with settler
colonialism in British Columbia came from a cultural discourse that
emphasized the gulf between civilization and savagery and the different
land uses associated with each.

The Management of Dispossession

As the years went by and settler society consolidated its power, physical
power moved into the background (while remaining crucial), and the
disciplinary strategies associated with the management of people, nature, and space came to the fore. British Columbia, a Canadian province
after 1871, was similar to other jurisdictions in this regard, although,
given its size and the central problematic of land in a new settler society,
the disciplinary focus was inflected towards the politics of land and
space. The reserve system itself was a spatial strategy of dispossession
and of population management.

The disciplinary strategies associated with modern states and economies have tended to simplify complex realities within narrow fields of legibility.[57] At the scale of the nation-state or the corporation, nature and space could not be managed otherwise, and state and capital, usually in close alignment, relied (whether consciously or not) on an array of disciplinary technologies to bring localities into focus by eliminating most of their detail. Of these many technologies – subsumed in Foucaultian terms within the concept of governmentality – those that bore particularly on the organization of land and reserves in British Columbia were probably maps, numbers, the common law, and the new geographies of settler colonialism.[58] I comment on each.

Maps. British Columbia could not have been reorganized into colonial space without something like the map. Maps enabled newcomers to locate themselves in this space and find their way around. More than this, maps conceptualized unfamiliar space in Eurocentric terms, situating it within a culture of vision, measurement, and management. Employing a detached vertical perspective, this cartography rendered space as a plan – as a surface. As such, Kenneth Brealey points out, maps comprised a system of territorial surveillance that "reached across vast distances, flattening space, compartmentalizing it, renaming it, and assimilating these representations into the geometry of the Cartesian grid."[59] By such means, newcomers found their bearings. Their early maps were often little more than outlines of coasts and rivers that erased almost all the contents of the space they depicted. It was not so much that outsiders using these maps then considered this space to be a *tabula rasa,* as a good deal of the literature on cartography and colonialism suggests, for settlers were drawn to resources not indicated on these maps, and colonial officials knew that Indigenous peoples inhabited many of the maps' empty spaces. In 1858, E.B. Lytton, secretary of state for the colonies, instructed the commander of the detachment of Royal Engineers he was sending to British Columbia as to his dealings with the "savage tribes" that "surrounded" the few white settlers – this after decades of cartography that, with few exceptions, had erased Indigenous peoples. Rather, this cartography introduced a geographical imaginary that ignored Indigenous ways of knowing and recording space, ways that settlers could not imagine and did not need as soon as their maps reoriented them after their own fashion. On the west coast of Vancouver Island, as Bruce Braun has shown, the space from which Indigenous knowledge had been subtracted would eventually be reconfigured within scientific classifications, industrial management strategies, and visions of wilderness.[60]

More explicitly, maps were tools in the process of land allocation. Property required a location, and maps were the means of establishing it. In the early years, when the demand for land exceeded the capacity to survey it and land could be acquired by preemption, these maps could be exceedingly crude. A few lines scratched on a page (Figure 17) sufficed to establish a preemption and, in the eyes of the law, to remove a piece of land from Indigenous control.

Eventually, preemptions would be surveyed, the basis of a more precise cartography and, sometimes, of scuffles between Indigenous peoples and survey parties. When villagers on the north coast resisted surveyors, the government deployed a gunboat, and surveying resumed in a theatre of power focused not, as in Foucault's famous analysis, on the sovereign's right to kill but on the government's right to lay out lines on the land. The surveyor reported, "I shall begin my survey at once, under the observation of Capt. Nicholls of the Cormorant ... in front of the village Church, immediately beside the Provincial Lock-up, and in full view of the entire village. Nothing shall be hidden, and there shall be no opportunity for saying the beginning of the Survey was 'surreptitious.'"[61] Guns, surveys, maps; commissions appointed to make final allocations of reserves depended on maps at every turn. They made rough cadastral maps, and they asked Chiefs to point out on maps the lands they sought. They pored over maps before making their decisions. Maps enabled them to locate these decisions in an abstract, geometrical space containing only what their own data collections and predilections inclined them to place there. They provided a measurable, transportable, and archivable record on which the commissioners were completely dependent. The maps that followed from their decisions ended up, eventually, in government files, often several outlines of small reserves mounted on a single sheet, rather like insects displayed on pins (see Figure 15, p. 194). A reserve had a name, an acreage, a location. It could be looked up. It was situated in a bureaucracy.

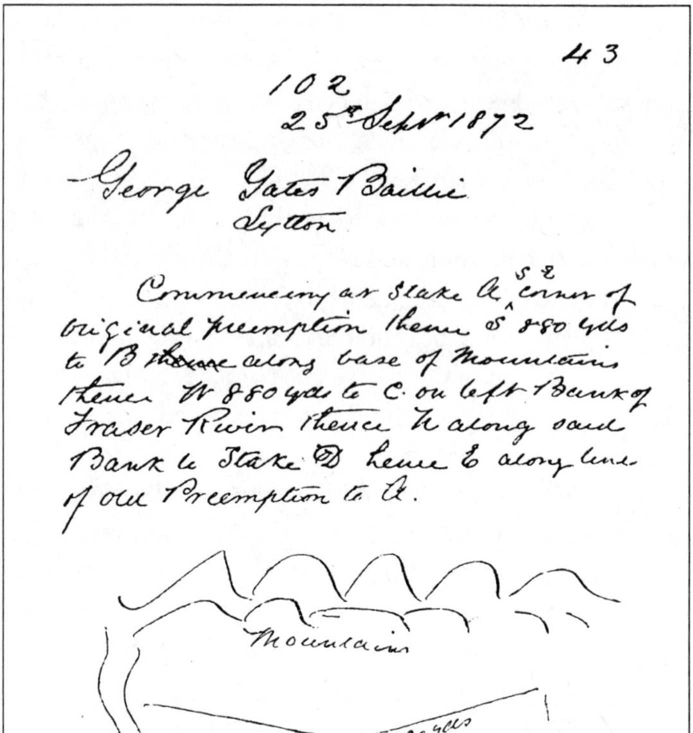

FIGURE 17
Property description and map accompanying
a preemption application, 1872

Numbers. The commissioners were equally dependent on numbers. Few of them knew much of British Columbia, and none was very familiar with Indigenous ways. They had been assigned an almost impossible task: to allocate reserves quickly over a huge territory. As they met and talked with Indigenous peoples about land, they began to encounter the deep local lore in which Indigenous lives were situated. Given the opportunity, the Chiefs could talk for days about the complexities of local land use – about how, as one Chief said, the landscape reflected "our work in past times" – in so doing, providing far more information than the commissioners had time for or wanted. Invariably, they rejected almost all such local knowledge. They could not process it. On the other hand, the commissioners avidly collected numbers. They wanted to know how many cultivable acres a band possessed and how many were actually being cultivated, how many school-age children were in the band and how many attended residential schools. This was firm quantitative information. The four-volume report of the last major reserve commission turned all such information into tables.[62] The commissioners had worked out, they said, a scheme for the "scientific analysis and tabulation of all information gleaned by the commission." They had replaced local knowledge with numbers. Earlier, reserve commissioners had tried to take censuses.

Numbers were powerful. They provided apparently objective information that could be analyzed by established procedures to reach verifiable conclusions. They enabled the commissioners to distinguish between "good Indians" (those who were cultivating their land and sending their children to school) and bad. The former might get a little more land. And they were transportable in a way that local knowledge was not. Like the simple cadastral maps the commissioners produced, they could be moved to a "centre of calculation," however distant. There, maps and numbers could be analyzed together and decisions made about the allocation of land. In this respect, they were both, in historian of science Theodore Porter's apt phrase, "technologies of distance,"[63] means of managing land and people from afar. Indigenous peoples soon understood this and refused census takers and the quantitative inquiries of reserve commissioners more frequently than they tried to disrupt surveyors. In such cases, the commissioners would seek the information from an Indian agent, or some other apparently knowledgeable settler. In one way or another, numbers were usually obtained. Like maps, they were at once egregious simplifications and effective colonial tools. They enabled a bureaucracy, essentially without local knowledge, to make decisions about localities.

The law. English common law was also an abstract, generalized means of normalizing and managing people and nature within the purview of the state and at the expense of local custom. But it had far more memory than maps or numbers and more ability to transpose complex ideas, values, and social relationships from one location to another. The product of accumulated social and legal understandings, it tended to hold on to time and, when shifted in space, to transfer these understandings with it. It was, therefore, historically rooted and geographically expansive. It had the capacity to overwhelm other ways of being in the world – as Don Mitchell has put it in another context, the capacity to annihilate space by law.[64] When English common law, a work of English centuries, was relocated overseas, a framework for the transplantation of English society had been introduced. Its influence was pervasive. The workings of capital in colonial settings depended on such law – as Indigenous fishers working for the salmon canneries at the mouth of the Fraser River found, for example, when charged with breaches of the terms of master and servant law.[65] Similarly, settlers' property rights depended on the law, first the right to exclude, then to alter, sell, will, and so on. Even more than this, the law expressed and constituted what some legal theorists call a legal consciousness, a matrix of ideas, ideologies, and values that tended to be assumed rather than debated.[66] Both law and popular mind, for example, constructed the rights of private property. So imbricated was law and the culture of legality in colonialism that some theorists consider them – perhaps too possessively – constitutive of colonialism itself.[67] Wide-ranging as the law was, and complicit as were some of its assumptions with popular values, it was also wrapped in a specialized professional language and in practices that were obscure to most people and set its detailed interpretation beyond their reach – what Pierre Bourdieu calls a juridical field.[68]

By the time that English common law was introduced to British Columbia, the triumph of a centralized, standardized law applicable to all of England was virtually complete. Nicholas Blomley has explored Sir Edward Coke's hugely influential efforts early in the seventeenth century to replace the variegated, decentred map of English law with an ordered, rational, national system based on the assumption of a unitary legal knowledge interpreted by experts.[69] The process of standardization had begun much earlier, however, as the mosaic of local legal practices of feudal England gradually gave way, at different times in different sectors of the law, to the common law.[70] At the top, the authority of the King was consolidated and then challenged and increasingly circumscribed by the landed elite. At the bottom, rights based on local custom, possession, and reciprocal feudal obligations slowly gave way to the normalized and relatively placeless understandings embedded in contracts and private property rights. The law that reached British Columbia was not a set of timeless legal truths but the product, rather, of these long, bitterly contested transformations.

In British Columbia (probably in all other settler colonies overseas) property law was the most immediately powerful component of the legal ideas, social values, and cultural understandings embodied in English common law. When a settler preempted land and met the terms of preemption, he (almost invariably "he") acquired title to the land in fee simple, an estate that had appeared in the thirteenth century, embodied a perpetual and indestructible right to the land potentially forever, and gradually became normative as the claims of overlords and of custom diminished. Well before the nineteenth century, free and common socage was the predominant English tenure and fee simple the predominant estate, both widely supported by legal theory and popular opinion. William Blackstone's *Commentaries on the Laws of England in Four Books,* published in 1765 and frequently reprinted, remained a guide through the nineteenth century. Blackstone held that society's principal aim was "to protect individuals in those absolute rights, which were vested in them by the immutable laws of nature." For Blackstone, property was such a right; it was "inherent in every Englishman," to the point that individuals gave up some of their liberty to enjoy the legal protection of property. "So great moreover is the regard of the law for private property, that it will not authorize the least violation of it; no, not even for the good of the whole community ... The public good is in nothing more essentially interested, than in the protection of every individual's private rights."[71] A long-contested and fairly recently popularized legal understanding had become an immutable law of nature. With Blackstone and his like in the background, no government or Indian reserve commissioner in British Columbia contested the rights of private property. When settlers complained that Indigenous people were trespassing on their property or had been given too much land, they assumed an Englishman's property rights, much as Blackstone had spelled them out. In the courts, as in the settler mind, the rights of property embedded in the common law tangibly legitimated the dispossessions and repossessions of land for which assumptions about civilization, savagery, and the progressive use of land had provided a more abstract justification.

From an Indigenous perspective, the lands they had lost were more than simply occupied by others. They had become defined by bundles of rights and values that were foreign to their ways and were defended by courts, the procedures of which were often impenetrable. Somewhat as in a much earlier England, Indigenous life in British Columbia was lived within networks of local customs, languages, and understandings. Indigenous law was embedded in locality and produced at many local sites, at none of which people could have begun to understand Blackstone. In a sense, a transition worked out over the centuries in England, had been compressed into the moment when native lands were preempted (or purchased, or leased from the Crown) and relocated in an alien legal regime. Indigenous peoples in British Columbia had experienced a particularly sudden and extreme form of a transition that the philosopher Jürgen Habermas describes as the system's penetration of the lifeworld and associates with emerging modernity.[72] They were suddenly exposed to, and increasingly regulated by, the common law of England and the Canadian Indian Act, not only as they expressed themselves formally in law but also as they were represented in the values of officials and settlers. Moreover, when they found themselves in court, they struggled, usually in translation, with another language and, in somewhat attenuated colonial form, with Bourdieu's juridical field of recondite legal procedures and customs, which many an ordinary English person, much less an Nlaka'pamux whom Coyote had placed on Fraser River, would not begin to understand.[73] Behind the law meted out in such incomprehensible circumstances were fines, jails, or gallows – ultimately, British military might.

The geography of resettlement. These disciplinary technologies, coupled with the more foundational colonial powers discussed above, enabled the resettlement of British Columbia. A settler society emerged and, with it, a new human geography (Figure 18). This new human geography – the survey lines, the property boundaries, the roads and railways, the farms, the industrial camps, the towns – became, from an Indigenous point of view, the most pervasive disciplinary technology of all. Superimposed on their former lands, it defined where they could and could not go. Made by newcomers, it was reinforced by property rights held by landowners (or renters or leasers) wary of trespassers, people who knew their rights and where, in their terms, "Indians" belonged. Theirs was a decentred gaze that emanated from the geography of resettlement itself. From their various vantage points, landowners watched and excluded. The courts, indeed, all the colonial powers that I have described, backed them up. Indigenous peoples could no longer go where they had. Their movements were blocked or channelled, and the resources on which they had always lived were increasingly out of reach. Severe malnutrition was common, at times to the point of starvation. Others, and the geographies of others, dominated the management of space, the essence, as Foucault knew, of disciplinary strategies.[74] To the extent that they made space for themselves (at quite different rates in different parts of the province), these others created an increasingly carceral environment for Indigenous peoples, of which the reserves were only the most obvious manifestation.

Concluding Observations

Such were probably the principal elements of the complex of power that settled around the Indigenous lands of British Columbia in the last half of the nineteenth century. Comprehensive and intricate, it quickly dispossessed one set of people and established another. But to emphasize

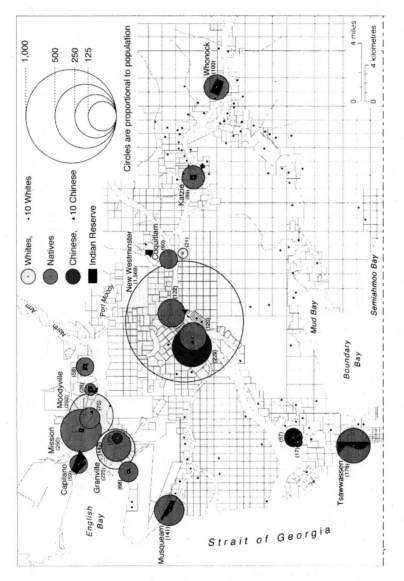

FIGURE 18

Land surveys and population, Lower Mainland, 1881

the complexity of colonial power, as the postcolonial literature tends to do, is not in itself particularly helpful. The challenge, rather, is to look inside the complex to establish how particular powers operated and to what particular effect. Different components of the colonial arsenal were not unrelated to each other, but nor were they blended in an amorphous imperial soup. They can be positioned somewhat and a measure of salience established. The geography of dispossession (Figure 18) is explained more precisely when the powers that effected it are disaggregated.

In this light, the following claims can be made, and scrutinized in other theatres of settler colonialism.

The momentum to dispossess derived primarily from the interest of capital in profit and of settlers in getting somewhat ahead in the world, both interests, in a new colony where land was the principal resource, dependent on the acquisition of land. Only the missionaries stood apart from this. They were drawn by a religious and cultural agenda and were not interested in land. Often, they supported Indigenous land claims, in so doing frequently alienating themselves from settlers, capital, and government. The initial ability to dispossess rested primarily on physical power and the supporting infrastructure of the state. Once the power of violence had been demonstrated, the threat of it was often sufficient. The colonial state sought and, backed by the British military, was often able to impose a monopoly on violence. It introduced the governmental framework of the modern state, within which colonization proceeded.

The legitimation of and moral justification for dispossession lay in a cultural discourse that located civilization and savagery and extolled the advantages for all concerned of replacing the latter with the former. The achievement of the colonial discourse literature has been to bring this discourse into focus, while its failing has been a tendency to neglect other forms of colonial power and, therefore, to decontextualize its own cultural arguments. The management of the dispossession of the colonized of their land rested with a set of disciplinary technologies of which maps, numbers, and law were perhaps the most important. All these disciplinary technologies were necessary, but law provided a far more comprehensive framework than did the others for recalibrating land and life on the colonizers' terms and without reference to Indigenous antecedents. All these powers facilitated the emergence of a new immigrant human geography, which became Indigenous peoples' most pervasive confinement. It follows that no one body of theory offers a sufficient interpretation of colonial power. Fanon was right about physical violence. It did underlie the whole colonial enterprise. In so doing, it created the opportunity for other forms of colonial power to come into play. Marx was right about the capacity of capital to detach people from land and right, too, about the landed opportunity that settler colonies offered ordinary people. Combine capital's interest in uncluttered access to land and settlers' interest in land as livelihood, and the principal momentum of settler colonialism comes into focus. The colonial discourse literature has impressively clarified the implicit and explicit assumptions that, in the minds of imperialists and colonists, validated the colonial enterprise. Foucault's analysis of the decentred disciplinary technologies associated with modern life is enormously suggestive in colonial settings. It leads to the analysis of the many technologies of power (four of which I have discussed here) that were associated less with the introduction of colonialism than with its ongoing operation.

There is one more point to make. Although Indigenous peoples were not able to contain this juggernaut of powers and stop the dispossession and repossession of their land, they did what they could to slow it down or to mitigate its effects. At times, as pointed out above, they considered war while knowing that, in the long run, they could not win. Over and over again, they told officials that they and their progeny would not be able to live on the patches of land reserved for them and pleaded, often eloquently, for more land. One Chief said that he would try kindness (which availed him nothing). Like oppressed people everywhere, they engaged in a virtually constant micropolitics of resistance: moving fences, not cooperating with census enumerators, sometimes disrupting survey parties. There was a stream of letters and petitions, often written with missionary assistance, to officials in Victoria, Ottawa, and London and meetings with cabinet ministers, prime ministers, and even, on one occasion, the King. Early in the twentieth century, they began to create intertribal Indigenous rights organizations[75] and, with the help of sympathetic non-Indigenous lawyers, to use the colonizers' law as a site of resistance. A legal case, elaborated in 1908 in a Cowichan petition intended for the judicial committee of the Privy Council in London and in a Nisga'a petition to the same body a few years later, argued that Indigenous peoples had never relinquished their title to the land, which therefore was still legally theirs.[76] By this time, some Indigenous leaders had emerged who spoke English fluently, understood a good deal about the complex of colonial power, and sought ways of bending it to their advantage. Indigenous peoples were not passive victims.

Nor was their resistance without effect. Reserve commissioners listened to Indigenous requests, and, if the land was not already taken by settlers, would allocate small reserves at some of the sites requested. A superintendent general of Indian affairs in Ottawa reestablished a reserve commission because a Chief urged him to do so.[77] A few politicians (particularly in Ottawa) and a small but growing number of settlers became convinced that Indigenous peoples had been poorly used and that, in justice, they deserved some redress. However, the legal challenge anticipated by the Cowichan and Nisga'a petitions had scared federal and provincial officials, and in 1927 an amendment to the Indian Act barred Indigenous peoples from raising funds for land claims, effectively isolating them from legal counsel and undermining their principal intertribal organization, the Allied Tribes. It disbanded in 1928. In the longer run, the colonizers' law has proved a durable site of Indigenous resistance, as it has in other colonized jurisdictions.[78] A version of the case laid out in the Cowichan and Nisga'a petitions reached the courts in the 1970s (*Calder*) and again in the 1990s (*Delgamuukw*), and, eventually, the Supreme Court of Canada established that Indigenous title had not been extinguished and laid out the terms by which it may be identified. Indigenous title is still before the courts.

But Indigenous agency in British Columbia has been exercised within the profound asymmetries of settler colonialism, a colonialism with relentless momentum and a comprehensive package of powers. For all their efforts, it dispossessed Indigenous peoples quickly of almost all their land and established other peoples in their ancestral territories. It is important to identify the powers in the settler colonial arsenal, map their positions, and sort out some of their linkages – which, in a preliminary way, I have tried to do here. The impact of these powers on those on the receiving end of them is another story, one of making do in and around the compartments created by colonialism. That story needs be told at least as much as the one I have sketched. In that telling, it will be important to remember that Indigenous peoples neither succumbed to colonialism's "fatal impact" nor interacted with newcomers on a basis of equivalency but coped as they could when confronted, as they were at virtually every turn, with one or more of the array of powers embedded in settler colonialism. From an Indigenous perspective, something like a desiring machine constructed of many parts had taken away their land.

Postscript:
The Boundaries of Settler Colonialism

I have suggested that settler colonialism is most inclusively studied on the ground, where it took place and where its causes and effects can be most readily discerned (see the previous essay). In these remarks on the relations of Indigenous peoples and settlers in Canada, I start from the same premise – that the relations between Indigenous peoples and others in Canada have always been and today remain inextricably tied to their varied uses of land. These relations turned, and continue to turn, on possession, on geographical patterns of settlement and economy, on values bearing on land. They differed greatly around the settler colonial world, as they did between Canada and the United States.

I begin with two basic maps, then consider the circumstances of settlers and Indigenous peoples at about the time of Confederation, then their changing relations over the ensuing century, and end with some observations about their relations now. The whole piece is a drastic précis, an extended glimpse.

We are all immigrants to this place even if we
were born here: the country is too big for anyone
to inhabit completely, and in the parts unknown
to us we move in fear, exiles and invaders.

– MARGARET ATWOOD, *THE JOURNALS*
OF SUSANNA MOODIE

THE PARTS OF BRITISH NORTH America at Confederation where the population density reached one or more persons per square mile are shown in Figure 19. There was a patch of settlement in the St. Lawrence–Great Lakes corridor and other smaller patches in the Maritimes. Elsewhere, the land appears unpopulated. The twelve thousand people, most of them Métis, living along the Red and Assiniboine Rivers in southern Manitoba and the sprinkling of miners and settlers in British Columbia barely show up at this scale. Figure 20 shows where in the United States, at the same date, the population density reached two or more people per square mile.[1] It shows largely contiguous settlement from the Gulf of Mexico, to the border with British North America, and west well beyond the Mississippi. By this measure, and across half the continental width of the United States, only a few patches of land appear to be uninhabited.

The European settlement of these adjacent political spaces confronted very different landed opportunities, a difference noted in some of the earliest European accounts of these lands.[2] Jacques Cartier, sailing in 1534 along the north shore of the Gulf of St. Lawrence – an edge of the Canadian Shield – could not see "one cartload of earth" and thought he had found the land "God gave to Cain"; a few years before, Giovanni de Verrazano, sailing along a coastal bar off what would become North Carolina, thought he had glimpsed Arcadia, a poetic space of harmonious natural bounty.[3] For the purposes of European settlement, the British North America that grew, ironically, out of Cartier's explorations, was severely bounded: a political border to the south, the Canadian Shield to the north, and, for years, no prospect of western settlement beyond the eastern shores of Lake Huron.

FIGURE 19
Population density, British North America, 1871 |
After Don Measner and Christine Hampton, "The Canadian Population, 1871, 1891,"
in R. Louis Gentilcore, *Historical Atlas of Canada*, vol. 2, *The Land Transformed,*
1800-1891 (Toronto, University of Toronto Press, 1993), plate 29

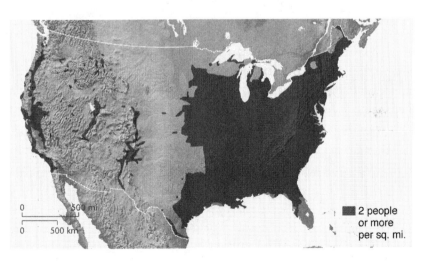

FIGURE 20
Population density, United States, 1870 |
After Charles Paullin, *Atlas of the Historical Geography of the United States*
(Washington, DC: Carnegie Institute and American Geographical Society, 1932), 76

Until the completion of the Canadian Pacific Railway in the 1880s, attempts to extend these boundaries had failed. In Quebec, the most ardent exponent of the colonization of the Canadian Shield (Curé Labelle) considered it land made by God for the Canadian people; in Ontario, the minister of agriculture held that the Huron Tract (the land between the Upper Ottawa Valley and Georgian Bay) could support 8 million settlers. Both were wrong. For those who tried to settle there, the fringe of the Canadian Shield produced failure. Most would soon leave, many of them for the United States. There, the Appalachians had been a surmountable barrier, the vast watershed of the Mississippi became one of the most productive agricultural regions on earth, and the limits of contiguous agricultural settlement, set by aridity, were reached only far to the west. When its Indigenous inhabitants were killed or relocated, as most of them were, a huge and bounteous land awaited American settlement. As Figures 19 and 20 imply, the landed experiences of these two adjacent transcontinental North American polities were essentially opposite.

The Settled Patches

At Confederation, some 3.5 million people lived in the occupied land identified in Figure 19, all of which were successful settler colonial spaces in which settlers and their governments were in control. Most people lived on family farms in established countrysides, but others lived in work camps and yet others in towns, the largest of which were rapidly industrializing. Wherever they lived, almost all of them spoke French or English and, although European social structures had been somewhat reworked overseas, lived within an array of transplanted values, customs, and artefacts. People were aware that they were part of the British Empire, but most of them lived locally – with their neighbours, their particular religious and ethnic communities, and their prejudices. For the great majority, the few Indigenous peoples living on small reserves within these settler colonial spaces were invisible.

The Canadian census of 1871 enumerated just over twenty-three thousand "Indians" in the four provinces (Ontario, Quebec, New Brunswick, and Nova Scotia) that first made up the Dominion of Canada, the great majority of them living within the settler colonial spaces identified in Figure 19. They comprised roughly 0.7 percent of the population of lands that, when Europeans first arrived, had had far more Indigenous inhabitants.[4] In the 1530s, Cartier found several villages of St. Lawrence Iroquoians near what is now Quebec City and a large palisaded village, Hochelaga, on Montreal Island. In Champlain's time (the early seventeenth century), some twenty thousand Wendat (Huron) and twice as many Petun and Neutral (all Iroquoian speakers) lived in what is now southern Ontario. In 1871, the only British North American remnants of these peoples were a few Wendat, descendants of refugees from the Iroquois Wars of the 1640s, who lived in Nouvelle-Lorette, a reserve not far from Quebec City. Anishinaabe (Ojibwe) had moved south into southern Ontario after its depopulation during the Iroquois Wars, but most of the Indigenous peoples enumerated in the St. Lawrence–Great Lakes corridor in 1871 were products of northward migrations provoked by the French-English wars, the expansion of American settlement, or the American Revolution.[5] Most of them were Kanyen'kehà:ka (Mohawk) or other (Haudenosaunee) Iroquoian peoples from what is now upstate New York. The small Indigenous populations in New Brunswick and Nova Scotia (after the census, 1403 in New Brunswick, and 1666 in Nova Scotia) comprised Mi'kmaq and Wolastoquiyik (Maliseet) who had long lived in the region.

The Indigenous peoples who settled along the lower St. Lawrence during the French regime lived in missions overseen by Sulpician or Jesuit priests, the first de facto reserves in Canada. After the Royal Proclamation of 1763, the legal means of land taking was by treaty and purchase, and in a series of treaties in Upper Canada (Ontario) the Anishinaabe ceded (or perhaps in their eyes shared) land they had occupied for more than a century in return for small payments, presents, and reserves. A fishing-hunting people living along rivers and marshes from spring to fall, they may have sought to protect their fisheries while sacrificing upland hunting territories. If so, the strategy failed. Their rivers were dammed, their fisheries encroached upon, and the Anishinaabe – weakened by disease, alcohol, and the loss of traditional leadership – found themselves on small reserves, which, as settlers eyed them, were often reduced or withdrawn altogether.[6] In New

Brunswick and Nova Scotia, the Mi'kmaq and Wolastoquiyik (Maliseet) also lived on reserves, portions of which settlers often claimed and took. On these diminishing reserve spaces, traditional economies based on hunting, fishing, and gathering were impossible and farming inadequate. People lived in wretched conditions. A Mi'kmaq Chief described the situation accurately in terms that would be repeated over and over again almost wherever Indigenous peoples living on small reserves were hemmed in by settlers. "My people," he said, "are poor. No Hunting Grounds – no Beaver – no Otter – no nothing. Indians poor – poor for ever. No store – no Chest – no clothes. All these woods once ours. Our Fathers possessed them all. Now we cannot cut a Tree to warm our Wigwaum in Winter unless the White Man please."[7]

In a widely read book, John Ralston Saul, writer and public intellectual, suggests that Canada is essentially a Métis nation formed out of the long mingling of Indigenous and non-Indigenous peoples and the partnerships forged between them.[8] He holds that only in the late nineteenth century, as Victorian society became increasingly imperial, self-righteous, and racist, would Canada deny its fundamental Métis nature. There is no doubt that military alliances with Indigenous groups in the interior supported the French and, briefly after 1760, the British position along the St. Lawrence, no doubt, especially in the early years, that there were liaisons, some of them enduring, within settler colonies between immigrant men and Indigenous women, but such interactions do not make a Métis society. In the settler colonies assembled in the new Dominion of Canada, numbers and social power rested overwhelmingly with the settlers. As some of the writings in this collection have shown, the societies they created did not precisely reproduce their Old World progenitors, but nor were they Métis societies. Within these settler colonies, Indigenous peoples were tucked away and, when seen, were marginalized and racialized. There could be no partnership when so much had been taken and so little respect accorded the survivors.

The Unsettled Space

Away from the settler colonial spaces identified in Figure 19 – that is, in most of the vast expanse of British North America – the situation was very different. The state had no purchase, there were almost no settlers, and in the Far North there were huge tracts that no white person had ever seen. For years, commercial capital in the form of the fur trade had penetrated large parts of this territory, fixing itself there in trading posts. Christian missionaries, most of them Roman Catholic or Anglican, a few Presbyterian or Methodist, had come – the first west of Lake Superior about 1820, most in the 1850s and 1860s – and had created missions. However, neither trading posts nor missions required many personnel – which, as a generous estimate, numbered not much more than two thousand across half a continent. Although their population densities were exceedingly low, beyond Red River, where most of the population was Métis, Indigenous peoples were, by far, the principal inhabitants of these vast lands. A few of them lived at the trading posts or missions; others, such as the Homeguard Cree, who lived near trading posts on Hudson Bay, had become middlemen in the fur trade; but most were on the land, living in small bands and still heavily dependent on hunting, fishing, and gathering.

Unlike settlers, fur traders did not seek land. Nor, other than to encourage Indigenous peoples to hunt and bring in furs, did they seek to transform Indigenous ways. But the traders were on their own, far from outside assistance, and dealing with people they considered barbarous. All their principal trading posts were well fortified, always locked down at night with watches posted. For the most part, traders felt safe in these outposts of commercial capital in an Indigenous world. Some Indigenous women usually lived in these posts, partners of lonely men, mothers of their children, and conduits of information across cultural boundaries. Men learned something of Indigenous languages, something of Indigenous ways. To some fair extent, a cultural middle ground emerged but always within the discipline and commercial objectives of the fur trade.[9]

Beyond the posts was an Indigenous world through which the goods and personnel of the fur trade moved and which, in the absence of institutional means of social control, the traders sought to manage as best they could. Their characteristic mode of social control was to instill fear – of their physical power, of quick corporal or capital punishment for any offences against their personnel or property, of the possibility that, if provoked, they would close a post. When iron knives, kettles, blankets, and cloth, and many other trade goods had become staples of Indigenous life, when tobacco and alcohol had created addictions, and when guns were required to fend off traditional enemies so armed, the threat to close a post was powerful. Supporting all these tactics was an ongoing theatre of control – expressed in dress, conduct, ceremony, and buildings – that had been worked out over the years and was usually effective. Broadly put, all these ways enabled the system of the fur trade to penetrate local Indigenous lifeworlds and establish itself among them.[10]

The fur trade depended on Indigenous peoples: their skills as hunters; their ability to travel long distances, summer and winter, through difficult terrain; and, because of the wide distribution of fur-bearing animals, their dispersed and mobile settlements. It also put intense pressure on many Indigenous ways, as did introduced infectious diseases. In the early 1780s, an epidemic of smallpox that originated in Mexico City devastated most of the northern continental interior – Samuel Hearne, the chief factor at Fort Churchill on Hudson Bay, estimated that it had killed 90 percent of the Dene (Chipewyan) nearby. Later, epidemics of smallpox, measles, whooping cough, influenza, and other often unidentifiable diseases cycled through Indigenous populations, many of them arriving, undoubtedly, along the expanding axes of the fur trade.[11]

The fur trade, and perhaps the epidemics, turned some Indigenous peoples into specialized traders operating between Indigenous hunters and company personnel in the posts. It shifted Indigenous hunting towards the procurement of marketable commodities. It created dependencies on introduced goods. It integrated subsistence and commercial economies to produce a dispersed fur-trade labour force sustained, in good part, by hunting, fishing, and gathering even as it produced a commercial product for an international market. By differentially introducing firearms, it increased the scale and intensity of Indigenous warfare. War and disease, and ensuing depopulations, shifted the location of many Indigenous peoples, and the boundaries between them. Most tellingly, perhaps, it tended to undermine the ecological basis of Indigenous livelihoods. Long before 1870 in many areas, beaver and marten, the furs most in demand, had become scare, also caribou, deer, and moose. Scarcity had become chronic rather than occasional. In these circumstances, there was less intergroup sharing, less local mobility, more local territorial defensiveness. People relied on small game, such as hare, that were subject to extreme population fluctuations. Some from the southern margins of the Canadian Shield moved into the parkland, thereby gaining access to bison; many others became dependent on the trading posts for food. In sum, the vast northern continental interior was not what it had been.[12] For many, starvation was not far away.

Yet, for all these difficulties, in 1871 Indigenous peoples remained the principal or only occupants of by far the largest part of British North America. Although the fur trade was more than two hundred years old in places, Indigenous peoples still spoke their languages, still practised many pre-fur trade ways, still had no doubt about who they were. They were not numerous: perhaps forty thousand to fifty thousand (including Métis) in the whole continental interior beyond the patches of successful settler colonialism and south of the tundra; perhaps twenty-five thousand to thirty thousand in the Western Cordillera;[13] perhaps a few thousand in the Arctic; not, in total, 100,000 people. But they were there, and apart from some two thousand fur traders, a handful of white settlers at Red River, and the beginnings of immigrant settlement on Vancouver Island and in a few valleys in the Cordillera, nobody else was.

The Subsequent Century

Figure 21 shows where in Canada in 1961 the population density was at least one person per square mile. By this date, a settler colonial population was well established on the Prairies and in many narrow valleys in British Columbia and had even found a few pockets of useful land in the Canadian Shield north of the St. Lawrence–Great Lakes corridor. The settled area on the 1871 map had been considerably expanded, but the pattern remained the same: patches of settlement in the south and, to the north, vast tracts of land that, by this measure and at this scale, appear unoccupied. As before, the patches were areas of successful settler colonialism where immigrants and their descendants and governments were in control and Indigenous peoples were tucked away on reserves.

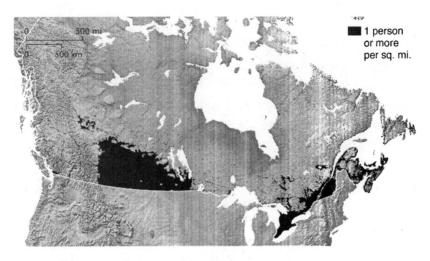

FIGURE 21
Population Density, Canada, 1961 |
After *The National Atlas of Canada* (Toronto and Ottawa: Macmillan Company
and Department of Energy Mines and Resources, 1974), 105-8

Where the population density was less than one person per square mile, there, as in 1871, almost all those living in these sparsely populated lands were Indigenous.

By this date, virtually all of Canada had been closely mapped and photographed and was broadly known to the outside world. Missionaries had expanded their reach. Remote places had become accessible to industrial capital, if only by bush plane, and their resources better known. Here and there, mines, camps, and mills had appeared. And the state had acquired some purchase over these vast lands: the provinces, by the terms of the British North America Act, over land and the federal government over Indigenous peoples. Laws and regulations promulgated in provincial capitals or in Ottawa had effect where, previously, no outside law had ever reached. In most places, the fur trade had collapsed and there were hardly any settlers, but Indigenous ways of life that had been refashioned during the fur trade years were again subjected to powerful pressures coming from far beyond their local lifeworlds.

The missionary enterprise that began early in the seventeenth century expanded onto the western plains in the early mid-nineteenth century and continued to advance into the boreal forest, the Mackenzie Valley, and well into the Cordillera. Wherever it went, the missionaries were hugely intrusive agents of cultural change. Almost all of them thought that Indigenous peoples, like anyone else, were children of God but children who lived in darkness yet could be brought to the light of true religion as reflected in upright Christian lives. They came, therefore, with both a theology and a transformative social agenda and with the confidence that they were right and that their gifts – basically the promise of eternal life – were of incalculable value. For Indigenous peoples, who understood that everything contained spirit power and whose cultural confidence had been weakened by disease and resource depletion, the missionaries seemed to offer access to white peoples' extraordinary spirit powers.

Most of these later missions were founded and served by Oblate priests, members of a Roman Catholic order that emerged in France early in the nineteenth century and bitterly opposed the secular, urban materialism of the times. The Oblate vision was retrospective: a peasantry living within the rhythm of the church calendar and the sound of the church bell. The Oblates strongly opposed the seasonal mobility of Indigenous life, which in their minds begot laziness and sin, and sought to settle their flocks in villages where they could be taught and watched. Often, they were successful; clusters of small log houses emerged close by a wooden church, each house, in Oblate eyes, a home for a nuclear family sanctioned by Christian marriage. They tried to teach the skills required for peasant farming. Always, they tried to stamp out shamanism and all forms of the Indigenous spirit world and replace them with Christian truth. Many of them gave their lives to their missions; they learned Indigenous languages, translated Catholic liturgy and hymns, and often urged settler governments to treat Indigenous peoples more generously, advice that these governments, frequently uneasy about missionaries, almost always ignored. In sum, however, the Oblates mounted a broad and sustained attack on Indigenous beliefs and ways. Because beliefs were always somewhat inscrutable, the most accessible measure of Christian conviction was the Christian life as the Oblates understood it. Therefore, they watched, particularly for sins of the flesh, and because there were more missions than priests, they appointed watchmen, even watchmen of the watchmen. In Anglican missions, the agendas of village formation and watching were much the same. In all missions, the attempt to remake Indigenous lives anticipated residential schools.[14]

Industrial capital usually arrived later and established itself at sites where a potentially profitable natural resource and transportation to the outside world could both be secured. Work camps and small resource-based towns appeared, their workers coming from away, the few Indigenous peoples nearby almost always disparaged and excluded. Later, and usually farther north, the labour force at these sites usually included Indigenous peoples who, as elsewhere, industrial capital transformed into workers. Suddenly, people who still lived partly off a well-known land found themselves in a workplace, under a boss, and subject to an unfamiliar time discipline in a radically unfamiliar work environment. They had moved into an economy that commodified land and labour and treated both as independent variables in an open market economy, assumptions that were byproducts of British industrialization and of arguments, recently advanced by economists, about the efficiencies of self-regulating markets. In Britain, a great many people struggled against the effects of these assumptions that detached labour and land from their social contexts[15] – and many Indigenous peoples, when suddenly confronted by them, found them altogether incomprehensible. They lived as they had been taught, did not "work," and had no concept of labour as an independent variable detached from land. As the German philosopher Habermas would have it, a system had penetrated a lifeworld.[16]

In an industrializing Britain, independent producers were transformed into factory hands in towns. In northern Canada, industrial capital developed work camps where Indigenous peoples were virtually the only inhabitants. There, they usually entered a labour market principally supplied from the south and, as they did not bring relevant skills, were commonly employed at the bottom of the workforce. Moreover, because it was a precarious gamble to cut ties with what remained of age-old subsistence economies, they would often quit when it was time to hunt or fish[17] – or when they could afford a skidoo and get out on the land. Bosses often considered them unreliable. However, the work camps themselves were unreliable, their existence tied to a quickly depleted resource, international commodity prices, and changing technologies of resource extraction. When they closed, there was no other wage work at hand, and after their brush with industrial capital, Indigenous peoples were left with the land, however depleted, and with parsimonious forms of welfare.

Often it came to this. On one side of many Indigenous lives in northern Canada was a collapsing fur trade and on the other unreliable industrial economies that, like the missionaries, contradicted most traditional Indigenous ways. The new settlements and their workplaces were sharply racialized places that reproduced elements of the outside world and expected Indigenous peoples to fit them. They imposed the social relations of industrial capital and the managerial bureaucracy of the state and, in so doing, massively assaulted older Indigenous ways. Even to live in a small house, its design and construction materials imported from the south, was to be assailed by difference. People struggled in these new circumstances: with high levels of substance abuse, sexual abuse, and cultural confusion; with violence; with mortality rates at or beyond third world levels; with the challenge of being a particular Indigenous people when the context of life had changed so drastically.

And for the first time in these vast lands, the state itself became a presence. As the Indian Act of 1876 made clear, "Indians" were wards of the state, in effect children whose lives were to be managed and civilized – an agenda that settler society largely took for granted. An understanding that people could be civilized and modern in different ways was not yet in the air; either Indigenous peoples would become civilized and assimilated into something like a modern, Western culture or they would probably die out.[18] Behind this wide consensus was evidence of the declining number (until the 1920s) of Indigenous peoples in Canada and, more basically, the same Christian beliefs that propelled the missionaries coupled with a universalizing understanding, rooted in the Enlightenment, of the common worth of all people. From both vantage points followed the premise that the "barbarous" could be improved – colonialism's civilizing mission. Some, convinced biological racists, flatly disagreed, and many others were doubtful,[19] but the impetus to civilize Indigenous peoples followed from the conviction that they shared a common humanity and, therefore, could be rescued from barbarism. It was easy, and often convenient, to assume a moral responsibility to do so.

These views, as is now well known, had horrendous consequences. From the 1890s the Canadian state provided the principal financing for church-run residential schools, most of which drew the majority of their pupils from beyond the boundaries of settler Canada. In 1920, it required all Indigenous children to attend such schools. It sent ships to pick up Inuit children on remote coasts in the Western Arctic and send them to schools far to the south, from where, years later, some would return whence they came, but now as outsiders speaking a different language. The residential schools were chronically underfunded, their teachers poorly paid and often unqualified, their students often traumatized, poorly fed, vulnerable to disease, bullied, and sexually abused. The Truth and Reconciliation Commission tells this story in agonizing detail.[20]

In the south, the state made treaties to acquire land wanted for agricultural settlement but hesitated to do so beyond the limits of agriculture until there was a perceived economic use for the land. As soon as there was, treaties followed: Treaty 8, 1899 (northern Alberta, northeastern British Columbia, and northwestern Saskatchewan); Treaty 9, 1905–6 (most of northern Ontario); Treaty 10, 1906–7 (northern Saskatchewan and a small portion of eastern Alberta); and Treaty 11, 1921 (eastern Yukon and western Northwest Territories). As written, in all these treaties Indigenous peoples surrendered title to vast territories in return for reserves (one square mile for a family of five), small initial payments and presents, small annuities (in Treaty 8, five dollars for all except Chiefs and Headmen, who received more; in Treaty 9, four dollars), medical services, and the right to hunt, fish, and trap as formerly – but subject to regulation and to the requirements of introduced economies. From the state's perspective, these treaties opened northern land for resource development. From an Indigenous perspective based on memories of oral agreements, they were thought to protect a way of life.

There were now officers of the Royal Canadian Mounted Police here and there in and well beyond these treaty lands. Hunting and trapping began to be regulated and registered trap lines introduced, many of them, with the advent of bush planes in the 1930s, taken up by white trappers. However, it was only after the Second World War that, apart from residential schools, the state seriously expressed itself in the largest part of these vast, thinly populated lands. It did so in particular instances because caribou herds were dwindling and people were starving but more generally in response to a set of widely circulating ideas that were, in many ways, the then contemporary heirs of the Enlightenment.

The clutch of postwar ideas that brought the state into the North turned around social management, development, and modernization.[21] The state, it was held, had the power and right to improve peoples' lives, build a more just society, and eliminate poverty. To do so required planning, top-down management, and scientific expertise; also a commitment to spatial justice through the equitable, universal distribution of social benefits. It sought to develop modern economies and weaken the constraints of tradition, in so doing creating more individualistic societies open to liberal democracy and capitalism. It encouraged mining capital to move into the North and encouraged, and often forced, Indigenous peoples to move to compact new settlements where services, medical attention, housing, and modern amenities could be more easily provided. When the North Rankin Inlet Nickel Mine closed, it flew some workers and their families to distant mines and sought to develop alternative economies, often introducing producer co-operatives that, officials thought, would blend traditional communal ways and the opportunity to acquire market experience. Some of this appeared to work, and some of it did not. An Inuk flown with her family and miner husband from Rankin Inlet on Hudson Bay to Yellowknife became a binge alcoholic because, as she said, "I have no place in this land."[22] The Inuit artists' co-op at Baker Lake, formed after the closure of the North Rankin Inlet nickel mine in 1962, generated local incomes and became world famous. Family allowance payments began in 1944, old age pensions a little later. Although officials tried to avoid Indigenous welfare dependency, in isolated locations where industrial wage work came and went, the low biological yield of the land provided few and uncertain commercial alternatives, and traditional economies no longer supported growing populations; a new economy based on welfare was emerging.[23]

All these systemic introductions massively altered Indigenous life-worlds that, previously, had been altered by the fur trade. Moreover, exotic diseases still circulated, their effects still devastating. Yet the stubborn realities of a harsh land had not changed. North of the patches of immigrant settlement, the land attracted outsiders at only a few sites, and there, usually, to work for a time and leave. Most who stayed had ancestors who had always lived there. Now, given the residential schools (in the Eastern Arctic, federal day schools with a residential capacity), most of them were no longer fluent speakers of their own languages. Most were no longer fully in charge of their own destinies or lived in ways that their ancestors could have imagined. But the basic fact of the matter is that they were there, still different, still the principal or only population in the largest part of Canada.

The Present and Beyond

In 1969 the Trudeau Liberal government introduced a white paper that proposed to repeal the Indian Act, wind up the Department of Indian Affairs and Northern Development, and treat Indigenous peoples the same as all other Canadian citizens. "The government," it stated, "believes in equality. It believes that all men and women shall have equal rights. It is determined that all shall be treated fairly and that no one shall be shut out of Canadian life."[24] Separate laws and administrative structures for Indigenous peoples were held to be discriminatory and racist. With its emphasis on individual rights, the White Paper was a classic liberal document, and it ran into a storm of protest from those who thought of rights more collectively. For Indigenous leaders, who considered that it ignored the destruction wrought by colonialism, the obligations embedded in treaties, and the distinctiveness of Indigenous cultures, it seemed the culmination of a long assimilative agenda.[25] Faced with their barrage, the government withdrew the White Paper a year later. Thereafter, the discourse shifted – from assimilation to respect for difference and reconciliation.[26] In 1982, section 35 of the Constitution Act recognized Indigenous and treaty rights.

Behind these developments has been the growing capacity of the empty spaces in Figure 21 to make themselves heard. Indigenous peoples have been speaking back to settler Canada as never before and in a great variety of ways: in the arts, in creative writing, in academic analyses of settler colonialism, in court challenges of colonial practices, in commissions on residential schools and missing and murdered Indigenous women, in blockades and other protests against resource developments, and perhaps, most basically, in their numbers. In 1961, according to the census of that year, some 220,000 Indigenous peoples in Canada were 1.2 percent of the population. In 2016, 1,673,000 Indigenous peoples comprised 4.9 percent of the population. Over the previous ten years, the Indigenous population had grown by 42.5 percent. With most Indigenous livelihoods no longer tied to the land, the ecological constraints that maintained low population densities throughout most of Canada no longer held.

This speaking back is taking place across the full span of the country because wherever there are settlers there is always land not far away to the north, where the population is largely or entirely Indigenous (Figures 19 and 21). In America, where immigrants found and took a huge and useful land (Figure 20), the relationship with Indigenous peoples is far less pressing. Canadians have little choice but to listen to the speaking back currently taking place. Here are four examples.

In a recent book, the work of many years, Marianne and Ronald Ignace, he a Chief and she a linguist, describe the traditional ways of the Secwépemc (Shuswap), an Interior Salish people in south-central British Columbia, and the challenges presented by settler colonialism.[27] Their picture of the precolonial Secwépemc world turns around an intimately known and managed territory; stories that provided moral instruction and laws; decentred, consensus-based social structures; and a language that grew out of and sustained the particular Secwépemc experience of land and life. All of this, in their view, is what it is to be Secwépemc, and their advice is clear: hold on to stories, land, and language. Yet the Ignaces know that many stories have been lost, that the Secwépemc control little more than 1 percent of their former lands, and that there are fewer than one hundred fluent speakers of their language. More generally, but close at hand, are the pressures that are weakening or obliterating local ways throughout the modern world. Their urgings are attractive – the Secwépemc will be more secure and

Canada culturally richer if their language survives – but not, as the Ignaces know, easily attained.

In a recent collection of her speeches over the last ten years, Jody Wilson-Raybould, member of the Kwakwaka'wakw nation (northern Vancouver Island), lawyer, Regional Chief of the British Columbia Assembly of First Nations, and the first Indigenous minister of justice and attorney general in Canada, argues for a rights-based reconciliation of Indigenous peoples and the Canadian state.[28] Law, in her view, was the "lifeblood" of colonialism, and the Indian Act of 1876 the legal means of transferring power away from Indigenous peoples. Now, the rights of self-determination and of self-government have to be returned so that Indigenous peoples can manage their own societies and lands and express their cultures. The recognition and affirmation of Indigenous and treaty rights in section 35 of the Constitution Act, 1982, seemed to open this door, but whereas the Charter of Rights and Freedoms was widely accepted, section 35 of the Constitution Act has been contested at every turn and rights only slowly established after long and expensive court cases. The whole country, in Wilson-Raybould's view, has been held hostage to uncertainty. The solution is to get beyond the Indian Act and implement the right of Indigenous self-government, also Indigenous courts and laws.[29] Already legally plural and built around co-operative federalism, the country will adjust to these developments and be stronger for them.

In an influential book published two decades ago, Mohawk scholar-activist Taiaiake Alfred argued that a politics of reconciliation only serves to perpetuate the grip of colonialism, a claim taken up more recently by, among others, Glen Coulthard (Yellowknives Dene) and Leanne Simpson (Anishinaabe).[30] In this view, the overriding legacy of colonialism has been to disconnect Indigenous peoples from the land and to colonize Indigenous minds. Reconciliation solves neither problem. Self-government can also be an empty shell because, in itself, it recovers neither land nor values. Cultures change, to be sure, and the challenge is not to try to re-create the past but to reclaim and build upon the best that can be found there. That best, in this view, has to do with the land, seen as a locus of relations and obligations that constitute the ethical foundation of life. Everything is interconnected; everything has spirit power. "All my relations." This, these scholars aver, is the heart of what it is to be Indigenous and, as such, stands as a striking alternative to the possessive individualism, aggressive materialism, and wanton destruction associated with the massive assault on North America that accompanied settler colonialism and commercial and industrial capitalism. Indigenous nations as detached as possible from the larger fabric of Canadian life are the geopolitical corollaries of these views.

In a book on Indigenous law in contemporary Canada, Anishinaabe legal scholar John Borrows suggests that rights-based approaches to citizenship and to Indigenous-state relations are insufficient because lives are situated in complex webs of interdependencies, which "rights" cannot identify, with the land and other peoples.[31] Indigenous peoples, he holds, now inhabit a "multifaceted, pluralistic world."[32] They are at once "traditional, modern, and postmodern," their identities variously constructed and reconstructed locally, nationally, and internationally. Moreover, they live within a federal state and "the constitutionally mandated inter-societal pluralism that lies at the heart of Canada's legal tradition." In these circumstances, the solution, in Borrows view, is not to turn inward and create defensive cells of Indigenous nationhood that would not reflect the reality of contemporary Indigenous lives, rather to inject Indigenous ways into the Canadian mainstream. He envisages more Indigenous peoples in command positions throughout Canadian society. He would refashion the law, particularly land law, to become increasingly Indigenous, in so doing reflecting Indigenous understandings of interdependence. He would extend citizenship to land. The whole country, in response, would become more Indigenous, and as it does so, the many boundaries between settler and Indigenous Canada would tend to slip away. A dream? Perhaps. But understanding that his proposals are situated within a constitutional tradition predicated less on first principles than on compromise, pluralism, and respect for others,[33] Borrows holds that a real option lies somewhere along this line of thought.

It is not for me, a product of settler colonialism, to suggest to Indigenous peoples how to deal with the effects of what I am a part. However I can, in conclusion, offer several brief and general observations. First, it seems very clear that the influence of Indigenous peoples in Canada will only grow, this partly because they are ever more sophisticated users of power in a modern society, partly because their numbers are growing rapidly, but most basically because settler colonialism in Canada has been a bounded enterprise. Settlers could not use most of the land, but Indigenous peoples could and did. However buffeted, they retained a presence that, circumstances permitting, would grow, as it now is. This, rather than resources, is the principal yield of the Canadian Shield and the rest of the sparsely inhabited North – the "empty" expanses in Figure 21. Second, it is clear that the fit of Indigenous peoples in this country is a matter of prime importance. The country will not be comfortable with itself, nor will decision making about land be more than a wrangle until a just and fair accommodation of Indigenous peoples and the Canadian state is worked out. Third, it may be helpful to recognize that the temptations of power are widely shared. Given the imbalance of power, the intensity in Europe of geopolitical rivalries, the pressures on European land, and the attractions of Indigenous land overseas, these lands drew Europeans as soon as they became visible and there were means to reach them. Indigenous peoples could not stop the taking. But it was also the case that when the balance of power favoured particular Indigenous peoples and adjacent lands were enticing, they too engaged in taking.[34] Fourth, much of what galls an Indigenous scholar like Taiaiake Alfred has also galled thoughtful Europeans, and for many of the same reasons. The enclosure of land, the spread of private property rights, the growing salience of market economies, the commodification of land and labour, the transformation of independent producers into factory hands, above all the progressive detachment of people from land – all this created enormous hardship and drove many people overseas. To some fair extent, the Indigenous critique of settler colonialism is situated within a larger critique of modernizing societies in the throes of deep structural changes. Fifth and finally, as it becomes increasingly clear how much, in recent centuries, the land has been abused and how serious the consequences of that abuse are likely to be, the significance of the Indigenous understanding of the dense web of interrelations that unite people and a teeming, animate land is increasingly obvious. Indigenous peoples are not, and probably never have been, impeccable environmental stewards,[35] but they have known the land far more intimately than have any others, have worked out enduring relationships with it, and hold very different values than those underlying the current environmental predicament. After many years of telling Indigenous peoples what to do, it has become necessary to listen to them.

The relationship between settlers and Indigenous peoples in Canada has shifted. Fifty years ago Northrop Frye, perhaps the most appreciated literary critic of his day, published *The Bush Garden,* a collection of his Canadian essays.[36] Most of them deal with poetry, two with painting. Frye considered them explorations of the Canadian imagination, an imagination in which Indigenous peoples barely appear, and then only as relics. The land, on the other hand, is treated as a dominating presence, and Frye's essential geography, like mine, identifies discontinuous patches of settlement close to the border – garrisons in his metaphor – with rock and cold beyond. Yet his land beyond comprised "empty spaces" where those who entered found "the loneliness of a deserted land." Given the sparseness of Indigenous populations, this error was easily made, one I have made myself.[37]

There is a huge difference, however, between a thinly populated and an empty land, a difference crucial to what Canada has become since Frye's day. Today, no one could write a book about the Canadian imagination and leave out Indigenous peoples. They extend almost everywhere, unsettle established ways, and pose many of the basic constitutional and legal questions with which the country has to deal: the extent of Indigenous rights to land, the nature and powers of Indigenous governments, the relationship of such governments to the Canadian state. As these matters are worked out, as it is now clear they have to be, Canada will become more Indigenous, more just, and, I would hope, more sensitively attuned to its vast lands. The country is being reimagined.

Notes and Further Readings

The Fraser Canyon Encountered

1 After fellow North-Wester David Thompson who, Fraser thought, was then exploring the upper reaches of this river. W. Kaye Lamb, ed., *The Letters and Journals of
Simon Fraser, 1806–1808* (Toronto: Macmillan, 1960), 86–92.

2 Kokwe'la (Thq'w'wíle), the son of Carrotroot, trained in the mountains and became
a magician with invincible powers. Pat Shaw and Dale Kinkade, Department of
Linguistics, UBC, kindly provided this identification.

3 J.A. Teit, "Mythology of the Thompson Indians," in *The Jesup North Pacific Expedition: Memoirs of the American Museum of Natural History,* vol. 8, part 2 (New
York: 1912), 416.

Imagining and Claiming the Land

For a summary of sixteenth-century exploration, see Richard Ruggles, "Exploring
the Atlantic Coast," in *Historical Atlas of Canada,* vol. 1, *From the Beginning to 1800,*
ed. R. Cole Harris, cart. Geoffrey J. Matthews (Toronto: University of Toronto Press,
1987), plate 19. For a short discussion of the early voyages, consult John L. Allen,
"From Cabot to Cartier: The Early Exploration of Eastern North America, 1497–
1543," *Annals of the Association of American Geographers* 82, 3 (1992): 500–21; and
for a more extended discussion, refer to Samuel Eliot Morison, *The European
Discovery of America: The Northern Voyages* (New York: Oxford University Press,

1971). The Cartier quotes are from Jacques Cartier, Henry Biggar, and Ramsay Cook, *The Voyages of Jacques Cartier* (Toronto: University of Toronto Press, 1993). For a survey of sixteenth- and early seventeenth-century cartography that includes fine reproductions of the principal maps, see Derek Hayes, *Historical Atlas of Canada: Canada's History Illustrated with Original Maps* (Vancouver and Toronto: Douglas and McIntyre, 2002), 7–56. For the principal documents relating to explorations before 1612, consult D.B. Quinn, *New American World: A Documentary History of North America to 1612* (New York: Arno Press, 1979). For Champlain's exploration and cartography, see Conrad Heidenreich, "The Beginning of French Exploration Out of the St. Lawrence Valley: Motives, Methods, and Changing Attitudes towards Native People," in Germaine Warkentin and Carolyn Podruchny, eds., *Decentring the Renaissance: Canada and Europe in Multidisciplinary Perspective, 1500–1700* (Toronto: University of Toronto Press, 2001), 236-51; Heidenreich, with Edward H. Dahl, "La cartographie de Champlain (1603–1632)," in Raymonde Litalien and Denis Vaugeois, eds., *Champlain: La naissance de l'Amérique française* (Sillery: Nouveau Monde and Septentrion, 2004), 312–32; and Heidenreich, "Early French Exploration in the North American Interior," in *North American Exploration*, vol. 2, *A Continent Defined*, ed. J.L. Allen (Lincoln and London: University of Nebraska Press, 1997), 65–148. On maps and power, consult Bruno Latour, *Science in Action: How to Follow Scientists and Engineers through Society* (Cambridge, MA: Harvard University Press, 1987), chap. 6; and J.B. Harley, "Maps, Knowledge, and Power," in Denis Cosgrove and Stephen Daniels, eds., *The Iconography of Landscape: Essays on the Symbolic Representation, Design and Use of Past Environments* (Cambridge and New York: Cambridge University Press, 1988), 277–312.

Voices of Smallpox around the Strait of Georgia

1 R.G. Thwaites, *The Jesuit Relations and Allied Documents*, vol. 3 (Cleveland, OH: Borrows Brothers, 1900), 105.

2 Interview by Gordon Mohs and Sonny McHalsie with Elder Jimmy Peters, September 29, 1986, Stó:lō Heritage, Book 11A, Oral History, Stó:lō Tribal Council, Sardis, BC. This essay owes much of its initial impetus to comments by Ruben Ware in *A Sto:lo Bibliography* (Sardis, BC: Coqualeetza Education Training Centre, 1983) and to the remarkable collection of research materials in the Coqualeetza Cultural Education Centre.

3 "Ethnological Report on the Stseelis (Chehalis) and Skaulits (Scowlitz) Tribes of the Halkomelem Division of the Salish of British Columbia," *Journal of the Royal Anthropological Institute* 34 (July–December 1904). Reprinted in Ralph Maud, ed., *The Salish People: The Local Contribution of Charles Hill-Tout*, vol. 3, *The Mainland Halkomelem* (Vancouver: Talonbooks 1978), 110.

4 On the medical implications of genetic similarity, see Francis L. Black, "Why Did They Die?" *Science* 258 (December 11, 1992): 1739–40.

5 For current estimates and reviews of estimates, see William Denevan, "Native American Populations in 1492: Recent Research and Revised Hemispheric Estimate," in *The Native Population of the Americas in 1492*, 2nd ed. (Madison: University of Wisconsin Press, 1992), xvii–xxxviii; and Douglas H. Ubelaker, "North American Indian Population Size: Changing Perspectives," in *Disease and Demography in the Americas*, ed. J.W. Verano and D.H. Ubelaker (Washington, DC: Smithsonian Institution Press, 1992), 169–78.

6 Jan Vansina, *Oral Tradition as History* (Madison: University of Wisconsin Press, 1985), 83.

7 Erna Gunther, *Klallam Ethnology*, University of Washington Publications in Anthropology, vol. 1, no. 5 (Seattle: University of Washington Press, 1927), 171–314; and H.G. Barnett, *The Coast Salish of British Columbia* (Eugene: University of Oregon Press, 1955).

8 Wilson Duff, *The Upper Stalo Indians of the Fraser River of B.C.*, Anthropology in British Columbia, no. 1 (Victoria: British Columbia Provincial Museum, 1952).

9 W.W. Elmendorf, *The Structure of Twana Culture with Comparative Notes on the Structure of Yurok Culture [by] A.L. Kroeber, Research Studies* 28, 3, Monographic Supplement no. 2 (Pullman: Washington State University, 1960), 272.

10 Wayne Suttles, "Post-Contact Culture Change among the Lummi Indians," *British Columbia Historical Quarterly* 18, 1–2 (1954): 42. In 1951, a Samish woman, Ruth Sheldon, then ninety-four years old, told Suttles that most of her people had been wiped out by smallpox "about 300 years ago," a date that, allowing twenty years per generation, Suttles revised to 1770–90. Other information about disease that he gathered in the late 1940s and early 1950s from Semiahmoo, Swinomish, and Katzie informants cannot be dated unambiguously to the eighteenth century. Suttles, personal communication, July 1993.

11 By "Hydahs" in this story, but Haida do not appear to have been on the South Coast before 1853. These raiders were probably Laich-kwil-tach, southern Kwakwa̱ka̱'wakw peoples.

12 E.C. Webber, "An Old Kwanthum Village: Its People and Its Fall," *American Antiquarian* 21 (September–October 1899): 309–14. "Dragon," presumably, is Ellen Webber's word.

13 E.C. Webber, *Museum and Arts Notes* 6, 3 (September 1931): 119.

14 Charles Hill-Tout, "Notes on the Cosmogony and History of the Squamish Indians of British Columbia," in *The Salish People: The Local Contribution of Charles Hill-Tout*, vol. 2, *The Squamish and the Lillooet*, ed. Ralph Maud (Vancouver: Talonbooks, 1978), (first published in *Transactions, Royal Society of Canada*, 2nd series, 3 (1897): sec. 2).

15 Maud, *Salish People*, 2:22.

16 Diamond Jenness, *The Faith of a Coast Salish Indian,* British Columbia Provincial Museum Anthropology Memoir, no. 3 (Victoria: British Columbia Provincial Museum, 1955).

17 Ibid., 34.

18 "Quimper's Journal," in Henry R. Wagner, *Spanish Explorations in the Strait of Juan de Fuca* (Santa Ana: Fine Arts Press, 1933), 129–32; see also Wayne Suttles, "They Recognize No Superior Chief: The Strait of Juan de Fuca in the 1790s," in *Culturas de la costa noroeste de America,* ed. J.L. Peset (Madrid: Sociedad Estatal Quinto Centenario, 1989), 251–64.

19 "Extract of the Navigation Made by the Pilot Don Juan Pantoja," in Wagner, *Spanish Explorations,* 185–88.

20 "Voyage of the Sutil and Mexicana," in Wagner, *Spanish Explorations,* esp. 254, 289, 293. On the Spanish route through Johnstone Strait, see Robert Galois, *Kwakwaka'wakw Settlements, 1775–1920: A Geographical Analysis and Gazetteer* (Vancouver/Seattle: UBC Press/University of Washington Press, 1994).

21 William Kaye Lamb, ed., *A Voyage of Discovery to the North Pacific Ocean and Round the World, 1791–1795,* 4 vols. (London: Hakluyt Society, 1984), 2:516–17, 538.

22 T. Manby Journal, December 1790 to June 1793, William Robertson Coe Collection, Yale University, 43, photocopy in W. Kaye Lamb Papers, Special Collections, University of British Columbia, box 1.

23 Puget Journal, Adm. 55, 27, 133–34, Public Record Office, London, photocopy in W. Kaye Lamb Papers.

24 James Johnstone Log Book, January 2, 1792, and May 20, 1792, 176, photocopy in W. Kaye Lamb Papers, box 4. This point, obviously, was discussed; Archibald Menzies, the expedition's botanist, put it this way: "In this excursion ... we saw only the few Natives I have already mentioned, silence and solitude seemed to prevail over this fine and extensive country, even the feathered race, as if unable to endure the stillness that pervaded everywhere had in great measure abandoned it and were therefore very scarce" (C.F. Newcombe, ed., *Menzies' Journal of Vancouver's Voyage: April to October, 1792* [Victoria, BC: n.p., 1923], 40).

25 Newcombe, *Menzies' Journal,* 53.

26 T. Manby Journal, June 12.

27 Lamb, *Voyage of Discovery,* 603–4.

28 Ibid., 613.

29 R.G. Thwaites, ed., *Original Journals of the Lewis and Clark Expedition, 1804–1806,* vol. 4 (New York: Dodd, Mead and Company, 1905), 240–41.

30 Barbara Belyea, ed., *Thompson's Narrative, 1774–1812* (Montreal/Kingston: McGill-Queen's University Press, 1994), 70.

31 Richard Glover, ed., *Thompson's Narrative, 1774–1812* (Toronto: Champlain Society, 1962), 367.

32 W. Kaye Lamb, ed., *The Letters and Journals of Simon Fraser, 1806–1808* (Toronto: Macmillan, 1960), 94.

33 Ross Cox, *Adventures on the Columbia River* (London: R. Bentley, 1831), 1:314.

34 John Work's Journal, November 18 to December 30, 1824, BC Archives, A/B/40/W89.2A.

35 John Scouler, "Dr. John Scouler's Journal of a Voyage to N.W. America," *Quarterly of the Oregon Historical Society* 6, 1 (1905): 303–4.

36 Ann F. Ramenofsky, *Vectors of Death: The Archaeology of European Contact* (Albuquerque: University of New Mexico Press, 1987), 130; and H.F. Dobyns, "Estimating Aboriginal American Population: An Appraisal of Techniques with a New Hemispheric Estimate," *Current Anthropology* 7 (1966): 395–416.

37 W. George Lovell, *Conquest and Survival in Colonial Guatemala: A Historical Geography of the Cuchumatán Highlands, 1500–1821* (Montreal/Kingston: McGill-Queen's University Press, 1992), 154–57; and Fernando Casanuava, "Smallpox and War in Southern Chile in the Late Eighteenth Century," in *Secret Judgments of God: Old World Disease in Colonial Spanish America,* ed. N.D. Cook and W. George Lovell (Norman: University of Oklahoma Press, 1991), 183–212.

38 S.F. Cook, "Smallpox in Spanish and Mexican California, 1770–1845," *Bulletin of the History of Medicine* 7 (1939): 153–94; M. Simmons, "New Mexico's Smallpox Epidemic of 1780–1781," *New Mexico Historical Review* 41 (1966): 319–26; Arthur J. Ray, *Indians in the Fur Trade: Their Role as Trappers, Hunters, and Middlemen in the Lands Southwest of Hudson Bay, 1660–1870* (Toronto: University of Toronto Press, 1974), 105–8; Jody F. Decker, "Tracing Historical Diffusion Patterns: The Case of the 1780–1782 Smallpox Epidemic among the Indians of Western Canada," *Native Studies Review* 4, 1–2 (1988): 1–24, and "Depopulation of the Northern Plains Natives," *Social Science and Medicine* 33, 4 (1991): 381.

39 Glover, *Thompson's Narrative,* 236.

40 Ibid., 235–36.

41 Rueben Gold Thwaites, ed., *Original Journals of the Lewis and Clark Expedition, 1804–1806* (New York: Dodd, Mead, 1904), 1:202, cited in Ramenofsky, *Vectors of Death,* 128–29. Lewis and Clark were told that "smallpox destroyed the greater part of the [Mandan] nation and reduced them to one large village and Some Small ones, all the nations before this maladey was afraid of them, after they were reduced the Seaux and other Indians waged war, and Killed a great many, and they moved up the Missourie" (Thwaites, *Original Journals,* 1:220).

42 Glover, *Thompson's Narrative,* 49.

43 Decker, "Tracing Historical Diffusion Patterns," 12.

44 William R. Swagerty, "Indian Trade in the Trans-Mississippi West to 1870," in *Handbook of North American Indians,* ed. Wilcomb E. Washburn, vol. 4, *History of Indian-White Relations* (Washington, DC: Smithsonian Institution, 1988), 352.

45 Clark Wissler, *Material Culture of the Blackfoot Indians*, Anthropological Papers of the American Museum of Natural History, vol. 5, no. 1 (New York: The Trustees, 1910), 13.

46 The quotes from Smith and Work are cited in Robert Boyd, "The Introduction of Infectious Diseases among the Indians of the Pacific Northwest, 1774–1874" (PhD diss., University of Washington, 1985), 78–80.

47 Gregory Mengarini, *Recollections of the Flathead Mission: Containing Brief Observations, Both Ancient and Contemporary, Concerning This Particular Nation* (Glendale, CA: A.H. Clark, 1977), 193–94.

48 Henry Dobyns has argued for a hemispheric smallpox pandemic in the 1520s – see *Their Number Became Thinned: Native American Population Dynamics in Eastern North America* (Knoxville: University of Tennessee Press, 1983) – but Reff's work on northwestern Mexico and the southwestern United States provides, I think, strong evidence against a sixteenth-century epidemic in the northern Cordillera. See his *Disease, Depopulation and Cultural Change in Northwestern New Spain, 1518–1764* (Salt Lake City: University of Utah Press, 1991). However, the case has been argued, see Sarah Campbell, "Post-Columbian Culture History in the Northern Columbia Plateau: AD 1500–1900" (PhD diss., University of Washington, 1989).

49 Rupert Brooke, *Letters from America* (New York: Scribner's Sons, 1916), chap. 13.

50 See note 2 above.

Acadia: Settling the Marshlands

The works referred to by Rameau de Saint-Père, Parkman, and Lauvrière are E. Rameau de Saint-Père, *Une colonie féodale en amérique, L'Acadie, 1604–1881*, 2 vols. (Paris: Librarie Plon, 1889); Francis Parkman, *A Half-Century of Conflict* (Boston: Little, Brown, 1892); and Emile Lauvrière, *La tragédie d'un peuple* (Paris: Bossard, 1922). Rameau de Saint-Père published several important documents that are not easily available elsewhere. For a more contemporary introduction to the Acadians, see Jean Daigle, "Acadian Marshland Settlement," in *Historical Atlas of Canada*, vol. 1, *From the Beginning to 1800*, ed. R. Cole Harris, cart. Geoffrey J. Matthews (Toronto: University of Toronto Press, 1987), plate 29. Although probably exaggerating the extent of Acadian commerce, A.H. Clark, *Acadia: The Geography of Early Nova Scotia to 1760* (Madison: University of Wisconsin Press, 1968), is the most thorough account of Acadian settlement and economy. A short and more political account by Naomi Griffiths is *Contexts of Acadian History, 1686–1784* (Montreal/Kingston: McGill-Queen's University Press, 1992). Griffiths's most recent and imposing book, *From Migrant to Acadian: A North American Border People 1604–1755* (Montreal/Kingston: McGill-Queen's University Press, 2005), is also primarily a political history but includes a wealth of social and economic information and fascinating accounts of the relationships between the Acadians and the various colonial administrations that attempted to govern them. See particularly chaps. 6, 7, 11, and 12. On Mi'kmaq-Acadian relations, consult William C. Wicken, "Re-examining Mi'kmaq-Acadian Relations, 1635–1755," in *Vingt ans après Habitants et marchands: Lectures de l'histoire des XVIIe et XVIIIe siècles canadiens,* ed. Sylvie Dépatie, C. Desbarats, D. Gauvreau, M. Lalancette, and T. Wien (Montreal/Kingston: McGill-Queen's University Press, 1998), 93–114. On Acadia in its imperial context, refer to Elizabeth Mancke and John G. Reid, "Elites, States, and the Imperial Contest for Acadia," in *The "Conquest" of Acadia, 1710: Imperial, Colonial, and Aboriginal Constructions,* ed. J.G. Reid, M. Basque, E. Mancke, B. Moody, G. Plank, and W. Wicken (Toronto: University of Toronto Press, 2004), 25–47; Elizabeth Mancke, "Imperial Transitions," in ibid., 179–202; and on Acadian political culture, Maurice Basque, "Family and Political Culture in Preconquest Acadia," in ibid., 48–63. There is no better short introduction to Louisbourg than Kenneth Donovan, "Île Royale, Eighteenth Century," in Harris and Matthews, *Historical Atlas of Canada,* vol. 1, plate 24.

Of Poverty and Helplessness in Petite-Nation

1 In St-Féréol behind the present settlement of Ste-Anne de Beaupré after the Séminaire de Québec had conceded all the land along the Côte-de-Beaupré.

2 See Michel Chamberland, *Histoire de Montebello, 1815–1928* (Montreal: Imprimerie des Sourds-Muets, 1929), chap. 7, for a description of early immigration to Petite-Nation. The data in Table 1 of the present volume (p. 77) are derived from the nominal census of 1851. The place of birth of approximately one-half the heads of households in St-André Avellin is given in the census.

3 Ibid., 58–59.

4 See, for example, J. Papineau to his son Benjamin, Île Jésus, May 1824, *Rapport de l'Archiviste de la province de Québec* (RAPQ), 1951–52, 194–96; and a letter of February 9, 1826, ibid., 231.

5 This process is described here and there in the Denis-Benjamin Papineau correspondence. See, for example, Denis-Benjamin Papineau à Louis-Joseph Papineau, February 1836, Bibliothèque et Archives nationales du Québec (BAnQ), Archives Personnelles (AP), P, 5, 2.

6 The physical geography of Petite-Nation is well surveyed in Paul G. Lajoie, *Etude pédologique des comtés de Hull, Labelle, et Papineau* (Ottawa: Ministère de l'Agriculture du Canada, 1968), 14–31.

7 A detailed description of the forest in Petite-Nation before very much of the seigneurie had been cleared is in Joseph Bouchette's "Field Book of the Line between the Seigniory of La Petite-Nation and the Augmentation of Grenville, beginning 1 October 1826," BAnQ, AP, P, 5, 48.

8 Joseph Papineau to his son Benjamin, Montreal, July 22, 1809, RAPQ, 1951–52, 173. Joseph Papineau does not give the date of the contract in this letter, but apparently it was made in the previous year or two.

9 Chamberland, *Histoire de Montebello*, 58–59.

10 "Vente de partie de la Seigneurie de Petite-Nation par J. Papineau, Ecr. à Robert Fletcher, Ecr.," January 17, 1809, BAnQ, AP, P, 5.

11 *La Gazette de Québec,* March 9, 1809, no. 2289.

12 This account of Fletcher's death is given by Judge Augustin C. Papineau in a short history of Petite-Nation written in 1912. Copy of original manuscript by J.T. Beaudry, October 1819, BAnQ, QP, P, 5.

13 Sale by Joseph Papineau to Louis-Joseph Papineau, May 2, 1817, BAnQ, AP, P, 5, 46. In this case the sale was for £5,000.

14 D.-B. Papineau to Mgr. Lartigue, Petite-Nation, February 25, 1828, BAnQ, PQ, P, 5, 29; Chamberland, *Histoire de Montebello*, 79–81, gives 512 people in 1825. Nominal Census of Petite-Nation, 1842, Library and Archives Canada (LAC), reel C-729.

15 Nominal Census of Petite-Nation, 1851, LAC, reels C-1131 and 1132; 1861, reel C-1304.

16 Tableau de la Censive de la Petite-Nation, 1818, BAnQ, AP, P, 5, 48.

17 J.-B.N. Papineau, son of Denis-Benjamin, pointed out in 1852 that rotures in Petite-Nation had been laid out "along the course of the Ottawa River or the Petite Nation River and its tributaries so that the rivers can be used for roads until such time as the censitaires are able to build them." Nominal Census of Petite-Nation, 1851, LAC, reel C-1132, remarks of enumerator on back of p. 131, March 6, 1852. See also, "Instructions de Denis-Benjamin Papineau sur l'arpentage," 1839, BAnQ, AP, P, 5, 46.

18 With inadequate surveying, there was always a good deal of confusion about property lines, particularly in the irregular pockets of cultivable land in the Shield for which the cadastral system of long lot and côte was quite ill suited.

19 During the French regime, seigneurs had been expected to build and the censitaires to maintain the roads. The title to Petite-Nation, however, did not specify the seigneur's responsibility to build roads, and there is no indication that the Papineaus built any roads in Petite-Nation other than a few short roads to mills.

20 Louis-Joseph Papineau to Benjamin Papineau, Montreal, November 22, 1829, BAnQ, AP, P, 5, 5 (folder 153a); and also Joseph Papineau to his son Benjamin, Île Jésus, May 1824, RAPQ, 1951–52, 194–96.

21 Louis-Joseph Papineau to Alanson Cooke, Petite-Nation, October 22, 1850, BAnQ, AP, P, 5, 48 (bundle Alanson Cooke).

22 Louis-Joseph Papineau to Benjamin Papineau, October 23, 1848, BAnQ, AP, P, 5, 5 (folder 185).

23 Louis-Joseph Papineau to Benjamin Papineau, October 11, 1848, ibid. (folder 184).

24 The legal position in this regard of the seigneur during the French regime is discussed in R.C. Harris, *The Seigneurial System in Early Canada: A Geographical Study* (Madison: University of Wisconsin Press, 1966), 106–8.

25 Louis-Joseph Papineau to Benjamin Papineau, Petite-Nation, October 22, 1850, BAnQ, AP, P, 5, 5 (folder 203). The title deed to the seigneurie of Petite-Nation, unlike most others, did not specify that the seigneur was required to subgrant land, but it is doubtful that an intendant during the French regime would have permitted Louis-Joseph to grant land as he did.

26 Louis-Joseph Papineau to Benjamin Papineau, October 11, 1848, ibid. (folder 184).

27 For an example of a roture contract in Petite-Nation, see "Concession de roture no 2, côte du Moulin ... à Alanson Cooke," October 20, 1846, BAnQ, AP, P, 5, 51.

28 In many seigneurial titles, even the seigneur had been forbidden to cut oak anywhere on the seigneurie.

29 Indeed, by an *arrêt* of the Conseil d'Etat of June 4, 1686, seigneurs during the French regime could lose their banal right if they did not put up a grist mill within a year.

30 Harris, *The Seigneurial System*, 63–69, 78.

31 All dollar values are given in Halifax dollars, such a dollar being worth five English shillings and approximately five and one-half livres tournois. Thus one livre tournois was worth approximately eighteen cents Halifax currency.

32 Louis-Joseph was fully aware that seigneurs who fixed their charges in money payments were not likely to prosper in the long run from their holdings. He discusses this matter at some length in "Tableau statistique des Seigneuries," ca. 1851, BAnQ, AP, P, 5, 55.

33 A graph of wheat prices during the French regime is in J. Hamelin, *Economie et société en Nouvelle France* (Quebec: Presses de l'Université Laval, 1960), 61, and a similar graph for the later period is in Fernand Ouellet, *Histoire économique et sociale du Québec, 1760–1850* (Montreal: Fides, 1966), 603.

34 In the seigneurial account books, the charge for each year was always listed in livres rather than in minots and depended on the price of wheat in that year. It was not possible for a censitaire to accumulate several years of debt and then, when the price of wheat was low, pay back his seigneur in kind.

35 *Pièce-sur-pièce* was the most common form of log construction during the French regime and was still widespread in the nineteenth century. Round-log construction probably had entered Quebec from New England in the late eighteenth century and was widely adopted in the Shield by both French Canadians and Irish. French Canadian and Irish houses in the Shield were often almost indistinguishable, both being essentially simple versions in wood of a Norman house, one brought from the St. Lawrence lowland, the other from southeastern Ireland. The heavily flared eaves, the porches, and the elevated ground storey, all characteristics of the vernacular French Canadian house of the nineteenth century, often did

not penetrate the Shield, presumably because of the additional work and cost associated with them.

36 In 1842 the median amount of cleared land per roture was ten arpents and by 1861 was 19 arpents (Nominal Census of Petite-Nation, 1842, LAC, reel C-729).

37 See, for example, Joseph Papineau to his son Louis-Joseph, Montreal, February 28, 1818, RAPQ, 1951–52, 182.

38 Denis-Benjamin Papineau to his uncle Frs. Papineau, Petite-Nation, February 29, 1812, BAnQ, AP, P, 5, 29.

39 These figures are calculated from data on yields in the Nominal Census, 1861, LAC. They assume that French Canadians sowed one and a half minots of grain per arpent. A good deal of land in 1861 was still within a few years of first cultivation. Later, without a change in agricultural technology, yields would have been substantially lower.

40 This lease was arranged sometime before 1822. There is a receipt, dated 1822, for £75 ($300) for lease of the mill in the Papineau Papers (BAnQ, AP, P, 5, 48).

41 "Lease from 1 November 1833 ... between the Hon. L-J. Papineau and the Hon. P. McGill, Sept 20, 1834," ibid. (bundle Alanson Cooke).

42 Nominal Census, Petite-Nation, 1851, LAC, reel C-1132.

43 This was a long-standing arrangement, its terms varying over the years. See, for example, D-B. Papineau to Stephen Tucker, February 10, 1844, BAnQ, AP, P, 5, 30.

44 Joseph Papineau to his son Louis-Joseph, Montreal, March 25, 1840, RAPQ, 1951–52, 299.

45 Nominal Census, Petite-Nation, 1851, LAC, reels C-1131 and C-1132.

46 An exact statement would be possible only if the records of all timber concerns operating in Petite-Nation had survived. As it is, there are, apparently, no such records.

47 Nominal Census, Petite-Nation, 1851, LAC. Some of the information given here is listed on the back of folio sheets and is not photographed on microfilm.

48 Ibid., 1861, reel C-1304. At this date, Gilmour and Co. and Stephen Tucker were the only major employers in Petite-Nation, and it can be taken that only just over two hundred men worked in forest industries in the seigneurie in 1861.

49 These figures are my estimates, which probably err on the side of more rather than fewer jobs. In much of the Ottawa Valley, the same men were hired to cut and square timber and then to raft it to Quebec. Stephen Tucker may well have hired in this way; if so, the 50 to 60 raftsmen given in these estimates were the same men as the 50 to 60 of those estimated to work in the logging camps.

50 The 1861 wages are given in the census (Nominal Census, Petite-Nation, 1861, LAC, reel C-1304). Wages at Hull, forty miles away, were $10 a month in 1820 and $12 a month in 1840, and there is no reason for those in Petite-Nation to have been different. See C.H. Craigie, "The Influence of the Timber Trade and Philemon Wright

on the Social and Economic Development of Hull Township, 1800–1850" (master's thesis, Carleton University, 1969), 94.

51 My estimate, probably too generous, is based on the wage scale and inventory of jobs given above.

52 Nominal Census, Petite-Nation, 1842, LAC, reel C-729.

53 "Tableau d'arrérages," 1822, BAnQ, AP, P, 5, 48. In 1825, forty-six rotures owed "over 20,000 livres" (ibid., 1825, BAnQ, QP, P, 48).

54 "État des dettes," November 11, 1832, BAnQ, AP, P, 5, 48. By this date, the seventy-three rotures along the Ottawa River owed approximately 40,000 livres.

55 "Tableau d'arrérages," 1822.

56 There are numerous indications in the documents that the Papineaus exercised this droit de retrait. See, for example, J. Papineau to his son Benjamin, Montreal, January 7, 1825, RAPQ, 1951–52, 198–99.

57 Accounts between D-B. Papineau and L-J. Papineau, 1825–37, BAnQ, AP, P, 5, 48.

58 At this date there was no court in the Ottawa Valley, and, as a result, minor disputes rarely reached a court. See D-B. Papineau to Philemon Wright, May 14, 1833, LAC, Wright Papers, MG24, D8, vol. 19, 8179.

59 Denis-Benjamin was always an easy-going seigneurial agent, often too much so for his brother's liking. Once, for example, when Louis-Joseph was determined to sue, Denis Benjamin would go only so far as to tell the censitaires in question that they would be taken to court if their debts were not paid in three years. "Je ne scais si cela conviendra à [Louis-Joseph] Papineau," he told his father, "mais je ne pense qu'à moins de déposséder les habitants l'on puisse exiger d'avantage" (J. Papineau to his son Louis-Joseph, St. Hyacinthe, September 27, 1838, RAPQ, 1951–52, 291–92).

60 Although he rarely sued, Papineau did expect to be paid, and he pushed his censitaires as hard as he could short of actual eviction. During one brief visit to the seigneurie, he wrote to his wife, "Je vois que je n'en retirerai rien, il est trop tard, leur grains sont mangés" (Louis-Joseph Papineau to his wife, Petite-Nation, April 9, 1828, RAPQ, 1953–54, 247–49).

61 "Oh il faudrait vivre ici pour réussir à une petite partie des améliorations que je rêve et pour forcer la rentrée des arrérages qui me permettraient de les tenter" (L-J. Papineau to Benjamin Papineau, October 23, 1848, BAnQ, AP, P, 5, 5 [folder 185]).

62 Louis-Joseph Papineau to Benjamin Papineau, Montreal, May 6, 1848, ibid. (folder 175).

63 Louis-Joseph Papineau to his son Amédée, April 28, 1952, BAnQ, AP, P, 5, 7 (folder 327).

64 Louis-Joseph Papineau to Benjamin Papineau, March 12, 1848, BAnQ, AP, P, 5, 5 (folder 173). In French law, the debts against land were not revealed at the time of its sale, and in this circumstance bidders were unwilling to pay more than a pittance

for rotures sold for the nonpayment of dues. The seigneur could acquire them for next to nothing.

65 Chamberland, *Histoire de Montebello*, 165. Denis-Benjamin did not, here, mention Tucker by name, but other reports about him and the fact he was the only Baptist merchant in Petite-Nation leave no doubt who was being described. There is some indication that his offer was not always rejected. In the nominal census of 1851, Aureole Gravelle and his wife, both French Canadians by birth, are listed as Baptists.

66 "Liste alphabétique des actes reçus par Andre-Benjamin Papineau, notaire à St-Martin ... transactions en la Seigneurie de La Petite-Nation de 1837 a 1845 inclusivement," BAnQ, AP, P, 5.

67 Stephen Tucker to Louis-Joseph Papineau, Papineauville, May 25, 1855, BAnQ, QP, P, 5, 48; and also, "Reciprocal Discharge and Acquittance from and to the Honorable Louis-Joseph Papineau and Stephen Tucker, July 14, 1858," BAnQ, AP, P, 5, 48. Tucker had not been paying the back dues on these rotures, and in 1858 he owed approximately £900 on them.

68 L-J. Papineau to Stephen Tucker, Montebello, May 27, 1858, ibid.

69 One priest, however, reported that there was "beaucoup d'animosité" between French Canadians and Irish in Petite-Nation (M. Bourassa to Mgr. Lartigue, March 23, 1839, cited in Chamberland, *Histoire de Montebello*, 174). And, of course, there were many accounts in the Ottawa Valley of strife between rival gangs of French Canadian and Irish workers.

70 One of these Protestants was a Lutheran, another, brother of the first, a Universalist, and the third, an Anabaptist.

71 This information is calculated from the nominal census of 1842.

72 Resident priests were not established in rural parishes until the 1720s, and before that time parishes were visited intermittently, as in Petite-Nation, by missionary priests.

73 Copies of all the correspondence between Joseph Raupe, the first missionary priest to visit Petite-Nation, and Joseph Papineau are preserved in the Papineau Papers (BAnQ, AP, P, 5, 49). Together, these letters give a vivid picture of the Ottawa Valley mission in its earliest years.

74 This intricate history is treated more fully in Chamberland, *Histoire de Montebello*, chaps. 9–11

75 M. Brady, Missionaire ambulante à l'évêque, Petite-Nation, November 4, 1838; cited in Chamberland, *Histoire de Montebello*, 171–73.

76 Chamberland, *Historie de Montebollo*, 188.

77 Corespondence between D-B. Papineau and Mgr. de Guiges, Bishop of Bytown, 1850–51, BAnQ, AP, P, 5; see also L-J. Papineau to his son Amédée, January 21, 1851, BAnQ, AP, P, 5, 7 (folder 299).

78 Chamberland, *Histoire de Montbello*, 135.

79 M. Brunet to Mgr. Lartigue, 1838, cited in ibid., 167.

80 "Procès verbal d'une assemblée des habitants de la Paroisse de Notre Dame de Bonsecours, 14 juil. 1844," BAnQ, AP, P, 5, 46. "Cette assemblée est d'opinion qu'en payant les dîmes de patates en sus des dîmes de tout grain, tel que pourvu par la loi, la subsistance du Curé de cette paroisse serait assurée."

81 M. Mignault to Mgr. Guigues, October 18, 1854, cited in Chamberland, *Histoire de Montbello*, 218–19.

82 Ibid., 155.

83 Mgr. Lartigue to D-B. Papineau, Montreal, July 15, 1833, BAnQ, AP, P, 5, 28 (folder 1).

84 There are many references to drunkenness. "Il faut dire," wrote one missionary, "que l'ivrognerie regne en maîtresse" (M. Bourassa a Mgr. de Telenesse, April 10, 1839, cited in Chamberland, *Histoire de Montbello*, 174).

85 *An Ordinance to Prescribe and Regulate the Election and Appointment of Certain Officers in the Several Parishes and Townships in This Province ...*, December 29, 1840; 4 Vic., c. 3; *Ordinances Passed by the Governor and Special Council of Lower Canada*, 1840 and 1841, 9–16. See also 4 Vic., c. 4.

86 In 1833, D-B. Papineau and the priest did attempt to raise money for a school. Although they obtained over forty pounds in subscriptions, the project apparently collapsed (D-B. Papineau to Louis-Joseph Papineau, Petite-Nation, May 17, 1833, BAnQ, AP, P, 5, 29).

87 *Ordinances Passed by the Governor and Special Council of Lower Canada*, 4–5 Vic., c. 18, 1841.

88 "Le goût de l'Education ... n'existe pas dans le classe qui en a le plus besoin ... plusieurs fois des parents ont été assez déraisonnables pour retirer leurs enfants de l'École sans aucune juste raison de plainte contre le maître; quelquefois par animosité à cause de quelque châtiment merité infligé aux enfants; quelquefois par pique personnelle contre quelque commissaire ou Syndic; d'autres fois par un motif ignoble de vengeance, qui les portait à faire tout en leur pouvoir pour faire manquer l'École" (D-B. Papineau to Governor General, Petite-Nation, May 22, 1843, BAnQ, AP, P, 5, 29). "You, nor no one else not being amidst our rural population could ever conceive the extravagant notions which they entertain respecting that Great Bug Bear 'The Tax' [the school tax] and designing Scoundrels are prowling about the Country raising still more the heated minds of the Habitants" (D.M. Armstrong to D-B. Papineau, April 8, 1845, BAnQ, AP, P, 5, 28 [folder A]).

89 L-J. Papineau to D-B. Papineau, September 26, 1846, Chamberland, *Histoire de Montebello*, 193–94. See also letters from Denis-Benjamin to Mgr. de Guiges, Bishop of Bytown, December 18, 1850, and 1851 (more specific date not given), BAnQ, AP, P, 5.

90 9 Vic., c. 27, 1846.

91 D-B. Papineau to Mgr. de Guigues, Bishop of Bytown, 1851, BAnQ, AP, P, 5.

92 In 1843, for example, the following men were parish officials in Petite-Nation. Parish clerk: J.B.N. Papineau. Assessors: Thomas Schryer, Charles Cummings, and Asa Cooke. Collector: Stephen Tucker. Inspector of roads and bridges: Ebenezer Winters. Inspector of the poor: Asa Cooke. Commissioners of schools: Mr. Sterkendries (priest), Asa Cooke, Stephen Tucker, Bazile Charlebois, and Charles Beautron. Road viewers: Jean Lavoie, Henry Baldwin, Antoine Gauthier, Franois Gravelle, Elezear Frappier, and Augustin Belile. Fence and ditch viewers: Louis Chalifoux, Edward Thomas, Paul Sabourin, Daniel Baldwin, Antoine Couillard, and Louis Beautron. "Book of Proceedings of the Civil Corporation of the Seigneurie of Petite-Nation Persuant of the Ordinance of the Special Council of the 4th Victoria, C. 3," BAnQ, AP, P, 5, 46.

93 "Et moi aussi je suis chef de colonie" (L-J. Papineau to Eugene Guillemot, Ex-ministre de France au Brésil, January 10, 1855; printed in Fernand Ouellet, ed., *Papineau* (Quebec: Presses d'Université Laval, 1959), 99.

94 The periods of office of all the elite can best be worked out from the "Book of Proceedings the Civil Corporation," BAnQ, AP, P, 5, 46.

95 Louis-Joseph's wife was especially uneasy about leaving Montreal and competent medical attention. In his later years, Louis-Joseph often took to task this or that member of the family for not spending more time in the seigneurie, where he most loved to be.

96 L-J Papineau to his son Amédée, June 26, 1848, BAnQ, AP, P, 5, 6 (folder 281).

97 L-J. Papineau to Mgr. Guigues, March 29, 1856; printed in Chamberland, *Histoire de Montebello*, 221–22. All these names have since been changed to saints' names.

98 This characterization of Louis-Joseph hardly does justice to the complex, manysided character of the man, although in his later years it is probably the single word that fits him best.

99 The tentative sketch of the social evolution of habitant Quebec that concludes this chapter was based largely on work I undertook after the publication of *The Seigneurial System in Early Canada.*

100 Changes in the rate of the cens et rente after 1760 cannot be described simply. In many seigneuries, they did not change, and in many others changes were spasmodic. As yet there is insufficient evidence to support the claim that English or French seigneurs, as a group, adjusted these changes in a certain way.

101 The Coutume de Paris had provided a base of civil law throughout most of the French regime, but it was a French law, evolved in conditions far different from those in early Canada, and some of its tenets were irrelevant to Canadian life for many years.

102 By the 1820s and 1830s, perhaps even earlier, the parish was undoubtedly a strong institution in rural French Canadian life, and this image of it, as of many aspects of French Canadian life in the early nineteenth century, has been projected back to the French regime.

The Settlement of Mono Township

1 See J.T. Lemon, *The Best Poor Man's Country* (Baltimore: Johns Hopkins University Press, 1972).

2 Nominal Census of Mono Township, 1842, Library and Archives Canada (LAC), reel C-1344.

3 W.H. Smith, *Canada – Past, Present and Future* 2 (1851): 61–62.

4 On the background and nature of nineteenth-century prefamine migration from Ulster, see, particularly, William F. Adams, *Ireland and the Irish Emigration to the New World from 1815 to the Famine* (New Haven, 1932; reprint, New York: Russell and Russell, 1967); S.H. Cousens, "The Regional Variation in Emigration from Ireland between 1821 and 1841," *Transactions of the Institute of British Geographers* 37 (December 1965): 15–29; Conrad Gill, *The Rise of the Irish Linen Industry* (Oxford: Clarendon Press, 1925); and Thomas W. Freeman, *Pre-famine Ireland: A Study in Historical Geography* (Manchester: Manchester University Press, 1956).

5 We are not arguing that these values were peculiar to Ulster; for our purposes, it is sufficient to show that they were widespread there.

6 R.H. Buchanan, "Common Fields and Enclosure: An Eighteenth-Century Example from Lecale, County Down," *Ulster Folklife* 15–16 (1970): 99–118, especially 110.

7 The early nineteenth-century social structure of rural Ulster is not yet well studied; the most perceptive comments are by John Mogey, "Social Relations in Rural Society," in *Ulster since 1800: A Social Survey*, ed. T.W. Moody and J.C. Beckett (BBC: London, 1957). Our remarks depend on his interpretation.

8 Elliott H. Leyton, "Spheres of Inheritance in Aughnaboy," *American Anthropologist* 72, 6 (December 1970): 1378–88.

9 E. Estyn Evans, "The Personality of Ulster," *Transactions of the Institute of British Geographers* 51 (1970): 13.

10 Gill, *The Rise of the Irish Linen Industry,* 23–30.

11 Freeman, *Pre-famine Ireland,* 140.

12 W.J. Smyth, "The Social and Economic Geography of 19th-Century County Armagh" (PhD diss., National University of Ireland, University College, Dublin, 1973), 181.

13 J.H. Johnson, "The Two 'Irelands' at the Beginning of the Nineteenth Century," in *Irish Geographical Studies in Honour of E. Estyn Evans,* ed. Nicholas Stephens and R.E. Glasscock (Belfast: Department of Geography, Queen's University of Belfast, 1970), 224–43.

14 Freeman, *Pre-famine Ireland,* 51.

15 E.R.R. Green, *The Lagan Valley, 1800–1850* (London: Faber and Faber, 1949), especially 59–61.

16 See, for example, Mr. and Mrs. S.C. Hall, *Ireland: Its Scenery, Character, etc.* (London: How and Parson, 1841–43), 2:453; cited in Freeman, *Pre-famine Ireland,* 287.

17 Henry D. Inglis, *Ireland in 1834: A Journey throughout Ireland, during the Spring, Summer and Autumn of 1834* (London: Whittaker and Co., 1835), 2:249–50, cited in Freeman, *Pre-famine Ireland*, 275–76.

18 Freeman, 269–71.

19 Many of the points in this paragraph emerged from discussions with W.J. Smyth and from his PhD thesis on County Armagh. See note 12.

20 An average figure is given in W.H. Smith, *Canadian Gazetteer*, 1846, 118, and there is more detailed information on land values in the Crown Land Papers, Archive of Ontario (AO).

21 In Armagh, for example, only 4.1 percent of all farms were larger than thirty acres (Smyth, "The Social and Economic Geography," 152).

22 Phoenix Diaries, AO, 1871.

23 The common pioneer rotation in south-central Ontario was wheat-fallow-wheat, but in Mono Township, where spring plantings are late and the growing season is short, wheat often did not ripen and oats was widely planted.

24 For a fuller discussion of these points, see Kenneth Kelly, "Wheat Farming in Simcoe County in the Mid-nineteenth Century," *Canadian Geographer* 15 (1971): 95–112. Kelly describes an agricultural system essentially similar to that in Mono.

25 James to David Rintoul, March 3, 1857, in J. Richardson, *The Story of Whittington* (Centennial publication of Whittington village, Amaranth Township, 1967).

26 The increasingly diversified activity of the produce speculators is revealed in advertisements in the Orangeville *Sun*. For example, *The Sun*, October 5, 1865.

27 James to David Rintoul, October 16, 1862.

28 Ibid., June 23, 1858.

29 *The Sun*, July 10, 1867.

30 James to David Rintoul, June 10, 1859.

31 *The Sun*, June 18, 1865.

32 Ibid., August 13, 1868.

33 James to David Rintoul, November 27, 1857.

34 W.F. Munro to Georgie, Horning's Mills, July 7, 1858, AO, W.F. Munro Papers.

35 Submission for George Hopkins, Mono, June 25, 1833, AO, Crown Land Papers, Mono Township, lot 1, 7th concession.

36 W.F. Munro to Georgie, Horning's Mills, June 11, 1858, AO, Munro Papers.

37 James to David Rintoul, December 26, 1865.

38 AO, Crown Land Papers, Mono Township. See, for example, lot 7, 3rd concession, or lot 14, 8th concession.

39 Oath of John Wiley and Joseph Patterson, March 15, 1866, AO, Crown Land Papers, Mono Township, lot 27, 4th concession.

40 The level of literacy among pioneers in Mono can be calculated from the signatures on land records in the Crown Land Papers. If a man signed a document, however badly, he may be considered literate; if he marked it with an "X," he may be considered

illiterate. On this basis, and considering only the first signed document for each lot before 1855, the following results are obtained: literate, ninety-six; illiterate, fifty-six. These figures correspond fairly well with the literacy levels that might be expected in early Mono. In the Irish counties from which settlers had principally come, illiteracy levels in the early nineteenth century were as follows: Armagh, 44 percent; Tyrone, 45 percent; Monaghan, 52 percent. See Freeman, *Pre-famine Ireland,* 136.

41 E. Bowers to the Commissioner of Crown Lands, May 1866, AO, Crown Land Papers, Mono Township, lot 24, 5th concession.

42 Thomas Bell to the Commissioner of Crown Land, July 19, 1849, AO, Crown Land Papers, Mono Township, lot 2, 4th concession.

43 The only way to give some quantitative measure to the rate of failure would be to build up a lot-by-lot inventory of data from the nominal censuses, the abstract index of deeds, the Crown Land Papers, inspection records, and all other sources relating to the progress of settlement in the township.

44 *The Sun,* August 28, 1862.

45 Ibid., October 22, 1874.

46 A sentimental passage in *The Yellow Briar,* John Mitchell's idyll of pioneering and the only literature of any consequence on Mono Township, accurately catches this expectation: "Coming to Canada, these women continued to suffer and endure as their menfolk cut homesteads on these stony hillsides – but there was a touch of hope thrown in ... One of the finest things Canada ever did was to put a kindly twinkle into the blue-grey eyes of those proud, poverty-stricken Irishwomen."

47 This tale is told by several old-timers and is recorded by Mrs. Russell Turnbull in a lively account of the early days. See *Orangeville Banner,* August 10, 1967.

48 James to David Rintoul, March 3, 1857.

49 Barn-raising bees were associated primarily with the large-frame barn (the central Ontario barn), which was built in Mono in the mid-late nineteenth century. The pioneer barn – a log building – was usually erected by the settler and his family.

50 W.F. Munro to Georgie, Horning's Mills, April 17, 1858, AO.

51 Nominal Census of Mono Township, 1861, LAC, reel C-1073.

52 *The Sun,* September 18, 1862. The phrase is used in a letter by John Avison praising two painters who had painted his house "in a manner becoming the progress of the times" and who, therefore, deserved other employment.

53 *The Sun,* July 17 and August 28, 1862.

54 An outstanding overview of this development is given by J.B. Bury, *The Idea of Progress: An Inquiry into Its Origin and Growth* (London: MacMillan, 1920).

55 The range of application is discussed by Arthur Ekirch in *The Idea of Progress in America, 1815–1860* (New York: Columbia University Press, 1944). There is no doubt that settlers in Mono were impressed by the progress of the British Empire; by the progress marked by the erection of a new, transcontinental dominion; and

by the progress of railways, cities, and settlement in southern Ontario and the Middle West. All of this served to fortify the sense of progress that grew out of their experience.

56 For an elaboration of this point, see Rush Welter, "The Idea of Progress in America," *Journal of Historical Ideas* 16 (1955): 401–15.

57 These changes can be established by spot drilling with a soil auger. Professor J. van der Eyk, pedologist in the Department of Geography at the University of Toronto, is thanked for his assistance in this regard.

European Beginnings in the Northwest Atlantic

1 E.P. Thompson, "The Grid of Inheritance," in *Family and Inheritance: Rural Society in Western Europe, 1200–1800,* ed. Jack Goody, Joan Thirsk, and E.P. Thompson (Cambridge: Cambridge University Press, 1976).

2 Cited by Juliet Clutton-Brock, "The Animal Resources," in *The Archaeology of Anglo-Saxon England,* ed. David M. Wilson (London: Methuen, 1976), 391.

3 For an example of the pressure on the forest and of the steps taken to protect it, see E.P. Thompson, *Whigs and Hunters: The Origin of the Black Act* (London: Allen Lane, 1975).

4 The recent literature on early New England emphasizes local variety and the transatlantic persistence of local English ways yet embodies a certain ambivalence. To take one example, in T.H. Breen, *Puritans and Adventurers: Change and Persistence in Early America* (New York: Oxford University Press, 1980), both the persistent localism of early New England and the influence of "the American environment" are stressed.

The Overseas Simplification of Europe

1 This essay owes a special debt to Leonard Guelke, for some of its central ideas coalesced during many discussions and arguments with him, and the section on South Africa depends on his study, "The Early European Settlement of South Africa" (PhD diss., University of Toronto, 1974). The central argument in this essay is adumbrated in R. Cole Harris and Leonard Guelke, "Land and Society in Early Canada and South Africa," *Journal of Historical Geography* 3 (1977): 135–53. Graeme Wynn is thanked for his comments on an earlier draft.

2 Louis Hartz, *The Founding of New Societies* (New York: Harcourt, Brace and World, 1964), 10.

3 Only, it seems to me, with some such model can we begin to develop a comparative historical geography of European overseas settlement. Andrew H. Clark's work is instructive in this regard. Undertaken with some comparative ambition, his work developed without quite asking the questions that could have generated

the data to achieve a comparative analysis. With the exception of James T. Lemon's *The Best Poor Man's Country: Early Southeastern Pennsylvania* (Baltimore, MD: Johns Hopkins University Press, 1972), the same can be said of all the writing by Clark's students on European settlement overseas. Donald Meinig has written a provocative "Macrogeography of Western Imperialism," in *Settlement and Encounter: Geographical Studies Presented to Sir Grenfell Price*, ed. Fay Gale and Graham H. Lawton (Melbourne: Oxford University Press, 1969), 213–40, but we do not have a basis for the rigorous comparison of data from different regions of European overseas expansion, and we do not because we have not asked common questions. Therefore, only the broadest emphases are common to us: an interest, for example, in man and environment or in spatial patterns in colonial settings. If comparative analyses of colonial studies are to be forthcoming, a tighter and more clearly emphasized body of ideas is essential.

4 In the vast debate generated by the frontier thesis there have been surprisingly few attempts to do this, for Turnerians and anti-Turnerians usually sought to defend or demolish Turner's propositions rather than to restate them more accurately. Perhaps they could hardly do otherwise when there were few detailed social studies on two sides of the Atlantic. Only in the last fifteen years or so are local studies of family and society beginning to create a basis for the more accurate interpretation of social change with overseas migration. Accompanying this work is a revived appreciation of the role of environment – so much so that the environment can again become an almost mystical presence. An unusually sharp and, I think, essentially accurate statement is in Chapter 1 of Jackson Turner Main's *The Social Structure of Revolutionary America* (Princeton, NJ: Princeton University Press, 1965), although Main is perhaps unnecessarily tied to a Turnerian frontier vocabulary. The continuing relevance of Turner is powerfully evaluated by Richard Hofstadter in *The Progressive Historians: Turner, Beard, Parrington* (New York: Random House, 1968), particularly 151–64. James A. Henretta, *The Evolution of American Society, 1700–1815: An Interdisciplinary Analysis* (Lexington, MA: D.C. Heath and Co., 1973), 23–31, develops an argument, with which I am in basic agreement, about the extension of an English sense of family into colonial environments.

5 A study by the French demographer Philippe Aries, *L'enfant et la vie familiale sous l'ancien régime* (Paris: Pion, 1960) has generated a huge literature on these topics. I am particularly influenced by Pierre Goubert, "Les cadres de la vie rurale," in *Histoire économique et sociale de la France, 1660–1789*, ed. Fernand Braudel and Ernest Labrousse (Paris: Presses universitaires de France, 1970), particularly 88–89; and by Peter Laslett, *The World We Have Lost*, 2nd ed. (London: Methuen, 1971), and *Household and Family in Past Time* (Cambridge: Cambridge University Press, 1972), particularly the Introduction.

6 This crucial point is at variance with much of the long debate about the different social characteristics of dispersed and agglomerated settlement. Many have con-

sidered that a "collective tradition" was associated with agglomerated settlement and collective agricultural practices, but there is mounting evidence that adherence to individual or collective agriculture depended less on social preference than on economic circumstances. Those with a measure of financial security tended to withdraw from collective agricultural practices whereas poorer and more vulnerable people did not because these practices afforded them some security. The ideal of the nuclear family was widely held, even where "collective constraints" on agricultural individualism remained strong. See particularly Goubert, "Les cadres de la vie rurale," particularly from 107.

7 Joan Thirsk, "Enclosing and Engrossing," chap. 4 in *The Agrarian History of England and Wales*, vol. 4, *1500–1640*, ed. H.P.R. Finberg (Cambridge: Cambridge University Press, 1967), 255. Thirsk asserts that commons and open fields "kept alive a vigourous co-operative spirit in the community," but the fact that no voices were raised to defend the community is surely a measure of the primacy of other values. Writing in the same volume, Alan Everitt points out that enclosure almost always increased the poorer peasant's dependence on his landlord, often turning him into a simple wage labourer. See chap. 7, "Farm Labourers," particularly 408–9.

8 For an effective discussion of the literature on this point, see W.R. Prest, "Stability and Change in Old and New England, Clayworth and Dedham," *Journal of Interdisciplinary History* 6, 3 (1976): 359–74.

9 When or wherever European conditions approached those in New World colonies, similar social responses could be anticipated. Thirteenth- and fourteenth-century plagues drastically reduced the population and depressed agricultural prices and land rents, but in the aftermath of the plagues the real income of ordinary peasants improved, the relative size of the labour force declined, and wealth was more evenly distributed in the countryside. In seventeenth-century England, opportunity for agricultural expansion was greatest in the wooded areas of the Midlands and West. Much as colonial officials inveighed against the insubordination of frontier societies, so many seventeenth-century Englishmen felt that forests harboured "the mean people [who] live lawless, nobody to govern them, they care for nobody, having no dependence on any body": John Aubrey, cited by Joan Thirsk, "The Farming Regions of England," chap. 1 in *The Agrarian History of England and Wales*, 112. The range of income in the woodlands appears to have been considerably less than in the mixed-farming regions to the south and east, where there was not land for agricultural expansion. Fernand Braudel's observation that mountain societies of the Mediterranean rimlands tended to be more independent and egalitarian than those of the plains is also worth keeping in mind. See *The Mediterranean and the Mediterranean World in the Age of Philip II* (New York: Harper and Row, 1972), from 39. Of course, neither woods nor mountains caused independence. In these areas, presumably, land was relatively cheap, and markets were relatively inaccessible, conditions somewhat like those in middle-latitude colonies of Europe overseas.

10 The chronic cost and uncertainty of white labour in colonial settings is a clear economic measure of the attraction of land for European settlers. Even where there was little nonagricultural work, a forest to clear before a farm could be established, and the possibility of returning to Europe, white labour was expensive and would remain so as long as employers had to compete with the accessible alternative of independent farming. Royal shipyards at Quebec near the end of the French regime, for example, always had trouble holding Canadian workers. "As he is a Canadian," wrote the intendant of a blacksmith who wanted to quit, "he prefers his liberty to being subjected to a clock." Cited in Jacques Mathieu, *La construction navale royale* (Quebec: La Société Historique de Québec, 1971), 57. In South Africa the situation was much the same. For Baron Van Imhoff, who inspected the Cape in 1743, it seemed "incredible that a mason and a carpenter each earns from eight to nine schellingen a day and in addition receives food and drink and withal does not do as much as a half-trained artisan in Europe": *Reports of Chavonnes and His Council and of Van Imhoff, on the Cape* (1918), 137, cited in Leonard Guelke, "Frontier Settlement in Early Dutch South Africa," *Annals, Association of American Geographers* 66 (1976): 33. In early New England, Winthrop noted that when the General Court passed wage regulations, labourers "would either remove to other places where they might have more, or else, being able to live by planting and other employments of their own, they would not be hired at all"; cited in S.C. Powell, *Puritan Village: The Formation of a New England Town* (Middletown, CT: Wesleyan University Press, 1963), 130.

11 The most detailed demographic study of one colonial community is Philip J. Greven Jr.'s *Four Generations: Population, Land, and Family in Colonial Andover, Massachusetts* (Ithaca: Cornell University Press, 1970), chap. 2. An excellent short survey of "pathology and the disease environment" in New England and the middle colonies is in Henretta, *The Evolution of American Society*, 9–15. A brief discussion of habitant living standards in early Canada is in R.C. Harris, *The Seigneurial System in Early Canada: A Geographical Study* (Madison: University of Wisconsin Press, 1966), 164–68.

12 Harris, *The Seigneurial System in Early Canada*, 117–19; and Louise Dechêne, *Habitants et marchands de Montréal au XVIIe siècle* (Paris and Montreal: Pion, 1974), part 3, chap. 4.

13 Philippe Guillot, "Etude économique et sociale du front de côte entre Orne et Seulles," in *A travers la Normandie des XVIIe et XVIIIe siècles*, ed. Michel Caillard (Caen: Université de Caen, 1963), 102, for an estimate of land prices in Normandy. On the value of land in Canada, see Harris, *The Seigneurial System in Early Canada*, ix, 57, 62, and 106.

14 Data on South African land prices can be obtained from the Transporten en Schepenkennis volumes (Deeds Office, Cape Town). On land prices in the Netherlands, see Jan de Vries, *The Dutch Rural Economy in the Golden Age* (New

Haven, CT: Yale University Press, 1974), 186–92. In the Netherlands, land improvements due to drainage were included in taxes, an additional financial burden on Dutch farmers.

15 See Petrus Johannes van der Merwe, *Die Trekboer in die geskiendenis van die Kaapkolonie (1657–1842)* (Kaapstad: Nasionale Pers., 1938) for a detailed analysis of the origin and operation of the leeningsplaats system at the Cape. In the early 1730s, the payment was increased to seventy-two guilders. Harris and Guelke, "Land and Society in Early Canada and South Africa," 137–38.

16 William Wood, cited in D.B. Rutman, *Husbandmen of Plymouth, Farms and Villages in the Old Colony, 1620–1692* (Boston: Beacon Press, 1967), 61. Francis Higginson, an important figure in early Salem, was convinced that because of land English poverty would not reappear in New England, where even "little children by setting of Corn may earn more than their own maintenance"; cited by R.P. Gildrie in *Salem, Massachusetts, 1626–1683: A Covenant Community* (Charlottesville: University of Virginia Press, 1975), chap. 1.

17 Main, *The Social Structure of Revolutionary America,* 9.

18 C.S. Grant, *Democracy in the Connecticut Frontier Town of Kent* (New York: Columbia University Press, 1961), 61.

19 Dechêne, *Habitants et marchands,* para. 3, chap. 4 and 521, for the best discussion of prices in early Canada and for a graph of wheat prices.

20 Guelke, "The Early European Settlement of South Africa," 264, 274; and Guelke, "Frontier Settlement in Early Dutch South Africa," 25–42.

21 Richard Bushman, *From Puritan to Yankee: Character and Social Order in Connecticut, 1690–1765* (Cambridge, MA: Harvard University Press, 1967), 30.

22 For a general survey of these later developments, see R. Cole Harris and John Warkentin, *Canada before Confederation* (New York: Oxford University Press, 1974), chap. 3.

23 Dechêne, *Habitants et marchands,* part 3, chap. 2; and Harris, *The Seigneurial System in Early Canada,* chap. 5.

24 This position contrasts sharply with the interpretation of trekboer settlement offered by S.D. Neumark in *Economic Influences on the South African Frontier: 1652–1836* (Stanford, CA: Stanford University Press, 1957). For a critical analysis of Neumark, see Guelke, "Frontier Settlement in Early Dutch South Africa."

25 Guelke, "The Early European Settlement of South Africa," 333.

26 Marcel Trudel, *La population du Canada en 1663* (Montreal: Fides, 1973), 49; also *The Beginning of New France, 1524–1663* (Toronto: McClelland and Stewart, 1973), from 257.

27 Here, my analysis agrees with Jackson Turner Main, *The Social Structure of Revolutionary America,* although I would not emphasize a distinction between "frontier" and "subsistence" society. Far more important is the extent of agricultural commercialization and, related to it, the cost of land. There is not yet a good study of the

relationship between distance and land prices in early New England, although the general nature of the relationship is probably fairly obvious and is frequently hinted at in the literature. For example, Gildrie, *Salem, Massachusetts, 1626–1683*, points out that in the 1640s agricultural land values were rising rapidly on the Salem peninsula but much more slowly farther inland.

28 John Demos, *A Little Commonwealth: Family Life in Plymouth Colony* (New York: Oxford University Press, 1970), points out that because the nuclear family was more transportable than the community, dispersion attacked the community head on. Agreed, but it is also true, as Greven points out in *Four Generations,* that stability as well as dispersion was part of early New England life. Family names stayed in some settlements generation after generation, and there extended family relationships became important parts of the social fabric of closely knit communities. Yet even such communities were built from a base of nuclear families. Most households were not extended, agricultural work was individual rather than collective, and a patriarchal society developed around the heads of individual households. I am not altogether convinced by Greven's arguments about the patriarch's control over his grown sons. Where it made economic sense to wait for an inheritance, the marriage age might have been substantially the same whether fathers were severe or mild. More critical would be their longevity.

29 Darret Rutman points out that in early Plymouth collective agriculture was required by the financial terms worked out with London merchants but that settlers moved away from this "common course and condition" as soon as they could; Rutman, *Husbandmen of Plymouth,* 5–6. All the detailed village studies undertaken so far show the rapid collapse of collective agriculture. On Dedham, see Kenneth A. Lockridge, *A New England Town: The First Hundred Years* (New York: W.W. Norton and Company, 1970); on Sudbury, see Powell, *Puritan Village*; on Andover, see Greven, *Four Generations*. Important recent work, still unpublished, by historical geographers at Clark University (under the direction of Martyn Bowden) and at Pennsylvania State shows that dispersion rather than nucleation was overwhelmingly characteristic of early rural New England. Farm families worked the land individually and settled well apart. Most nucleated villages appeared late in the eighteenth century; the stereotype village on the green became common only by the beginning of the nineteenth century. Interestingly enough, this timing is very close to that along the lower St. Lawrence, where most of the agricultural villages in the older seigneurial lowlands were established within twenty years of 1800.

30 In New England this process has not been well studied, but there is some reference to it in, for example, John J. Waters' treatment of the convergence of East Anglians and West Countrymen, "Highman, Massachusetts, 1631–1661, an East Anglian Oligarchy in the New World," *Journal of Social History* 1 (1968): 351–70; and also in Powell, *Puritan Village*. A good study of the diffusion of vernacular housing would be singularly revealing.

31 On social levelling see, for example, Bushman, *From Puritan to Yankee,* 41.

32 "In communities an ocean apart from England communities which were, likely, several days' travel even from Boston, and communities which had no staple economy – the skills by which one man sustained himself and his family were much the same skills by which other men around him did the same. Few were possessed of anything sufficiently exotic to separate themselves very far from their fellows, and few sought such separation anyway. If political and economic inequality existed, definite social distance did not. Deference in such a society was just a dimly remembered dream from the other country": Michael Zuckerman, *Peaceable Kingdoms: New England Towns in the Eighteenth Century* (New York: Knopf, 1970), 219. See also Norman H. Dawes, "Titles as Symbols of Prestige in Seventeenth-Century New England," *William and Mary Quarterly,* third series, 6 (1949): 69–83. A strenuous attempt was made to maintain titular honours, but soon the niceties of titular designations were blurred or lost. Of course, as the Bergers point out, a sense of honour requires a traditional institutional setting. Weaken the institutional setting and the sense of honour will give way to a sense of dignity stressing individual rights and worth. Peter L. Berger, Brigitte Berger, and Hansfried Kellner, *The Homeless Mind: Modernization and Consciousness* (New York: Random House, 1973), chap. 3.

33 I am not arguing that a social hierarchy had disappeared but that its range had diminished sharply while it became more flexible. Township records contain few references to institutions of English social control (Powell, *Puritan Village,* 182–83), and within New England the power of the General Court gave way to a remarkable town-level autonomy. Within townships where agricultural land was cheap and markets were poor, the economic range was not great. Some men were leaders, and the community imposed certain regulations. A measure of community regulation fostered individual interest (Bushman, *From Puritan to Yankee,* 31), and leadership usually depended less on wealth or inheritance than on personal qualities.

34 In one form or another, this conflict is a central theme in all the township studies mentioned above.

35 Kenneth Lockridge, "Land, Population, and the Evolution of New England Society, 1630–1790," *Past and Present* 39 (1968): 62–80. See also Greven, *Four Generations,* chap. 8. Greven argues that, in Andover, land scarcity increased the percentage of poor and landless without benefitting the rich. Apparently, land prices fell in Andover after 1750, perhaps because of the availability of land elsewhere. However, the long-run implications of scarce land – rising land and falling labour costs – can only have strengthened the position of landowners and employers.

36 Grant, *Democracy in the Connecticut Frontier Town of Kent,* 102.

37 These quotations from Winthrop are cited by Darret B. Rutman in *Winthrop's Boston: Portrait of a Puritan Town, 1630–49* (Chapel Hill: University of North Carolina Press, 1965), chap. 1.

38 Cited in Bushman, *From Puritan to Yankee,* 3.

39 For a thoughtful elaboration of this point, see Northrop Frye, "Conclusion," in *Literary History of Canada: Canadian Literature in English,* ed. C.F. Klinck (Toronto: University of Toronto Press, 1965).

40 Rutman, *Winthrop's Boston,* 243.

41 Both Lockridge and Powell attach too much importance, I feel, to the communal roots of peasant experience. According to Lockridge, "the utopian communities of the select are rooted in the ethos of peasant tradition as much as in Calvinist theology and sectarian purification." In pressing this argument, social disintegration and the assertion of the individual have to be seen as a fundamental break with Old World tradition. The argument returns to Turner's "new man" and to the mystical influence of environment. It is simpler and more accurate to suggest that a common European aspiration had found a setting for its fuller expression.

Creating Place in Early Canada

1 The word "Canada" creates anachronisms that cannot be simply resolved in a discussion ranging across several centuries. Before 1760, Canada was the French colony focused along the St. Lawrence River and extending inland. After the Constitutional Act of 1791, Lower Canada became the southern part of what is modern Quebec and Upper Canada the southern part of Ontario. With Confederation, Canada became the new transcontinental dominion. The word, particularly with "early" attached, can also be used (as in the title above) to indicate the territory that eventually became modern Canada. In this essay, I use "Canada" in all these senses and rely on readers' contextual savvy to figure out which Canada is intended.

2 After its foundation as a trading post some seventy years earlier.

3 See my more ample consideration of observations such as these in *The Reluctant Land: Society, Space, and Environment in Canada before Confederation* (Vancouver: UBC Press, 2008), and *Le pays revêche: Société, espace et environnement au Canada avant la Confédération* (Quebec: Presses de l'Université Laval, 2012).

4 As did the large European cities such as London or Paris.

5 Louise Dechêne, *Le peuple, l'État et la guerre au Canada sous le Régime français* (Montreal: Éditions du Boréal, 2008).

6 Elizabeth Mencke, "Another British America: A Canadian Model for the Early Modern British Empire," *Journal of Imperial and Commonwealth History* 25, 1 (1997): 1–36.

7 Harold Innis, *The Fur Trade in Canada: An Introduction to Canadian Economic History* (New Haven: Yale University Press, 1930); and Harold Innis, *Problems of Staple Production in Canada* (Toronto: Ryerson University Press, 1933).

8 This is American environmental historian Richard White's thesis in *The Middle Ground: Indians, Empires, and Republics in the Great Lakes Region, 1650–1815* (Cambridge: Cambridge University Press, 1991).

9 Maize, he wrote, yielded more than a thousand-fold. Quoted in R.G. Thwaites, ed., preface to and *The Jesuit Relations and Allied Documents,* vol. 69 (Cleveland, OH: Burrows Brothers, 1899), 22.

10 As, considerably, they still do. In more investigated forms, they survive in literature and scholarship.

11 On British patriotism and local regionalism, see Linda Colley, *Britons: Forging the Nation, 1707–1837* (New Haven, CT: Yale University Press, 1992). Even in the early nineteenth century, Colley points out, the British Isles were still a patchwork of regional cultures and identities on which was superimposed a measure of patriotism born of wars and Protestantism.

12 Years ago, I worked out land charges in Canada during the French regime. See R.C. Harris, *The Seigneurial System in Early Canada: A Geographical Study* (Madison: University of Wisconsin Press, 1966). Some years later, Louise Dechêne tackled the matter more thoroughly. See *Habitants et marchands de Montréal au XVIIe siècle* (Paris and Montreal: Pion, 1974). See also Alan Greer, *Peasant, Lord, and Merchant: Rural Society in Three Quebec Parishes, 1740–1840* (Toronto: University of Toronto Press, 1985).

13 John Clarke, *Land, Power, and Economics on the Frontier of Upper Canada* (Montreal/ Kingston: McGill-Queen's University Press, 2001); and Peter A. Russell, "Upper Canada: A Poor Man's Country? Some Statistical Evidence," in *Canadian Papers in Rural History,* ed. D.H. Akenson (Gananoque, ON: Langdale, 1982), 3:129–47.

14 The writer had purchased a partially developed farm; hence its price.

15 Terry McDonald, "A Door of Escape: Letters Home from Wiltshire and Somerset Emigrants to Upper Canada, 1830–1832," in *Canadian Migration Patterns from Britain and North America,* ed. Barbara J. Messamore (Ottawa: University of Ottawa Press, 2004), 103.

16 Marvin McInnis, "Marketable Surpluses in Ontario Farming, 1860," *Social Science History* 8, 4 (1984): 407.

17 Gordon Darroch and Lee Soltow, *Property and Inequality in Victorian Ontario: Structural Patterns and Cultural Communities in the 1871 Census* (Toronto: University of Toronto Press, 1994), 200.

18 Ibid.

19 For a well-known and ideologically inflected Pennsylvanian version of this analysis, see J. Hector St. John Crèvecoeur's frequently reprinted *Letters from an American Farmer* (London: Thomas Davies, 1782), particularly Letter II: "The instant I enter my own land, the bright idea of property, of exclusive right, of independence exalt my mind ... No wonder that so many Europeans who have never been able to say that such portion of land was theirs, cross the Atlantic to realize that happiness" (21).

20 Hubert Charbonneau and Normand Robert, "The French Origins of the Canadian Population, 1608–1759," in *Historical Atlas of Canada,* vol. 1, *From the Beginning*

to 1800, ed. R.C. Harris, cart. G.J. Matthews (Toronto: University of Toronto Press, 1987), plate 45.

21 Associating urbanité with conservative social reproduction in the towns of New France, and territorialité with social change in the countryside, Serge Courville offers an analysis fairly similar to mine. See Serge Courville, "Espace, territoire, et culture en Nouvelle-France: Une vision géographique," *Revue d'histoire de l'Amérique française* 37, 3 (1983): 417–29.

22 On Heidegger as a philosopher of place, see Jeff Malpas, *Heidegger's Topology: Being, Place, World* (Cambridge, MA: MIT Press, 2006).

23 Karl Marx, *The German Ideology* (London: Lawrence and Wishart, 1965).

24 Karl Marx, *Capital*, ed. Friedrich Engels, trans. Samuel Moore, Edward Aveling, Marie Sachey, and Herbert Lamm, Great Books of the Western World, vol. 50 (Chicago: Encyclopedia Britannica, 1952), 381.

25 Ibid., 383.

26 French civil law provided for the partible inheritance of land held *en censive* (at the lowest rank of the feudal hierarchy), and in law, therefore, the son who took over the family farm assumed debts to his siblings for their equal shares of its value.

27 Henry David Thoreau, "Walking," in *The Major Essays of Henry David Thoreau*, ed. Richard Dillman (Albany: Whitston, 2001), 169–70.

28 Michael B. Katz, Michael J. Doucette, and Mark J. Stern emphasize the transience of the industrial workforce and its large number of recent immigrants in *The Social Organization of Early Industrial Capitalism* (Cambridge, MA: Harvard University Press, 1982), 131–57.

29 Samuel V. LaSelva, *The Moral Foundations of Canadian Federalism: Paradoxes, Achievements, and Tragedies of Nationhood* (Montreal/Kingston: McGill-Queen's University Press, 1996), 38.

The Struggle with Distance

1 Among the most imposing of this literature are Edward W. Said, *Orientalism* (New York: Vintage, 1979); Edward W. Said, *Culture and Imperialism* (New York: Vintage 1994); Homi K. Bhabha, ed., *Nation and Narration* (London: Routledge, 1990); Homi K. Bhabha, *The Location of Culture* (London: Routledge, 1994); Gayatri Chakravorty Spivak, *In Other Worlds: Essays in Cultural Politics* (London: Routledge, 1988); Gayatri Chakravorty Spivak, *The Post-colonial Critic: Interviews, Strategies, Dialogues* (London: Routledge, 1990); and Robert Young, *White Mythologies: Writing History and the West* (London: Routledge, 1990). A striking engagement with some of these ideas in British Columbia is Daniel Clayton's "Islands of Truth: Vancouver Island from Captain Cook to the Beginning of Colonialism" (PhD diss., University of British Columbia, 1995).

2 Innis's main writing is collected and his thought summarized in Harold Adams Innis and Daniel Drache, ed., *Staples, Markets, and Cultural Change: Selected Essays* (Montreal/Kingston: McGill-Queen's University Press, 1995).

3 Daniel R. Headrick, *The Tools of Empire: Technology and European Imperialism in the Nineteenth Century* (New York: Oxford University Press, 1981); and Daniel R. Headrick, *The Tentacles of Progress: Technology Transfer in the Age of Imperialism, 1850–1940* (New York: Oxford University Press, 1988).

4 Among the large literature on this topic, see particularly Stephen Kern, *The Culture of Time and Space, 1880–1918* (Cambridge, MA: Harvard University Press, 1983), chaps. 8 and 9; and Said, *Orientalism*, particularly chap. 1, parts 1 and 2.

5 See Neil Smith, *Uneven Development: Nature, Capital and the Production of Space* (Oxford: Basil Blackwell, 1984), 102–5.

6 Harold A. Innis, *The History of the Canadian Pacific Railway* (London: P.S. King and Son, 1923), 139; J.H. Hamilton, "The 'All-Red Route,' 1893–1953: A History of the Trans-Pacific Mail Service between British Columbia, Australia, and New Zealand," *British Columbia Historical Quarterly* 20 (January–April 1956): 1–126.

7 Said, *Orientalism*, 92.

8 See, particularly, Michel Foucault, *Discipline and Punish: The Birth of the Prison* (New York: Vintage, 1979).

9 Gilles Deleuze and Félix Guattari, *Anti-Oedipus: Capitalism and Schizophrenia*, trans. Robert Hurley, Mark Seem, and Helen R. Lane (New York: Viking, 1977).

10 David Harvey, *The Limits to Capital* (Oxford: Basil Blackwell, 1982).

11 David Harvey, *The Condition of Postmodernity: An Enquiry into the Origins of Cultural Change* (Oxford: Basil Blackwell, 1989), 238.

12 For a fuller summary of Deleuze and Guattari's thinking about desire, capitalism, and spatiality, see Robert J.C. Young, *Colonial Desire: Hybridity in Theory, Culture, and Race* (London: Routledge, 1995), especially 166–74.

13 Jean and John Comaroff, *Of Revelation and Revolution: Christianity, Colonialism, and Consciousness in South Africa*, vol. 1 (Chicago: University of Chicago Press, 1991), 309–14.

14 In some cases, Indigenous people adapted very quickly. In 1866, less than two years after the telegraph arrived, Nlaka'pamux people sent a telegram in Chinook to the Anglican missionary J.B. Good at Yale, inviting him to establish a mission at Lytton. Good went, interpreting the telegram as a call from God. Brett Christophers, "Time, Space and the People of God: Anglican Colonialism in Nineteenth Century British Columbia" (master's thesis, University of British Columbia, 1995).

15 Richard Mackie, *Trading Beyond the Mountains: The British Fur Trade on the Pacific, 1793–1843* (Vancouver: UBC Press, 1997).

16 Consider the analogous relationship of St. Louis and Chicago, admirably described by William Cronon in *Nature's Metropolis: Chicago and the Great West* (New York: W.W. Norton, 1997), 295–309.

17 As subsequent events in British Columbia have shown, colonial theorist Robert Young is correct in saying that prior cultures were not so much destroyed as layered over, and the layers increasingly imbricated with each other. See Young, *Colonial Desire*, 174.

18 Kay Anderson, *Vancouver's Chinatown: Racial Discourse in Canada, 1875–1990* (Montreal/Kingston: McGill-Queen's University Press, 1991).

19 Said, *Orientalism*, 93.

Indigenous Space

1 See, for example, J.M. Bumsted, *The People's Clearance: Highland Emigration to North America 1770–1815* (Edinburgh: Edinburgh University Press, 1982); James Hunter, *The Making of the Crofting Community* (Edinburgh: John Donald, 1976); and S.J. Hornsby, *Nineteenth-Century Cape Breton: A Historical Geography* (Montreal/Kingston: McGill-Queen's University Press, 1992).

2 E.P. Thompson, *Whigs and Hunters: The Origin of the Black Act* (New York: Pantheon, 1975), 207.

3 Ibid., 241.

4 For a magisterial survey of these issues in Britain and overseas, see Thompson's essay "Custom, Law and Common Right," in his *Customs in Common* (London: Merlin, 1991).

5 A vivid discussion of such changes in the American South is provided by Richard White in *The Roots of Dependency: Subsistence, Environment, and Social Change among the Choctaws, Pawnees, and Navajos* (Lincoln: University of Nebraska Press, 1983).

6 J.M. Neeson, "The Opponents of Enclosure in Eighteenth-Century Northamptonshire," *Past and Present* 105 (1984): 138.

7 For a discussion of the application of such rhetoric to Spanish American society, see Mary Louise Pratt, *Imperial Eyes: Travel Writing and Transculturation* (London: Routledge, 1992), chap. 7.

8 Michel Foucault, *Discipline and Punish: The Birth of the Prison*, trans. Alan Sheridan (New York: Vintage, 1979). Originally published as *Surveiller et punir: Naissance de la prison* (Paris: Gallimard, 1975).

9 Ibid., 203, also 143.

10 Ibid., 219.

11 Frantz Fanon, *The Wretched of the Earth*, trans. Constance Farrington (New York: Grove Press, 1963). Originally published as *Les damnés de la terre* (Paris: François Maspero, 1961). Fanon, however, attributed the compartmentalization of colonized societies basically to violence rather than to a decentred disciplinary regime operating through myriad local capillaries.

12 Foucault, *Discipline and Punish*, 294–95.

13 Ibid., 303.

14 There were many residential schools, of course, and different modes of instruction therein. Not all drew on the type of procedures that Foucault associated with Mettray. For a discussion of a much more permissive residential schooling, see Paige Raibmon, "'A New Understanding of Things Indian': George Raley's Negotiation of the Residential School Experience," *BC Studies* 110 (1996): 69–96.

15 On surveillance by Oblate (Roman Catholic) priests, see, for example, Margaret Whitehead, *They Call Me Father: Memoirs of Father Nicolas Coccola* (Vancouver: UBC Press, 1988), especially 15–16; Elizabeth Furniss, "Resistance, Coercion, and Revitalization: The Shuswap Encounter with Roman Catholic Missionaries, 1860–1900," *Ethnohistory* 42 (1995): 231–63; and Lynn A. Blake, "Let the Cross Take Possession of the Earth: Missionary Geographies of Power in Nineteenth-Century British Columbia" (PhD diss., University of British Columbia, 1997). On Anglican practices in this regard, see Brett Christophers, *Positioning the Missionary: John Booth Good and the Confluence of Cultures in Nineteenth-Century British Columbia* (Vancouver: UBC Press, 1998), 103–4.

16 Foucault, *Discipline and Punish*, 306–7.

17 Ibid., 290–92.

18 Simon Ryan, *The Cartographic Eye: How Explorers Saw Australia* (Cambridge: Cambridge University Press, 1996). Also Kenneth Brealey, "Travels from Point Ellice: Peter O'Reilly and the Indian Reserve System in British Columbia," *BC Studies* 115–16 (1997–98): particularly 182–84; and Kenneth Brealey, "Mapping Them 'Out': Euro-Canadian Cartography and the Appropriation of the Nuxalk and Ts'ilhqot'in First Nations' Territories, 1793–1916," *Canadian Geographer* 39 (1995): particularly 149–50.

19 This regime of decentred surveillance, backed by the law, and the management of movement associated with it, was not implanted immediately. Gilbert Malcolm Sproat, Indian reserve commissioner, warned in 1878 that settlers who stood on their legal rights to land might not be permitted by Indigenous people to exercise them. "A government, of course, is supposed to protect the legal rights of citizens, but we all know that in the upper country a practical view has at present been taken of this Gov't obligation, so far as Indians are concerned in some places at any rate." Sproat to John Clapperton [Justice of the Peace, Nicola], May 19, 1878, Library and Archives Canada (LAC), Sproat Letterbooks, 2, Federal Collection, I, 117–18.

20 Seton Lake hearings, November 5, 1914, LAC, RG 10, vol. 11025, file AH7, 18–40 (reel T-3963).

21 Lillooet hearings, November 4, 1914, ibid., 4–17.

22 Bridge River hearings, November 7, 1914, ibid., 62.

23 Fountain hearings, November 9, 1914, ibid., 70–73.

24 Ashcroft hearings, November 1, 1913, LAC, RG 10, vol. 11024, file AH4, 737ff (reel T-3962).

25 Johnny Chillihecha to Mr. Shaw and Associates, Douglas Lake, October 23, 1913, LAC, RG 10, vol. 11021, file 524B, 496–501 (reel T-3958).

26 Koskimo hearings, May 26, 1914, LAC, RG 10, vol. 11025, file AH6, 1020ff (reel T-3962).

27 Alert Bay hearings, June 1, 1914, ibid., from 1102.

28 Coldwater hearings, October 17, 1913, ibid., from 836.

29 Fanon, *Wretched of the Earth*, 39. Fanon writes that the first thing a colonized Indigenous person learns is to stay in one's place in a hemmed-in world (52).

Making an Immigrant Society

An earlier draft benefitted from comments by Brett Christophers, Daniel Clayton, Jeanne Kay, Audrey Kobayashi, Nadine Schuurman, and Graeme Wynn.

1 Derived from Ethel Wilson, *The Innocent Traveller* (Toronto: Macmillan, 1949).

2 Derived from Nan Bourgeon, *Rubber Boots for Dancing and Other Memories of Pioneer Life in the Bulkley Valley* (Smithers, BC: T. and J. Hetherington, 1979).

3 Derived from Denise Chong, *The Concubine's Children* (Toronto: Penguin, 1994).

4 This literature focuses on the colonized and on European attitudes towards them and seldom deals with the most successful of all colonizing strategies: the creation of new societies made up of the colonizers. For an anthropological response to these issues, see Ann Laura Stoler, "Rethinking Colonial Categories: European Communities and the Boundaries of Rule," *Comparative Studies in Society and History* 31, 1 (1989): 134–61. The geographer Derek Gregory provides a broad discussion of current orientations in the literature on colonialism/resistance in *Geographical Imaginations* (Cambridge and Oxford: Blackwelll, 1994), particularly 168–203.

5 For example, Jack Hodgins, *The Invention of the World: A Novel* (Toronto: Macmillan, 1977).

6 This terminology is from Gilles Deleuze and Félix Guattari, *Anti-Oedipus: Capitalism and Schizophrenia*, trans. Robert Hurley, Mark Seem, and Helen R. Lane (New York: Viking, 1977).

7 For a fairly straightforward elaboration of this position, see Anthony Giddens, *The Constitution of Society: Outline of the Theory of Structuration* (Berkeley and Los Angeles: University of California Press, 1984).

8 The word "simplification" has caused problems in the past, but I cannot find an acceptable alternative. I do not mean that New World societies were somehow simpler than Old World societies, a proposition that can hardly be analyzed and that is intuitively implausible. I use the word to refer to the paring back of, or the deletions from, particular Old World traditions that occurred with migration and resettlement. Only elements of the ways of one setting were reproduced in another. Against this "simplification" of particular traditions were the many new experiences

and relationships that immigrants encountered in new settings. In short order, an immigrant society became another creation, probably neither simpler nor more complex than its Old World antecedents, but clearly different. I suggest that the character of such societies had a good deal to do with the loss (simplification) of a great many Old World ways, and the incorporation of many new ways associated with a new setting broadly conceived.

9 Edward Gibbon Wakefield, *A View of the Art of Colonization, with Present Reference to the British Empire; in Letters between a Statesman and a Colonist* (London: J.W. Parker, 1849). Among the most astute comments on Wakefield are those by his near contemporary Herman Merivale, *Lectures on Colonization and the Colonies* (London: Longman, Green, Longman, and Roberts, 1861). Turner's famous article "The Significance of the Frontier in American History," published in 1893, dominated two generations of American historiography. Turner's frontier was a complex, somewhat mystical space where, following one of his most central metaphors, free land emphasized a changed and far more accessible relationship with property.

10 Louis Hartz, *The Founding of New Societies* (New York: Harcourt, Brace and World, 1964).

11 Cole Harris, "The Simplification of Europe Overseas," *Annals of the Association of American Geographers* 67, 4 (December 1977): 469–83; and "European Beginnings in the Northwestern Atlantic: A Comparative View," in *Seventeenth-Century New England*, ed. David D. Hall and David G. Allen (Boston: Colonial Society of Massachusetts, 1984), 119–52.

12 R. Byron Johnson, *Very Far West Indeed: A Few Rough Experiences in the Northwest Pacific Coast* (London: S. Low, Marston, Low and Searle, 1872), chap. 9.

13 For general accounts of the changed gendering of places of work and residence, see Barbara Laslett, "Gender and Social Production: Historical Perspectives," *Annual Review of Sociology* 15 (1989): 381–404; and Gillian Rose, *Feminism and Geography: The Limits of Geographical Knowledge* (Minneapolis: University of Minnesota Press, 1993), chap. 2.

14 On the domestic image of women in the imperial imagination, see Anna Davin, "Imperialism and Motherhood," in *Patriotism: The Making and Unmaking of British National Identity*, ed. Raphael Samuel, vol. 1 (London: Routledge, 1989); Anne McClintock, *Imperial Leather: Race, Gender and Sexuality in the Colonial Context* (New York: Routledge, 1995); and, more specifically on British Columbia, Adele Perry, "'Oh I'm Just Sick of the Faces of Men': Gender Imbalance, Race, Sexuality, and Sociability in Nineteenth-Century British Columbia," *BC Studies* 105–6 (Spring-Summer 1995): 27–45. For an example of the frontier male tendency to put women on a pedestal of civility, see Gordon Gibson, *Bull of the Woods* (Vancouver: Douglas and McIntyre, 1980), esp. chap. 1.

15 In his novel *Woodsmen of the West* (Toronto: Edward Arnold, 1908; reprint, Toronto: McClelland and Stewart, 1964), M.A. Grainger describes the confident,

never-say-can't attitude of western labour, what he calls "Western Spirit," an attitude formed where extended apprenticeships and close surveillance were out of the question.

16 Nelson Riis, "The Walhachin Myth: A Study of Settlement Abandonment," *BC Studies* 17 (1973): 3–25.

17 On the missionary politics of space, see Jean and John Comaroff, *Of Revelation and Revolution: Christianity, Colonialism, and Consciousness in South Africa* (Chicago: University of Chicago Press, 1991), chap. 6. More specifically, Jean Usher, *William Duncan of Metlakatla: A Victorian Missionary in British Columbia* (Ottawa: National Museums of Canada, 1974); and Brett Christophers, "Time, Space, and the Judgement of God: Anglican Missionary Discourse in British Columbia" (master's thesis, University of British Columbia, 1995).

18 "Imaginative geography of the 'our land-barbarian land' variety does not require that the barbarians acknowledge the distinction. It is enough for 'us' to set up these boundaries in our own minds; 'they' become 'they' accordingly, both their territory and their mentality are designated as different from 'ours.'" Edward Said, *Orientalism* (New York: Vintage, 1979), 54. Said suggests that the power of this simple "imaginative geography and of the dramatic boundaries it draws" has been enormous.

19 Address of His Excellency the Governor to the Inhabitants at Fort Yale, September 12, 1858, BC Archives (BCA), Douglas Papers.

20 For an admirable discussion of this evolution, see Catherine Hall, "Imperial Man: Edward Eyre in Australasia and the West Indies 1833–66," in *The Expansion of England: Race, Ethnicity and Cultural History*, ed. Bill Schwartz (London: Routledge, 1996). Also, Comaroff and Comaroff, *Of Revelation and Revolution*, chap. 3; and Robert J.C. Young, *Colonial Desire: Hybridity in Theory, Culture, and Race* (London: Routledge, 1995), chap. 2.

21 Kay Anderson, *Vancouver's Chinatown: Racial Discourse in Canada, 1875–1980* (Montreal/Kingston: McGill-Queen's University Press, 1991). Anderson is right about the territorial ambitions of white racist attitudes, but she discounts Chinese agency, which may have been more active than she allows in the making of Chinatowns.

22 As a young man, Teit became an associate of Franz Boas; out of this association, plus his marriage to a Nlaka'pamux woman, came a series of magnificent ethnographies of the Interior Salish, still the standard works. Teit, a Shetland Islander and a socialist, never identified with mainstream white British Columbia and, fluent in several Interior Salish languages, admired Indigenous societies and was a confidante of many Indigenous people.

23 G. Bramhall, "That They Might Have Life: An Autobiography of the Late Stanley E. Higgs," BCA, AMS 1332.

24 Young, *Colonial Desire*, 174. As I pointed out above, the postcolonial literature largely ignores European settlement overseas; as a result, the literature is prone to

statements such as Young's, which, for all their authors' intentions to the contrary, embody a form of orientalism.

How Did Colonialism Dispossess?

The preparation of this essay has greatly benefitted from comments by Karen Bakker, Trevor Barnes, Nicholas Blomley, Bruce Braun, Daniel Clayton, Douglas Harris, Robert Mitchell, Geraldine Pratt, Robert Wilson, and Graeme Wynn. Versions of it were presented, to my great benefit, to the Department of Geography at the University of California, Los Angeles (Alexander von Humboldt Lecture), and to the Faculty of Law at the University of Victoria (McLean Lecture).

1 Michel Foucault, *The Archaeology of Knowledge and the Discourse on Language* (New York: Pantheon Books, 1972). Originally published as *L'archéologie du savoir* (Paris: Gallimard, 1969).

2 Edward Said, *Orientalism* (New York: Vintage, 1979).

3 Frantz Fanon, *The Wretched of the Earth* (New York: Grove Press, 1963). Originally published as *Les damnés de la terre* (Paris: F. Maspero, 1961).

4 For example, Nicholas Thomas, *Colonialism's Culture: Anthropology, Travel and Government* (Princeton, NJ: Princeton University Press, 1994).

5 Catherine Hall, *Cultures of Empire: A Reader* (Manchester: Manchester University Press, 2000), 5.

6 Dipesh Chakrabarty, *Provincializing Europe: Postcolonial Thought and Historical Difference* (Princeton, NJ: Princeton University Press, 2000), 16.

7 Peter Hulme, "Including America," *Ariel* 26, 1 (1995): 117–23; and Thomas, *Colonialism's Culture*, 172–73.

8 Patrick Wolfe, *Settler Colonialism and the Transformation of Anthropology: The Politics and Poetics of an Ethnographic Event* (London: Cassell, 1999), 1.

9 Ranajit Guha, *Dominance without Hegemony: History and Power in Colonial India* (Cambridge, MA: Harvard University Press, 1997).

10 For example, Stephen Slemon, "The Scramble for Post-colonialism," in *De-Scribing Empire: Post-Colonialism and Textuality*, ed. C. Tiffin and A. Lawson (London: Routledge, 1994), 15–32; and Anne McClintock, "The Angel of Progress: Pitfalls of the Term 'Postmodernism,'" in *Colonial Discourse/Postcolonial Theory*, ed. F. Barker, P. Hulme, and M. Iversen (Manchester: Manchester University Press, 1994), 253–66.

11 Benita Parry, "The Postcolonial: Conceptual Category or Chimera?," *Yearbook of English Studies* 27 (1997): 3–21.

12 Daniel Clayton, "Colonialism, Culture and the 'Postcolonial Turn' in Geography," in *A Companion to Cultural Geography*, ed. J. Duncan, N. Johnson, and R. Schein (Oxford: Blackwell, 2003), 447–68.

13 Felix Driver, *Geography Militant: Cultures of Exploration and Empire* (Oxford: Blackwell, 2001).

14 Frank Tough, "As Their Natural Resources Fail": Native Peoples and the Economic History of Northern Manitoba, 1870–1930 (Vancouver: UBC Press, 1996).

15 Derek Gregory, Explorations in Critical Human Geography, Hettner Lecture 1997 (Heidelberg: University of Heidelberg, 1998), 21.

16 Robert J.C. Young, Postcolonialism: An Historical Introduction (Oxford: Blackwell, 2001), 16–17.

17 For example, Daniel Clayton, Islands of Truth: The Imperial Fashioning of Vancouver Island (Vancouver: UBC Press, 2000); and Alan Lester, Imperial Networks: Creating Identities in Nineteenth-Century South Africa and Britain (London: Routledge, 2001).

18 Edward Said, Culture and Imperialism (New York: Vintage, 1994), 78.

19 Fanon, Wretched of the Earth, 37–40.

20 Wolfe, Settler Colonialism, 1–3.

21 Cole Harris, Making Native Space: Colonialism, Resistance, and Reserves in British Columbia (Vancouver: UBC Press, 2002).

22 Bruno Latour, Science in Action: How to Follow Scientists and Engineers through Society (Cambridge, MA: Harvard University Press, 1987), chap. 6.

23 Clayton, Islands of Truth.

24 Ibid., 236.

25 Harris, Making Native Space, 15–16.

26 Ibid., chap. 6; and James R. Gibson, Otter Skins, Boston Ships, and China Goods: The Maritime Fur Trade of the Northwest Coast, 1745–1841 (Montreal/Kingston: McGill-Queen's University Press, 1992), 163, 170.

27 Harris, Resettlement, chap. 2.

28 Barry M. Gough, Gunboat Frontier: British Maritime Authority and Northwest Coast Indians, 1846–1890 (Vancouver: UBC Press, 1984).

29 Harris, Making Native Space, 206.

30 Henry George Grey, The Colonial Policy of Lord John Russell's Administration, vol. 1 (London: Richard Bentley, 1853), letter 1.

31 Thomas R. Metcalf, Ideologies of the Raj (Cambridge: Cambridge University Press, 1996); and Andrew Porter, "Trusteeship, Anti-slavery, and Humanitarianism," in The Oxford History of the British Empire, vol. 3, The Nineteenth Century, ed. A. Porter (Oxford: Oxford University Press, 1999), 198–221.

32 Harris, Making Native Space, 108.

33 For example, Patricia Seed, Ceremonies of Possession in Europe's Conquest of the New World, 1492–1640 (Cambridge: Cambridge University Press, 1995); Peter Hulme and Ludmilla Jordanova, The Enlightenment and Its Shadows (New York: Routledge, 1990); Stephen Buckle, Natural Law and the Theory of Property: Grotius to Hume (Oxford: Clarendon Press, 1991); and Barbara Arneil, John Locke and America: The Defence of English Colonialism (Oxford: Clarendon Press, 1996).

34 John Locke, "An Essay Concerning the True Original Extent and End of Civil Government," reprinted in *Social Contract: Essays by Locke, Hume, and Rousseau,* ed. Sir E. Barker (London: Oxford University Press, [1690] 1947), chap. 5.

35 Michael Adas, *Machines as the Measure of Men: Science, Technology, and Ideologies of Western Dominance* (Ithaca, NY: Cornell University Press, 1989).

36 Daniel R. Headrick, *The Tools of Empire: Technology and European Imperialism in the Nineteenth Century* (New York: Oxford University Press, 1981).

37 Mark Francis, "The 'Civilizing' of Indigenous People in Nineteenth-Century Canada," *Journal of World History* 9, 1 (1998): 51–87.

38 Robert Galois and Cole Harris, "A Population Geography of British Columbia in 1881," *Canadian Geographer* 38, 1 (1994): 43–60.

39 David Harvey, *The Condition of Postmodernity: An Enquiry into the Origins of Cultural Change* (Oxford: Basil Blackwell, 1989), 264.

40 Karl Marx, *Capital,* trans. from 3rd German ed. (New York: International Publishers, 1967), part 8, chap. 27.

41 Ibid.

42 Gilles Deleuze and Félix Guattari, *Anti-Oedipus: Capitalism and Schizophrenia,* trans. R. Hurley, M. Seem, and H.R. Lane (New York: Viking Press, 1977). Originally published as *Capitalisme et schizophrénie,* vol. 1 (Paris: Editions de Minuit, 1972).

43 Thomas, *Colonialism's Culture,* 171–72.

44 Henri Lefebvre, *The Production of Space* (Oxford: Basil Blackwell, 1991); and Neil Smith, *Uneven Development: Nature, Capital and the Production of Space* (Oxford: Basil Blackwell, 1990), 90.

45 David Harvey, *The Limits to Capital* (Oxford: Basil Blackwell, 1982), chap. 13, and "The Geopolitics of Capitalism," in *Social Relations and Spatial Structures,* ed. D. Gregory and J. Urry (London: Macmillan, 1985), 150, 156.

46 Harris, *Making Native Space,* 241.

47 James Hunter, *The Making of the Crofting Community* (Edinburgh: John Donald, 1976); and Stephen J. Hornsby, *Nineteenth-Century Cape Breton: A Historical Geography* (Montreal/Kingston: McGill-Queen's University Press, 1992), chap. 2.

48 E.P. Thompson, *Whigs and Hunters: The Origin of the Black Act* (New York: Pantheon, 1975), 241.

49 Jeanette Neeson, "The Opponents of Enclosure in Eighteenth-Century Northamptonshire," *Past and Present* 105 (1984): 138; and M. Huitema, B. Osborne, and M. Ripmeester, "Imagined Spaces, Constructed Boundaries, Conflicting Claims: A Legacy of Postcolonial Conflict in Eastern Ontario," *International Journal of Canadian Studies* 25 (2002): 87–112.

50 Mary Louise Pratt, *Imperial Eyes: Travel Writing and Transculturation* (London: Routledge, 1992), chap. 7.

51 Marx, *Capital,* part 8, chap. 33.

52 Harris, *Resettlement*, chap. 8.

53 Wolfe, *Settler Colonialism*, 2.

54 Herman Merivale, *Lectures on Colonization and Colonies Delivered before the University of Oxford in 1839, 1840, & 1841, and reprinted in 1851* (London: Oxford University Press, 1928), lecture xviii.

55 Gilbert Malcolm Sproat, *Scenes and Studies of Savage Life* (London: Smith, Elder, 1868).

56 Ibid., chap. 1.

57 James C. Scott, *Seeing Like a State: How Certain Schemes to Improve the Human Condition Have Failed* (New Haven, CT: Yale University Press, 1998).

58 Michel Foucault, "Governmentality," in *The Foucault Effect: Studies in Governmentality*, ed. G. Burchell, C. Gordon, and P. Miller (Chicago: University of Chicago Press, 1991); and Matthew G. Hannah, *Governmentality and the Mastery of Territory in Nineteenth-Century America* (Cambridge: Cambridge University Press, 2000), chap. 1.

59 Kenneth Brealey, "First (National) Space: (Ab)original (Re)mappings of British Columbia" (PhD diss., University of British Columbia, 2002), 10; Simon Ryan, *The Cartographic Eye: How Explorers Saw Australia* (Cambridge: Cambridge University Press, 1996); and M. Huietma, B. Osborne, and M. Ripmeester, "Imagined Spaces, Constructed Boundaries, Conflicting Claims: A Legacy of Postcolonial Conflict in Eastern Ontario," *International Journal of Canadian Studies* 25 (2002): 87–112.

60 Bruce Braun, *The Intemperate Rainforest: Nature, Culture, and Power on Canada's West Coast* (Minneapolis: University of Minnesota Press, 2002), chap. 2.

61 Cited in Harris, *Making Native Space*, 204–5; and Matthew H. Edney, *Mapping an Empire: The Geographical Construction of British India, 1765–1843* (Chicago: University of Chicago Press, 1997).

62 British Columbia, Royal Commission on Indian Affairs, *Report of the Royal Commission on Indian Affairs for the Province of British Columbia* (Victoria: Acme Press, 1916).

63 Theodore M. Porter, *Trust in Numbers: The Pursuit of Objectivity in Science and Public Life* (Princeton, NJ: Princeton University Press, 1995), ix.

64 Don Mitchell, "The Annihilation of Space by Law: The Roots and Implications of Anti-homeless Laws in the United States," in *The Legal Geographies Reader*, ed. N. Blomley, D. Delaney, and R. Ford (Oxford: Blackwell, 2001), 6–18.

65 Douglas C. Harris, *Fish, Law, and Colonialism: The Legal Capture of the Aboriginal Fishery in British Columbia* (Toronto: University of Toronto Press, 2001), 49–55.

66 Nicholas K. Blomley, *Law, Space, and the Geographies of Power* (New York: Guilford Press, 1994), chap. 1.

67 John L. Comaroff, "Colonialism, Culture, and the Law: A Foreword," *Journal of the American Bar Foundation* 26, 2 (2001): 309.

68 Pierre Bourdieu, "The Force of Law: Toward a Sociology of the Juridical Field," *Hastings Law Journal* 38 (1987): 814–53.

69 Blomley, *Law, Space,* chap. 3.

70 S.F.C. Milsom, *Historical Foundations of the Common Law* (London: Butterworths, 1969); J.H. Baker, *An Introduction to English Legal History,* 2nd ed. (London: Butterworths, 1971); and Harold J. Berman, *Law and Revolution: The Formation of the Western Legal Tradition* (Cambridge, MA: Harvard University Press, 1983).

71 William Blackstone, *Commentaries on the Laws of England in Four Books,* 15th ed. (London: A. Strahan, [1765] 1809), 138.

72 Jürgen Habermas, *The Theory of Communicative Action,* vol. 2, *Lifeworld and System: A Critique of Functionalist Reason* (Boston: Beacon Press, 1989), part 6.

73 Hamar Foster, "'The Queen's Law is Better Than Yours': International Homicide in Early British Columbia," in *Essays in the History of Canadian Law,* vol. 4, *Crime and Criminal Justice,* ed. J. Phillips, T. Loo, and S. Lewthwaite (Toronto: University of Toronto Press, 1981), 41–111.

74 Michel Foucault, *Discipline and Punish: The Birth of the Prison* (New York: Vintage, 1979), 141. Originally published as *Surveiller et punir: Naissance de la prison* (Paris: Gallimard, 1975).

75 Paul Tennant, *Aboriginal Peoples and Politics: The Indian Land Question in British Columbia, 1849–1989* (Vancouver: UBC Press, 1990).

76 Hamar Foster, "Letting Go the Bone: The Idea of Indian Title in British Columbia, 1846–1927," in *Essays in the History of Canadian Law,* vol. 6, *British Columbia and the Yukon,* ed. H. Foster and J. McLaren (Toronto: Osgoode Society for Canadian Legal History/University of Toronto Press, 1995).

77 Harris, *Making Native Space,* 133–34.

78 Comaroff, "Colonialism, Culture, and the Law," 306–7.

Postscript: The Boundaries of Settler Colonialism

This postscript has greatly benefitted from comments and suggestions from Trevor Barnes, Daniel Clayton, Julie Cruikshank, Douglas Harris, Conrad Heidenreich, Stephen Hornsby, Samuel LaSelva, Frank Tester, Wendy Wickwire, and Graeme Wynn.

1 From a map in Charles Paullin's *Atlas of the Historical Geography of the United States* (Washington, DC: Carnegie Institute and American Geographical Society, 1932), 76.

2 For my more elaborated thoughts about many of the aspects of pre-Confederation Canada that are touched on in this postscript, see Harris, *The Reluctant Land: Society, Space, and Environment in Canada before Confederation* (Vancouver: UBC Press, 2008).

3 Marcel Trudel, "Cartier," *Dictionary of Canadian Biography,* vol. 1, *1000 to 1700* (Toronto: University of Toronto Press, 1966), 166.

4 A small fraction of the "Indians" enumerated in Ontario and Quebec lived in the Canadian Shield north of the settled area shown in Figure 18. In 1871, Quebec and

Ontario were far smaller than they are now, but each included southern parts of the Canadian Shield.

5 These migrations were numerous and complex. For a summary, see Bruce G. Trigger, "Resettling the St. Lawrence Valley," in *Historical Atlas of Canada*, vol. 1, *From the Beginning to 1800*, ed. R.C. Harris, cart. G.J. Matthews (Toronto: University of Toronto Press, 1987), plate 46.

6 Michael Thoms, "Ojibwa Fishing Grounds: A History of Ontario Fisheries, Law, Science, and the Sportsmen's Challenge to Ojibwa Fishing Rights, 1630–1900" (PhD diss., University of British Columbia, 2004).

7 Chief Pemmeenauweet to Queen Victoria, January 1841, in I.F.S. Upton, *Micmacs and Colonists: Indian-White Relations in the Maritimes, 1713–1867* (Vancouver: UBC Press, 1979), 190.

8 John Ralston Saul, *A Fair Country: Telling Truths about Canada* (Toronto: Penguin Canada, 2008), part 1.

9 The phrase "middle ground" is from Richard White, who argues in *The Middle Ground: Indians, Empires and Republics in the Great Lakes Region, 1650–1815* (Cambridge: Cambridge University Press, 1991) that a cultural middle ground developed west of Lake Michigan after the Iroquois Wars of 1649–50.

10 My thoughts in this vein are elaborated in "Strategies of Power in the Cordilleran Fur Trade," in *The Resettlement of British Columbia: Essays on Colonialism and Geographical Change* (Vancouver: UBC Press, 1997), chap. 2.

11 The most comprehensive study of these epidemics is Paul Hackett, *A Very Remarkable Sickness: Epidemics in the Petit Nord, 1670–1846* (Winnipeg: University of Manitoba Press, 2002).

12 The essential works, on which this brief account of the influence of the fur trade on Indigenous peoples is largely based, are, by Arthur Ray, *Indians and the Fur Trade: Their Role as Trappers, Hunters, and Middlemen in the Lands Southwest of Hudson Bay, 1660–1870* (Toronto: University of Toronto Press, 1974; reprint, 1998) and "Periodic Shortages, Native Welfare, and the Hudson's Bay Company, 1670–1930," in *The Sub-Arctic Fur Trade: Native Social and Economic Adaptations* ed. Shepard Krech III (Vancouver: UBC Press, 1984), 1–20; and, by Frank Tough, *"As Their Natural Resources Fail": Native Peoples and the Economic History of Northern Manitoba, 1870–1930* (Vancouver: UBC Press, 1996), chaps. 1 and 2.

13 The first federal census of British Columbia, in 1881, enumerated 26,849 Indigenous people.

14 This account of the missionaries relies on Lynn Blake, "Let the Cross Take Possession of the Earth: Missionary Geographies of Power in Nineteenth-Century British Columbia" (PhD diss., University of British Columbia, 1997); and Brett Christophers, *Positioning the Missionary: John Booth Good and the Colonial Confluence of Cultures in Nineteenth-Century British Columbia* (Vancouver: UBC Press, 1998).

15 Karl Polanyi, *The Great Transformation: The Political and Economic Origins of Our Time* (first published in 1944 and frequently reprinted), deals magnificently with these matters, which first affected the British Isles then spilled into the world. See particularly chaps. 14 and 15.

16 Jürgen Habermas, *The Theory of Communicative Action*, vol. 2, *Lifeworld and System: A Critique of Functionalist Reason* (Boston: Beacon Press, 1987), part 6.

17 Frank James Tester, Drummond E.J. Lambert, and Tee Wern Lim, "Wishful Thinking: Making Inuit Labour and the Nanisivik Mine Near Ikpiarjuk (Arctic Bay), Northern Baffin Island," *Inuit Studies* 37, 2 (2013): 15–36.

18 The early ethnographers along the West Coast had little interest in the Indigenous societies around them, which they thought were becoming civilized, and sought, rather, to retrieve information about precontact ways. Even they, close students of Indigenous ways, had no sense of a continuing, separate Indigenous presence and identity.

19 It is often held that the humanistic understanding of the inherent worth of all people gave way in the latter half of the nineteenth century to an increasingly strident racism, but it is clear, I think, that the humanist view had a long life, largely, perhaps, because it served the purposes of settler colonialism. For a comparative analysis of its early durability, see Kenton Storey, *Settler Anxiety at the Outposts of Empire: Colonial Relations, Humanitarian Discourses, and the Imperial Press* (Vancouver: UBC Press, 2016).

20 Truth and Reconciliation Commission of Canada, *Honouring the Truth, Reconciling for the Future: Summary of the Final Report of the Truth and Reconciliation Commission of Canada* (Ottawa: The Commission, 2015).

21 Tina Loo, *Moved by the State: Forced Relocation and Making a Good Life in Postwar Canada* (Vancouver: UBC Press, 2019), intro. and chap. 1.

22 Ibid., 44.

23 Frank Tester and Peter Kulchyski, *Tammaniit (Mistakes): Inuit Relocation in the Eastern Arctic, 1939–63* (Vancouver: UBC Press, 1994). See also Tester, "Serializing Inuit Culture: The Administration of 'Relief' in the Eastern Arctic, 1940–1953," *Canadian Social Work Review* 10, 1 (1993): 109–23.

24 Government of Canada, "Statement of the Government of Canada on Indian Policy, 1969" (the White Paper), Summary, 1, "Background."

25 The most prompt and influential among these Indigenous voices was Harold Cardinal's *The Unjust Society: The Tragedy of Canada's Indians* (Edmonton: G.M. Hurtig, 1969).

26 Alan Cairns, *Citizens Plus: Aboriginal People and the Canadian State* (Vancouver: UBC Press, 2000), especially chap. 2.

27 Marianne Ignace and Ronald E. Ignace, *Secwépemc People, Land, and Laws* (Montreal/Kingston: McGill-Queens University Press, 2017).

28 Jody Wilson-Raybould, *From Where I Stand: Rebuilding Indigenous Nations for a Stronger Canada* (Vancouver: Purich Books, 2019).

29 A position advanced by the Royal Commission on Aboriginal Peoples, *Aboriginal Self-Government: Restructuring the Relationship*, vol. 2, part 1 (Ottawa: Minister of Supply and Services Canada, 1996).

30 Taiaiake Alfred, *Peace, Power, Righteousness: An Indigenous Manifesto* (Don Mills, ON: Oxford University Press, 1999; reprint, 2009); Glen Coulthard, *Red Skin White Masks: Rejecting the Colonial Politics of Reconciliation* (Minneapolis: University of Minnesota Press, 2014); and Leanne Simpson, *Dancing on Our Turtle's Back: Stories of Nishnaabeg Re-creation, Resurgence, and New Emergence* (Winnipeg: Arbeiter Ring Press, 2011).

31 John Borrows, *Recovering Canada: The Resurgence of Indigenous Law* (Toronto: University of Toronto Press, 2002), chap. 6.

32 This and other quotations in this paragraph are from ibid, chap. 6.

33 A constitutional interpretation greatly elaborated in Samuel V. LaSelva, *Canada and the Ethic of Constitutionalism* (Montreal/Kingston: McGill Queen's University Press, 2018).

34 As, for example, did the Thule when, in the last major pre-European migration into northern North America, they displaced the Dorset across the High Arctic. Later, when the differential availability of firearms undermined former balances of power, fighting often ensued. In 1649–50, the Iroquois League, obtaining firearms from the Dutch, defeated and dispersed large Wendat, Neutral, and Petun populations in southern Ontario. Late in the eighteenth century, the Niitsitapi (Blackfoot), armed by the fur trade before the Kutenai, pushed the latter across the Rockies.

35 John Borrows suggests that Indigenous knowledge of the interrelations of all parts of the land is both "imperfect and incomplete" and "insightful and wise": *Recovering Canada*, 147.

36 Northrop Frye, *The Bush Garden: Essays on the Canadian Imagination*, (Toronto: University of Toronto Press, 1971).

37 Cole Harris, "Industry and the Good Life around Idaho Peak," *The Canadian Historical Review* 66, 3 (1985): 325-43.

Index